Everybody Came to Tana's

Tana's DINNER MENU

Dinners

Antipasto · Soup · Spaghetti

LOBSTER FRA DIAVOLO, Calcio or Broiled	5.75
SHRIMPS MARINARA, Scampi or Diavolo	5.25
VEAL SCALOPPINE, Saute with Peppers	4.95
VEAL SCALOPPINE, Marsala	4.95
VEAL SCALOPPINE, Francaise	4.95
VEAL SCALOPPINE, Picata	4.95
VEAL CUTLET, Parmigiana	4.95
VEAL CUTLET, Milanese	4.50
CHICKEN CACCIATORA	4.50
CHICKEN MARSALA or LISBON	4.50
CHICKEN VESUVIUS	4.50
CALF'S LIVER, Veneziana	4.50
ITALIAN SAUSAGE	4.50
LINGUINI CLAMS, white or red	4.25
HOMEMADE RAVIOLI	4.25
HOMEMADE LASAGNA	4.25
SPAGHETTI, Meat Balls	4.25

Coffee & Tea

Sales Tax will be added to retail price on all taxable items.

We reserve the right to refuse service to anyone

Everybody Came to Tana's

AN AMERICAN DREAM COME TRUE

DAN TANA

DIVERSION BOOKS

To my family, my friends, my employees,
and everyone who came to Dan Tana's.
You are in my heart.

Radius Book Group
A division of Diversion Publishing Corp.
www.radiusbookgroup.com

For more information, email info@radiusbookgroup.com

First Radius Book Group Edition: June 2026
Hardcover ISBN: 979-8-89515-109-9
e-ISBN: 979-8-89515-110-5

Design by Westchester Publishing Services
Cover design by Libby Kingsbury

Printed in the United States of America
1 3 5 7 9 10 8 6 4 2

Table of Contents

Introduction

A good restaurant has a good bar, and a good bar has ghosts.

It is late afternoon, the autumn sky changing from light to dark. The traffic on Santa Monica Boulevard in West Hollywood is hard and heavy when I arrive at the Italian restaurant that bears my name. I haven't owned it for years. Movie posters and pictures of athletes on the walls, paintings by my ex-wife, Chianti bottles hanging from the ceiling, red leather booths, red-and-white checked tablecloths. It's small and cozy—only twenty tables. A joint. A place with history. Ghosts.

You get the picture.

I am an old man, recently turned ninety. I live nearly full-time in Belgrade, Serbia, near where I was born and raised and fled after the war as a soccer-playing teenager. But I visit one of my two daughters in Los Angeles several times a year. And every visit, whether I am there for three days or three weeks, includes dinner every night at Dan Tana's.

I am Dan Tana.

I have been a soccer player, an actor, a film producer, a soccer team owner, and a restaurateur. I have survived a war, three marriages, and two daughters. I have friends in more countries than I can count. I have experienced the ups, the downs, and the in-betweens, and I have not only survived but thrived by embracing them all with joy and gratitude for being here, for living life.

I always refer to myself as the luckiest man alive. I feel that way this evening as I walk into my restaurant.

I enter through the back, straight into the kitchen, where I am engulfed by the sweet aroma of butter and garlic simmering, and the sound of marinara sauce burbling on the stove and of vegetables being washed and chopped. Dinner has not yet started. It's the calm before the storm. One of the cooks, looking up without interrupting his prep, says, "Hello, boss." He has worked at the restaurant for more than thirty years. Inside the dining room, a waiter finishing setups spots me and shakes hands. "Good to see you, boss." He has also worked here for nearly thirty years.

The maître d', spying me across the dining room, serves up a welcoming grin. I receive a hug from him. He's a newbie with only ten years at the restaurant.

"Dan Tana himself," he says.

"I have friends coming later," I say.

In reality, friends of mine are already there. The ghosts. I walk over to the bar, letting the palm of my hand skim the long, polished wooden bar top. It was here before this place became Dan Tana's and I am sure it will be here long after. The average diner might not see the ghosts, but I do, all of them crowded together—Bert Schneider, Dennis Hopper, Dabney Coleman, Bob Rafelson, Lakers owner Jerry Buss, John Drew Barrymore Jr.—drinking, talking, laughing, complaining, arguing, flirting with some of the women, eyeing others with designs on them for later in the evening, having a good time.

By the end of the bar, closest to the kitchen, the best perch in the whole place, is the guy who calls Dan Tana's his home: Harry Dean Stanton.

"Hi, Harry. Good to see you tonight."

"Hey, you're in town."

"Yeah."

"How're the girls?"

"Good. Everyone's good."

Harry died in 2017, but he never left Tana's. His weathered face and half-lidded eyes are as clear to me as the three shelves of liquor bottles rising behind the bar. Calling him a regular somehow falls short of capturing his presence. If he was in town, he was at the far end of the bar five nights a week. For forty years he was here.

He said he showed up one day and kept coming back. It was that simple.

"They stayed open until two o'clock and served food until one o'clock in the morning," he once told a paparazzo camped outside the restaurant. "You could order anything off the menu. Can't beat that."

Harry knew everyone: all the restaurant's maître d's—Giovanni, Bruno, Guido, Jimmy, and Craig; the waiters; even a couple of the busboys, Miguel and Raphael. He used to hang out with the guys after the restaurant closed at night. Drinks were poured. Cigarettes were smoked. Stories were told.

"Boss, should you be talking about this?"

"It's okay, Mike."

"But the after-hours stuff. We don't need—"

Mike Gotovac. He was Dan Tana's bartender from 1968 until his death in 2020. He was famous, beloved, celebrated for more than fifty years of pouring drinks and keeping secrets. He had a word for everyone—actually, a few words. My name was on the restaurant, but Mike was the person everyone who walked through the door knew. Sometimes I had to tell him to go home. Now he's behind the bar all the time. Another ghost.

"Don't worry, Mike. It's just you and me. No one can hear us."

For a long time, Harry came in with Johnny Depp. They brought their guitars and sometimes stayed until three or four in the morning, playing music, drinking, smoking, and telling the kind of fantastic tales that would keep a person up all night. More than a few times, I found Harry still there when I opened up the next morning. He drank Manhattans. Someone once asked him if the drinks were good at Tana's.

"As good as any place," he said.

That was so Harry. I remember a guy next to him once asked if Tana's had changed much. This was around 2004.

"Everything changes," he mused from behind a cloud of cigarette smoke even though it was against the law to light up indoors. "Every moment changes."

"But the restaurant, Dan Tana's, has it changed?"

"Actually, not that much," Harry said. "The food's still good. The décor is still the same. Even the bartender, Mike, he's been here forever. The only thing that's changed is guys like me. We got older sitting right here."

Harry looked around at some of the other regulars.

"But that's okay. A lot of shit happened here."

* * *

That's a perfect description of Dan Tana's. A lot of shit happened here. George Clooney, John Travolta, Jack Nicholson, Madonna, Brad Pitt, Michael Douglas, Arnold Schwarzenegger, Lew Wasserman, Fred Astaire, Larry King, Elizabeth Taylor, Magic Johnson, Linda Ronstadt, Drew Barrymore, Leonardo DiCaprio, John Wayne, Bob Newhart, Don Rickles, Barack Obama . . . Joni Mitchell, John Belushi . . . all regulars. All with stories.

The same is true for countless others who nobody has heard of outside of their families and the maître d's taking reservations and negotiating where to seat people. Some complained about having to wait. Others enjoyed their drinks at the bar. It was never supposed to be easy to get a table, but I always treated everyone the same, famous or not. When Barbara Sinatra offered me $25,000 to close for one night so she could throw her husband, Frank Sinatra, a surprise birthday party, I told her no, I couldn't do that to my regulars. They come three or four times a week. I couldn't lock them out. Barbara and Frank never set foot inside the restaurant again. But his daughters, Nancy and Tina, did—and so did everyone else.

That's the restaurant business, and as Harry would likely attest were he still among us, it had little to do with famous people. Of course, they played a crucial role in creating the word of mouth that led to a full reservation book and enough of a profit to keep Dan Tana's going for decades.

But making a restaurant work, especially one as small as Dan Tana's, is hard work, requiring long hours lasting late into the early morning. It is about serving good food. It is also about people and family. People become regulars because the restaurant feels like home. Indeed, it becomes a home away from home.

The same is true for the waiters, the busboys, and those in the kitchen. For this cast of characters, it's also home. The work is the opposite of glamorous. Those who make it a career are usually characters, not your normal nine-to-fivers, but they are among the most passionate on the planet. They are also probably unfit for anything else.

Most people don't choose to go into the restaurant business. It finds them.

Indeed, it found me. It saved me. And it made me.

Part One

The Appetizer

1

We Don't Want to Lose Our Lunch Spot

It was 1964—the year the Beatles appeared for the first time on *The Ed Sullivan Show*, boxer Cassius Clay changed his name to Muhammad Ali, and the US surgeon general issued a warning that smoking cigarettes might be bad for your health. I was a young man at the time, only a year shy of turning thirty, and I was eager to make my mark on the world. I wanted to make money, too.

I had come to Hollywood a few years earlier as a professional soccer player. The sport had saved my life and taken me around the world, ultimately leading me to this storied land of glitz and glamor. Along the way I had learned the hard way that human nature came in all shades and colors. I was naïve and trusting, a refugee who had survived numerous close calls with disaster while bouncing across Europe and Canada, until I finally landed in California.

My inexplicable streak of luck put me in the same orbit as some of Hollywood's biggest stars: among them, Frank Sinatra, Dean Martin, Cary Grant, and Lana Turner. I took acting classes with Natalie Wood, Angie Dickinson, Kim Novak, Carol Eastman, and Judy Exner and appeared in movies with Robert Mitchum and Glenn Ford. But always I was guided by my love of football. My identity was wrapped up in the sport. It had brought me to Hollywood. It had literally saved my life.

Now, in this same year when the St. Louis Cardinals win the World Series and the Cleveland Browns capture the NFL championship, I was trying to do the impossible: start a professional soccer league in the United States.

Yes, it was a dream, but it was not so far-fetched. I partnered in this endeavor with two wealthy and powerful men, Dan Reeves, the owner of the Los Angeles Rams, and his friend, Clarence Martin, who had served as the undersecretary of commerce for transportation in the Kennedy and Johnson administrations. Both were smart, tough Irish Americans who had done very well in their careers. I had proven myself tough and resilient, and perhaps luckier than I was smart, and I was good with people.

I had helped fund a new youth soccer league, AYSO, hoping to interest kids in the sport that obsessed the rest of the world and to develop future fans for our league. Dan Reeves had started something similar with a program called Free Football for Kids. I worked on my soccer business in a small office at one end of a busy block on Santa Monica Boulevard. The Troubadour nightclub was at the other end of the block. In the middle was a restaurant. Dan, Clarence, and I ate there every other Friday and discussed our upstart league.

The restaurant had at various times been named Black's Lucky Spot and then as Domenico's. Its new proprietors, the art gallery owner Chuck Feingarten and his girlfriend, Cyril Futterman, had renamed it the Ringer. The restaurant was just two small rooms with a long wooden bar dividing the two in the middle. Sawdust covered the floor. The lunch and dinner menus were the same: hamburgers, sandwiches, and salads.

Chuck and Cyril knew little about running a restaurant. Even though their bartender was from Chasen's, a favorite among the Beverly Hills social set (in 1962, Elizabeth Taylor had Chasen's famous chili delivered to her in Rome, where she was filming *Cleopatra*), his presence wasn't enough to draw a crowd. After a year, Chuck and Cyril wanted to sell.

Clarence Martin was eating there one day on his own and heard that actress-dancer Cyd Charisse had approached Chuck about taking over the lease and turning the restaurant into a dance studio. Clarence must have mentioned this to Dan Reeves on his own because when the three of us met for lunch the next Friday, I found out that they had already made an offer to buy the restaurant for $30,000. When I expressed surprise, they looked at me like I was missing something obvious.

"We don't want to lose our lunch spot," Clarence said.

"We'll be partners," Dan said.

I thought they meant the two of them were going in as partners. I was wrong.

"Each of us will put in $10,000," Dan continued, talking to me. "And you can run it. You're here in the office every day anyway."

* * *

My head spun and my stomach turned queasy. For a moment or two I lost track of whatever else Dan and Clarence were telling me. I took a drink of water. I put down my fork in case my hands started to shake more than they already were. Men like Dan and Clarence did not appreciate indecision or weakness. Dan's family had made a fortune in the grocery business while he was still a young man, giving him the resources to buy the struggling Cleveland Rams in 1941. Four years later, they won the league championship. The next year he moved the Rams to Los Angeles, the first professional sports franchise to set up on the West Coast, and he won his second league championship in 1951. His eyes reflected his fierce competitiveness.

Clarence was a vice president of the Rams, a position I suspected he occupied for his brilliance and connections, though he had his own impressive resume as a successful businessman. The son of a Washington state governor, he played football and was president of the Flying Club at Harvard University. His 1938 graduating class included Arthur Schlesinger Jr., Theodore White, Casper Weinberger, Randolph Hearst, and Joseph P. Kennedy Jr. He was a naval aviator in World War II. In 1950, he moved to LA, made a fortune owning car dealerships, and helped get his former classmate's younger brother, John F. Kennedy, elected to the White House. A cabinet position followed, which he maintained for two years after President Kennedy's assassination before returning to his business and community ventures in LA.

Both Dan and Clarence had money and power, the right club memberships, and ties to influential men like themselves. My circle of friends was a mix of actors, restaurateurs, athletes, and hustlers, none of particular social standing. I had a wife and an infant daughter, and a small home that I rented within walking distance of my office. I had made nearly $100,000 co-owning a short-lived dance club in Hollywood called The Peppermint West. It capitalized on the dance craze that grew out of the Chubby Checker hit song "The Peppermint Twist." But I had lost most of that money in the stock market and soccer promotion.

Reluctantly, but matter-of-factly, I told Dan and Clarence that I wasn't in a position to risk the little I had left.

"Don't worry about it," Clarence said, taking a bite of his lunch.

I didn't know how to interpret that comment. Dan, who had fought to regain control of the Rams after a falling-out with his partners, picked his napkin up from his lap, wiped his hands, and set it down on the table next to his plate. He was finished with lunch.

"Look, we've already committed three million dollars to your soccer league, and we don't even know if it will ever form, never mind whether it will survive. We're gambling on you. And you don't want to put in $10,000 with us?"

I had no choice. I was in. I was buying a restaurant.

* * *

Dan and Clarence shared the same attorney, Eugene L. Wyman. He was the senior partner at Wyman, Bautzer, Rothman & Kuchel, one of the city's most powerful law firms and also head of the California Democratic Party. We met in his large office on Wilshire Boulevard. I brought my lawyer, Richard Millen, a friend of my father-in-law.

"I don't want to do this," I told him before we went inside. "You have to find a way to get me out of this."

He gave me a reassuring pat on the back.

"I'll do everything possible."

To his credit, once all of us were seated around Wyman's large conference table, my attorney did try to screw things up, and for a moment I was hopeful that he might succeed in creating a graceful exit for me. But Wyman had other, greater concerns, and with a simple shake of his head, he redirected the discussion to his client.

"Dan, as the owner of the Los Angeles Rams, you can't own a bar where characters of possible disrepute might congregate. This contract needs to be in his name."

He gestured toward me. That same sinking feeling I had when this whole situation began returned. I saw the way this was going to unfold. I wanted to say something, but I was intimidated and couldn't find the right words. I considered getting up and going to the men's room in the hope some bright idea would come to me. Instead, I sat in my chair, frozen and overmatched, and resigned myself to listening while a plan was worked out around me. It all happened very fast. Finally, Dan turned to me with an explanation of the legalese.

"If the restaurant doesn't make it, Clarence and I will give you $10,000," he said. "What this means is, in a worst-case scenario, you won't lose any money. In the best case, you will own 100 percent of the restaurant."

Like many wealthy, powerful businessmen, they saw the world the way they wanted to see it, and what they saw in this instance was a done deal. I saw no way out, especially since I did not want to jeopardize the soccer league. We shook hands, and I arranged a meeting with Chuck and Cyril to finalize the purchase of the restaurant. Both were partners in the Ringer, but Cyril had put in $15,000 to Chuck's $5,000, making her the majority stakeholder in this transaction.

The three of us and our attorneys met in the restaurant and sat at a table next to the bar. My attorney had prepared the papers, which he took out of his briefcase and set in front of the others while I outlined my proposal. I wanted to put one dollar down and give Chuck and Cyril $10,000 after the first year. At the end of the second year, I would give them another $10,000. And after the third year, I would write them a check for the final $10,000.

From my perspective, the offer was a good idea. I might be able to afford the payout without risking everything on one roll of the dice. I assumed my partners, Dan and Clarence, did not expect the restaurant to last more than two or three years. It was just a feeling, nothing articulated. But restaurants, even good restaurants, went under all the time. The business was hard. The hours were long. The margins were as thin as the soles on my shoes. Chuck and Cyril's desire to sell after owning the Ringer for only a year was proof. I was using that to my advantage.

"Okay, I'll sign," Cyril said when I finished. "Dan's a very capable man. He's going to do this, and I can tell he's going to do his best to make it work."

Chuck nodded in agreement. He was ready to get out. But their lawyer's face turned red. He put his hands over his eyes and took a deep breath before looking at his clients with an expression of contempt and dismay.

"If you sign this, you are the stupidest people in the world," he said. "That's my professional legal opinion."

Cyril glanced around her restaurant. She offered me a reassuring smile. Her lawyer not so much.

"I trust Dan," she said.

Her lawyer stood.

"He's giving you one dollar and paying you $10,000 a year from now, that is if he has the money. And maybe, maybe, maybe you'll get the rest of the money in the future. I don't like this at all."

"I'm going to sign," Cyril said, still steadfast in her decision.

"Go ahead," her lawyer said. "But I will not witness this stupid decision. It's the dumbest deal I've seen in my life. I'm going out on the sidewalk."

My lawyer, silent up until this point but still looking for a way to screw up the deal and get me out of it, and thinking the moment had finally arrived, also got up, feigning the same disgust as his counterpart.

"I agree," he said. "Let's go."

The three of us signed the papers and clinked water glasses. I walked over to the pay phone on the wall near the bathrooms, dropped in two dimes, and called my partners. I told them the papers were signed, the deal was completed. After they congratulated me, there was silence. I stood still, looking across the room at Chuck and Cyril, who were smiling at each other. Then my gaze moved to the empty restaurant.

The phone was still pressed to my ear as I waited for one of my smart, successful, wealthy partners to offer advice. When nothing was forthcoming, I blurted out the question I had dared not ask this whole time, fearful of this very moment when the restaurant became mine.

"What now?"

2

Don't Go Into the Restaurant Business

Clarence Martin and his family resided in a mansion on one of the twisting, tree-lined streets in Bel Air. He had moved there after leaving the Johnson administration in Washington, DC. His personal staff included the two private chefs. One cooked Italian food. The other specialized in Chinese.

Many times while we were working on promotions for the soccer league, I heard Dan rave about the meals he had eaten at Clarence's house. The chefs were superb, he had said. Better than at the best restaurants. I was able to corroborate those reviews myself after I ate there. The first time I had Chinese. The next time it was Italian. Both meals were fantastic.

I was not a gourmet, but I knew good food when I ate it. When I first got to LA, I fell in with the people who worked at Patsy D'Amore's Villa Capri, the best Italian restaurant in the city. I loved their fresh, handmade pasta, roasted meats, and homemade sweets. The meal Clarence's Italian chef prepared for us was on that same delicious and memorable level.

A day or two after I assumed ownership of the Ringer, I met with Dan and Clarence and let them know I had asked Cyril, the former co-owner, to stay on as the office manager, and she had agreed. She would go on salary, and I would take over responsibility for paying for the food, the liquor, and everything else necessary to operate the restaurant. We were starting from zero. To that point, Dan asked my thoughts about creating a new menu. The three of us had already agreed the Ringer's humble offerings needed a complete revision if we were to improve the restaurant's meager lunch business and practically nonexistent dinner crowd.

I hadn't thought about a new menu. I had mostly thought about getting out of the deal. Now I had a restaurant, and it needed a menu. We began to put together a plan. Dan said to Clarence, "Listen, you have two cooks on your payroll. They don't do anything on the weekend. You go out, and they sit around fighting with each other. They're bored. Why don't you loan one of them to our partner here for a few months? Whichever one you choose can help Dan start something new in the restaurant."

Clarence turned to me. "How about Italian?" I said okay, and that's how we came to have Italian food.

His chef was named Michela Diguglio. He was admired by the many Washington, DC insiders who had dined at Clarence's home. Prior to working for Clarence, Michela had been in southern Italy, cooking for General Mark Clark, who led the American Fifth Army in liberating Italy from the Axis forces in World War II. And before that, he had been one of Mussolini's private chefs in Florence. He was the perfect choice to create the new menu.

I had kept the cook from the Ringer on the payroll. His name was Constantino, and he was an excellent and experienced restaurant cook. But he was not a chef. And there's a difference. Michela worked with him. He made each dish on the new menu while Constantino watched, and then Constantino replicated them while Michela supervised. After one dish was perfected, they moved on to the next.

* * *

One day Michela and I were talking in the kitchen and he asked, "What are you calling the restaurant?"

That was a good question, and one for which I didn't have a ready answer. Once I accepted ownership of the Ringer, I wanted to change the name as much as I did the menu. If this was going to work, the name would be more important than anything, even the food, and not just because I wanted to differentiate it from what was there before. I needed a name for the liquor license. Good food and service brought people into the restaurant, but the bar was where the money was made. I suggested the name Roma, but the man from the Department of Alcoholic Beverage Control said it was already taken. My second choice was Trieste. That was taken, too.

I returned to the restaurant and sat with Cyril and my attorney. Constantino made us some chicken and pasta. Cyril and my attorney sent their compliments to the kitchen. I picked at the food. I was out of ideas and that was ruining my appetite.

"Call it Dan Tana's," Cyril said.

"No," my attorney said without a second of hesitation. "He can't call it Dan Tana's. Or Dan's. Or Tana's. Nothing with his name in it. There's too much liability."

I didn't see the point of worrying about liability if there wasn't a restaurant, and there wasn't going to be a restaurant if we didn't have a liquor license, and we weren't going to get that unless we came up with a name.

"Just say Dan Tana's," I said. "Put that down. If that's already taken, I don't know what to call it."

I printed the name—my name—in big block letters in the space provided for the restaurant's name and then added my signature at the bottom of the document. I ordered a new neon sign for out front. I also had to get menus printed. There was so much to do, and I hadn't even started. I thought of my father, who had owned a restaurant and worked sunup to midnight at least; then I heard my mother's voice—something she had said to me when I was still a young child: "*Dragi moj sine, ne idi u restoranski posao.*" Translation: *My darling son, do not go into the restaurant business.*

* * *

My father fell in love with my mother the first time he saw her. She was one of the most beautiful women ever, an Ava Gardner lookalike. Her name was Lenka. She was from an honest, hard-working peasant family. He was Radojko Tanasijević—"Rubi" for short. He was a city slicker, a restaurateur from Belgrade, the capital of Yugoslavia. Rubi had a sense about this seemingly simple village girl, that there was more to her than good looks, and he was right.

Although Rubi's family wanted him to marry an educated girl from a rich family, he proposed to Lenka the day he met her. She turned him down. He waited awhile before returning to the village, and this time he left with Lenka at his side. It was 1934, and they got married at the Church of Saint George in Čibutkovica. Afterward, they settled in Belgrade. They were two people with very different backgrounds and beliefs who spent the rest of their lives together, in love.

Lenka needed time to adjust to her new life in the big city, where she did not have a single friend or even an acquaintance. My grandfather tried to lift her spirits by telling her she lived on the most beautiful street in all of Belgrade. "At one end you have a market, and at the other a church. And in between you'll find everything you could possibly need, including one of the best restaurants in town, a hotel, a maternity hospital, and a school. You never have to leave Queen Natalia Street. Everything that's good is already here!"

Despite these benefits, Lenka's new life was hard. Being far away from home was difficult for her. My father loved bars, drinking, and beautiful women, and marriage didn't change his habits. His father owned two grocery stores and the popular Složna Braća restaurant, so Rubi would leave home before dawn to go to the market to buy stock for the restaurant, where he toiled until midnight or later. This was my grandfather's shrewdness. He reckoned that if his son was going to spend all his time in inns and taverns, he might as well do so in one of his own.

Mother might have grappled with her new life, with its unfamiliar ways and strange customs, but she remained devoted to her husband and the home they built together. My father was the same in his own way.

Early in 1935, my father was called up to serve king and country and left Belgrade to join the Yugoslavian army. My mother was six months pregnant at the time, but she told my father not to worry about anything but staying safe and returning sound. Two months later, she set off to visit her family in the village, riding the shaky Lajkovac railway until she arrived at the station, where she saw one of her brothers waiting to take her home in a carriage.

Given her blessed state, her family could not have been happier to see her. Eager to spoil her with comfort and care, they told her to rest, but, headstrong and restless, Lenka set to work around the homestead. A few weeks later, she was in the field, taking food and water to the workers preparing the first harvest of the spring, when she realized the moment she had been waiting for had arrived. With the nearest hospital miles away, she had put her faith in the village's midwives, but by the time they arrived, Lenka had given birth in the middle of the field.

My cries echoed far and wide. It was May 26, 1935. One of the women working in the field cut my umbilical cord with a scythe. Some said I would become a good harvester. Others said I might make a good shepherd because I was born in the field. None were right. Even in their wildest dreams, the path I would follow was impossible to imagine.

3

In War, There Is No God

Late one night Harry Dean Stanton was still at the bar as the last customers were lingering in a corner booth over their after-dinner drinks. The waiters and busboys were already involved in the nightly closing routine. I joined Harry at the bar and asked how his night had been. He looked up from his drink with those eyes that had more stories and characters in them than a Russian novel.

"I miss Giovanni," he said.

"What do you miss about him?" I asked.

"His energy," Harry said.

"What energy? The man could barely breathe."

We laughed. I understood both the irony and the sentiment of his comment.

Giovanni was my first maître d'. He worked the lunch shift at the Nickodell restaurant next to Paramount Studios. They did a big lunch business with those who worked on the studio lot. Giovanni was a star, in his way as popular as some of the famous names you saw at the tables. He knew who was important, where to seat them, and all their special needs. Some insisted on a quiet table. Others wanted to be seen. Still others called ahead to see who else was going to be there so they could have an "accidental" meeting—or avoid one.

He was already old when I persuaded him to work nights at Dan Tana's. Married and the father of eight, he had asthma and frequently struggled to breathe. Sometimes he arrived for work looking like he had taken his last breath just before walking through the kitchen door. Then he tightened his tie and put on his black suit jacket and appeared to shed twenty years and all his health problems.

He loved restaurant life, with all its camaraderie. Restaurant people judge their co-workers very simply. Do they work hard? If you do that, you can come from any background and will be accepted. You will find a home. Giovanni was at home at Dan Tana's. He had managed the Croatian embassy in Berlin during the Second World War. He had studied the hospitality business in school and spoke Italian, German, French, and English. After the war, he brought his family to the United States. Without him, I could have been wiped out. He knew how to set up the restaurant, my restaurant. He worked tirelessly. At the end of the night, he loosened his tie and wheezed like he might expire before he reached his car.

One day he complained that he was having trouble taking out a loan. He needed $24,000 to repair and remodel his home out in Pasadena. His place was worth around $100,000. After getting turned down by two banks, he asked me for help. I had no money myself, but my banker, an Italian guy, was a good customer at the restaurant, and the three of us sat in a booth one afternoon. He listened attentively as I described the situation, but he also denied Gio the money. Turned him down right in front of me. Gio got up and left, defeated. I was incensed.

"This country is unbelievable," I said to him. "You bankers are so cruel. This man has eight kids, he's working two jobs, the roof of his house is leaking, and he's not going to miss a payment. Yet none of you have the sense to loan him the money."

My banker picked up his spoon and twirled it in his fingers. "Dan, it's not that," he said. "The man is sick. He has eight kids. What if he dies? Who's going to pay back the loan?"

"Well, you take the house," I said.

"No bank wants to take a house from a widow with eight kids," he said. "The only way I can give him a loan is if you co-sign."

"Okay, I'll co-sign," I said without hesitation.

The bank was still open. We got in our cars and drove there. I co-signed the papers, and Gio got his money. As we walked out to the parking lot, the banker ran after me. He had forgotten to tell me about an insurance policy that was available.

"It's fifty dollars," he said. "If he dies, you aren't responsible."

That sounded good to me. We went back in, did the paperwork, and guess what? Two months later, Gio dropped dead. It wasn't unexpected given his health issues, but still, it was terrible. I saw in Gio a man like myself. He had a beautiful family. He loved his work. Gio and I were different ages and nationalities, but both of us had survived the war, found our way to LA, and thrived. We came to work. He was one of the lucky ones, and he made me think back to how lucky I was, too.

* * *

In 1938, my father returned from the army and resumed his old ways of bars, women, and basketball games. I was not yet three years old. As far as I knew, our family home at 10 Queen Natalia Street—a quiet part of the suburban settlement south of the Kalemegdan Fortress, overlooking the river—was happy and stable. Then one day, my father returned from work with news of the conflict engulfing Europe. Grandpa, who owned the only radio on the street, immediately found BBC radio station and shook his head distressingly at the news.

He had lived through the First World War, and his memories were still fresh as he attempted to explain what war was really like, just how terrible it was. He kept muttering: "In war, there is no God!" The whole neighborhood was in the habit of gathering around our radio to listen to radio shows and news, which would soon feature the frontlines in far-flung places of the world.

War came to Yugoslavia three years later. One night toward the end of March 1941, I woke to the clamor of the crowd marching in the street below. People were shouting slogans, the words of which I could make out but not quite understand: *Better war than the pact! Better grave than a slave!* By the next day, the demonstrations were over, and life resumed its everyday course. I went back to running around the streets with my friends, chasing rag balls and waiting patiently for Easter.

On the evening of April 5, we had dinner together as a family and I found out that I would have a brother or a sister. Father didn't seem happy about it. He kept repeating to Lenka that "this is not a time for babies, tough times are ahead." Mother responded tersely that we had to make do somehow and did not let slip the opportunity to berate him for his constant absences and bohemian lifestyle.

The next day Belgrade was heavily bombed by the German Air Force. We were awakened in the predawn darkness by thunder of airplane motors, followed by deafening explosions. As the earth shook under our feet, Father hastily gathered us together and led us to the basement. He remained calm, though I remember being terrified and confused.

We huddled together in the dark for what seemed like an eternity. We were lucky; the bombs missed our house and we survived. Not everyone was as fortunate. When we emerged from the basement, a devastating scene awaited us. Several houses nearby were completely destroyed. Whole families were wiped out. More than four thousand people were killed in the city that night. Among them was my friend Saša, who I had played with only the day before. He and his family lived next door. All of them were killed.

We were lucky.

On April 13, an unfamiliar army marched into our town—the Germans. This was two years after Hitler had invaded Poland and gone to war with Britain and France. Within days of their surprise attack, bodies of those they executed were hung in front of Hotel Moskva for all to see. Belgrade citizens walked about as if nothing was happening, covertly glancing up at the bodies of the "five martyrs," as they secretly called them, swaying from the candelabras above the promenade. The Yugoslav army surrendered to the Germans on the eighteenth of April, and the entire country was occupied.

By the time Mother gave birth to my brother Bora a few months later, the streets were plastered with German directives designed to scare people into submission. Reprisals were savage: fifty citizens for a wounded German, a hundred for a dead one. The inhabitants of Belgrade responded with a flyer: *No Fear—But Righteous Anger; No Submission—But a Burning Desire for Revenge.* They called on people to rise up and fight.

Mother tried to persuade Father to take us to the village. We would be safer there, she said, but he would not hear of it.

* * *

At the end of 1941, my father disappeared. He simply failed to come home from work one day. As the curfew came and went and he was not back, Mother and Grandpa grew concerned. Grandpa was in the possession of an *Ausweis*, a pass that let him move about the city even after curfew, but my father had no such document. Mother was sure he had fallen asleep at the home of one of his many mistresses, to which Grandpa just said: "God willing, you will be right!"

A police informer who frequented my father's inn, as they did in those days, listening in wherever people gathered and talked, came over the next day to tell Grandpa that Father had been arrested by the Germans and taken to a notorious holding prison, from which we knew prisoners were dispatched either to the concentration camps or to their graves. The informer suggested a way to get him out but said we had only a couple of days to do it. He offered to mediate.

My grandpa naturally jumped at the opportunity to save his only son. The ransom had to be paid exclusively in gold. Grandpa came up with the goods somehow—he put in all he had and for the rest collected gold coins and jewelry from family and friends. My father was released but never came home from prison. He simply vanished. Then, in 1942, Grandpa died, and Mother, baby brother Bora, and I were left to fend for ourselves.

In my father's absence, the inn he owned was run by a certain Luka, who used to help Grandpa with his businesses. He continued to supply us with essentials, which were hard to find in the occupied city. A short while after Grandpa's death, two German officers lodged in our home, naturally without consulting us. They moved into Grandpa's part of the house. They were always in uniform and behaved decently—each time they passed Mother they would click their heels and greet her with a slight nod.

Out of curiosity, we children often rummaged through the trash the officers discarded into a large barrel behind the house. We hoarded everything that took our fancy: colorful chocolate wrappings, empty cream pots, tins. One day we found discarded razor blades among the trash. We played with them and I got injured. When my mother saw my bleeding hands, she flew into a rage. She found the German officers and started shouting at them in Serbian. They looked at her in astonishment, understanding nothing, until she dragged me out and showed them the razors and my injured hands. They tried to calm her down, apologizing in German and looking for bandages to dress my wounds. The next day, they brought chocolate for me and flowers for Mother.

Several mornings later, we woke to find them gone. They disappeared as suddenly as they had arrived.

4

We Didn't Have Money to Buy Anything

Eventually, I was packed off to the village where my mother's family lived while she was joined in Belgrade by her younger sister, Radmila, later better known as Lola. Lola married a tailor from Belgrade and moved to the city. Mother finally had one of her own close by.

I have only good memories of the village school. I learned to read and multiply, and about "nature and society," as one of the subjects was called. I helped farm the land and keep cattle. I learned to respect farmers' life during my stay in the village. My guide through farming "nature and society" was my grandmother Stanka. I was her favorite, probably because I was her only grandchild living away, in the city. She was convinced that city folk knew nothing of farmers' life and did her best to teach me. She showed me how to milk cows, how to make cheese and cream, and how to feed the animals and collect chicken eggs.

While the rest of the family called me by my nickname, Bata, she called me "her sunshine." Thanks to her, I enjoyed my time on the farm. I felt safe.

The most interesting thing that happened in the two years I spent in the village took place on a seemingly ordinary morning. We were at school when, around midday, we saw through the open window a surprising number of people rushing to the main village square. Our teacher, being curious, took us out of class to see what was happening. In the square, we found villagers clustered around a wonder they said had fallen out of the sky.

It turned out that a farmer from nearby Dudovica, taking a shortcut to his field, had found a man hanging from a mulberry tree next to the path. The man was an American pilot whose plane had apparently been shot down by German anti-aircraft fire. He'd had to bail out of his burning plane, and his parachute had gotten tangled in the tree. The farmer pulled him down and took him to the village, where he was surrounded by curious villagers.

Confused and frightened, the pilot tried to speak to them in his strange language, but no one could understand him. The villagers gawked at him as if he were an alien, clad as he was in a tawny leather jacket with cream fur collar, the flaps of his leather cap hanging over his ears and round aviator goggles pushed high up on his forehead.

Soon after, a group of armed men with long beards appeared out of nowhere—the Chetniks (fierce Serbian nationalists)—and took the man away. But they were not the only ones looking for the pilot. Soon German army vehicles rolled into the village. Their leader was riding pillion on a motorcycle and was so caked in dirt that he reminded me of a village miller covered in a thick layer of oat flour. He wore a round green helmet and goggles. Through an interpreter, the German officer tried to discover the pilot's whereabouts from the people still gathered at the square. They shrugged their shoulders and pointed in different directions but never revealed the truth.

I doubt that the villagers knew where the pilot had been taken, but I know that they would not have told the Germans even if they did. I returned to Belgrade after liberation, and Father followed a few months later.

* * *

In the aftermath of World War II, Yugoslavia was a country remade almost overnight. Josip Broz Tito's Communist Partisans emerged victorious, abolished the monarchy, and tightened their grip on power. In Belgrade, loyalty was no longer something you proved by what you did, but by what you had *always* been believed to be. My father was politically neutral, and in those days, that was the most dangerous position to take. He never expressed any political views, never joined a party, he was not a traitor or collaborator, and he was not a communist. It would turn out he was not lucky either.

The Germans imprisoned him during the war, and after being released, he had to spend three years in hiding. Now, just as he thought he was free to resume his life, the Communists accused him of having collaborated with the enemy during the war, and he was arrested again. Allegations such as these were common, even if most were completely baseless. But this time there was no Grandpa to save him.

The trial took place six months later. It was held in public and my mother, brother, and I attended, along with many others. Such public trials were commonplace. The courtroom was crammed with people who took every opportunity to shout out slogans and accusations. "HE FED THE ENEMY! DEATH TO FASCISM! LONG LIVE COMMUNISM! JUSTICE FOR THE WORKING CLASS! DOWN WITH BOURGEOISIE! ENGLAND AND AMERICA WILL BE PROLETARIAN!"

This was as far as it was possible to be from a place where a man's guilt or innocence could be determined. I was too young to know that my father had been condemned in advance and the mob was there to hide the real nature of the communist farce before us, in which justice was dispensed not with regard to truth but according to ideology.

The whole spectacle was traumatic for my family and me. It was clear that Father would not come out of there a free man, despite the lack of any credible evidence against him. He was represented by a lawyer assigned to him by the government. I remember thinking that odd: the government charged you, and then that same government defended you. It seemed strange.

The trial took all of thirty minutes, and then, without considering the evidence or even recording the proceedings properly, the judge passed the sentence: twelve years of hard labor! And in addition, a confiscation order seizing all property. Finally, the judge announced that Father had a right to appeal, but if he did, the sentence could be doubled. The lawyer rushed to accept the verdict, while my father bellowed at the judge: "I appeal the sentence! You will not be in power for twelve days if you continue passing sentences like this!"

The lawyer had his work cut out to get Father to calm down and then they led him out of the courtroom. Once more, Father was denied the opportunity to be with his family. He was taken back to the prison in Ada Ciganlija, and from there to somewhere in Bosnia to serve out his sentence, they told us.

Without Grandpa to help us and without my father's income, our life in the new Communist regime took a dramatic turn for the worse. There was less food on the table, clothes were worn for longer, even after they became threadbare and full of holes, and our shoes started getting "eyes"—worn-down circles in the leather of the soles.

I can still recall the smell of wood in the kitchen as Mother prepared *popara*, a mixture of old bread and water, cooked into a paste and seasoned with salt. I remember the taste of the potato I baked in its skin on the old stove. And my mother's words, which she repeated like a mantra: "Son, become a doctor, a lawyer, anything you want, but don't end up running a restaurant. Promise me!"

* * *

After the trial my mother went knocking on doors, frantically looking for a way to help Father, while I minded my younger brother and played with friends around the neighborhood. The focal point of all our entertainment was the market, Zeleni Venac. We didn't have money to buy anything, so we had to think of ways to get to the goods. We developed quite an elaborate technique of obtaining fruit, especially watermelons.

The oldest of us would approach the seller—with some coins in hand for authenticity—and while he would bargain with the man, we smaller kids would fall in line behind him. With the seller occupied with the sale, the boy in front would kick the nearest watermelon and pass it down the line like a soccer ball, all the way to the last boy, who would grab it and run to the designated meeting place—a bench in the nearby park.

One day while we sat on the bench enjoying the spoils of our efforts, a young man approached us and said: "How's the watermelon? Sweet? I saw you buying it. Next time you do it, buy me one for the same price." He chuckled, turned around and left.

Our "operation" must have coincided with him buying a watermelon at the same stall. We had no idea who he was, so we continued enjoying our plunder, until a neighbor approached us, the cantankerous Mr. Roga, who this time seemed curiously elated.

"Don't you know who that was?" he asked. We shrugged, but before we could say anything he yelled at us: "Shame on you, you chase your rag balls all day long and break our windows, but you don't recognize Rajko Mitić! That man is the captain of the Red Star!"

Rajko Mitić, the soccer star! That seminal encounter was the first time Rajko and I met. Later, our paths would cross often and in very different circumstances.

* * *

Life was hard without Father. My mother found a job in a sweet factory in Zemun, a municipality of Belgrade, and my brother Bora and I were often minded by her sister Lola. Lola was rumored to have been a communist informer in the war—her way of fighting the enemy was spying on the Germans and helping the Partisans.

Lola was in fact her nom de guerre. Unlike my mother, she was skillful in navigating Belgrade society circles and did well out of her marriage to Svetislav, a tailor with an expanding business specializing in peasant attire. He was well connected; all sorts of people passed through his atelier. As a young man, Svetislav had been apprenticed together with a certain Aleksandar Ranković, known as Leka, and Leka had introduced him to his new wife. Ranković was a close associate of President Josip Broz Tito, both before and during the war. After the war, he became the third most powerful man in Yugoslavia and held the post of the minister of the interior. He also served as vice president.

Lola doggedly pursued Ranković, who by this time was very difficult to reach, until she succeeded in seeing him. She managed to persuade him of my father's innocence, and Leka agreed to intervene. My father was duly released from his hard sentence. This time he escaped not with a ransom paid in gold, but on the order of the highest authority. The Communists convicted him, and the Communists saved him—one of the many paradoxes of that time.

Upon his return from prison, my father was given the job of managing the restaurant he used to own, but which was now owned by the government. My father was undaunted. He resumed his old ways as if nothing had happened. He was a fighter, my father. He survived the Germans, he survived the Communists, he survived imprisonment, and loss of property, but he kept his spirit, the same spirit with which he pursued my mother at the village fair all those years ago.

Maybe that is the reason he never quite managed the role of a father—perhaps being a typical father simply wasn't in his genes. He loved us and took care of us, but that was as far as our relationship went.

5

My Light in the Darkness

The Danube and the River Sava flowed past, their murky waters fast and turbulent like our lives. The Soviet and Russian movies that were supposed to serve as entertainment—with their highly charged narratives of brotherhood, unity, and heroic common struggle set against the backdrop of grisly reality of a country ravaged by war—mirrored the misery of our own postwar years.

Then, in 1948, Tito loosened Yugoslavia's ties to the Soviet Union and looked westward for both support and identity. American films soon filled Belgrade cinemas, projecting a version of freedom and modern life that quietly contrasted with Communist control. Tanks and explosions were replaced on movie screens by elegant and romantic film divas, like Jane Wyman, Jean Simmons, and Esther Williams.

Movies helped my friends and me realize that the world we knew was not the whole world, that there was much more to experience beyond our immediate surroundings. With the arrival of movies from the West, the ranks of cinemagoers in the city swelled and tickets for shows became a sought-after commodity. Older guys from our neighborhood saw an opportunity there and set out to seduce ticket-office girls in cinemas around the city.

Most were handsome, charming rogues and had no trouble illegally obtaining packs of a dozen tickets before they went on the market for syndicates—who at that time had a priority—to buy. The rogues passed the tickets to us younger boys—I was thirteen or fourteen—to sell to enamored couples or lonely gentlemen, anyone who wanted to see the movie. We made a healthy profit from this touting; there was always someone desperate for one more ticket.

The deal was this: Retail price of a ticket was fifteen dinars; we usually sold them for sixty dinars but for some movies, the price went up to a hundred dinars. We were given 25 percent of the retail price of every ticket we sold, with the rest going to the organizers. Tickets sold like crazy and the pile of money in my drawer grew thicker by the day. There were days when I didn't manage to sell all my tickets, but I did not consider that a failure because on those evenings I could sneak into the theater after everyone else using an unsold ticket and set out on a journey of my own.

Little by little, movies from the West helped us build a picture of a much more stimulating world than the one we knew or read about in books. It was in the movie theater that I fell in love for the first time. Not with a girl from my neighborhood, but with the enchanting Jane Wyman. I saw her playing a deaf-mute girl in *Johnny Belinda* and was smitten.

* * *

However, my only real-life love was soccer. Even so, it never crossed my mind that I could play professionally one day. At that time, every street in the neighborhood had a team and we played against each other. Boys from Sarajevo Street would play against the team from Narodni Front Street, or Lomina Street would play Balkan Street and so on.

When not playing soccer, my friends and I mostly hung around "our" bench in the park and talked about the future and what it might hold for us. With certainty typical of children, each of us knew exactly what he wanted to be when he grew up—a doctor, a pilot, a soccer player. I always joked that I would become an actor in Hollywood, although I had no idea how one went about becoming one in Belgrade, much less in Hollywood, but in my young imagination, this was the only way I could get closer to the enchanting Jane Wyman.

Movies opened our horizons and awakened the desire to see the world. We were fascinated by stories of "defectors" who had supposedly managed to escape across the border. The veracity of these stories was questionable, but managing to cross the border became something my friends and I considered the ultimate endeavor. We looked up to those who had as heroes.

The only story of escape we knew to be true was that of the North water polo team. They had gone to take part in a competition in Austria and most never returned. There were ten players and the trip leader, a man called Fedor Rajić, who was assigned to the team by the government and instructed to keep a close eye on them. His job was to ensure that they did not say or do anything that might be deemed subversive or unpatriotic. When eight of the players defected, Rajić did not dare return without them, so he stayed in Vienna, too.

Playing soccer was our passion, but my friends and I loved all sports and joined the Swimming Club North, so we could use the pool for free. That is how we got to know the water polo players who absconded. They weren't exactly friends. They were older than us and already accomplished sportsmen, but we all knew them for who they were—talented young men with successful careers in front of them. Their departure was a huge loss for Yugoslav water polo, and a gain for Canada and America, where most of them ended up.

The swimming pool was also where, aged fourteen, I fell in love with a "real" girl for the first time. Her name was Mirjana and she was Russian. Her family had left Russia and settled in Serbia after the October Revolution. We shared our first kiss in the middle of the pool of all places. But being a Russian was not easy in Yugoslavia after the country broke relations with its "big brother" Russia in 1948. After the breach, anyone who seemed connected with Russia found themselves persecuted by a Kafkaesque state machine. Consequently, our budding love affair was cut short when Mirjana's family emigrated to London to ensure their safety.

* * *

I recall a time many, many years later, after I was already involved with Dan Tana's restaurant, when I stopped to catch my breath and asked myself how one person could be involved in so many things: acting, producing, politics, football, the restaurant business, a wife and ex-wives, children. But life was no different when I was a teenager in school. There was math, history, chemistry, girls, swimming, selling movie tickets on the black market, chores at home, and the activity that consumed most of my time and energy, soccer.

Everyone finds that thing that propels them forward in life and, though I did not know this would be the case, for me it was soccer. One day, a smartly dressed gentleman appeared at our playground. He was smoking a cigarette in a long cigarette holder and obviously not from our part of town. He found a spot by the sideline and settled down to watch the game. None of us recognized him so we continued playing as we did any other day.

Bursting with youthful energy, we gave our all in every kick. We took the game seriously: It was important to play, but also to win. After the game, the gentleman called over my friend Toma and me and told us he was from Crvena Zvezda FC (Red Star FC) and that they were in the process of selecting candidates for the apprentice team.

The man was Dr. Aca Obradović, the famous Dr. O. He invited us to a training session on the following Sunday. We were quite surprised by this turn of events but felt wildly elated—our childhood dream was about to come true. We were going to play for the biggest club in town. I was too excited to sleep that night, convinced that we were destined to become new Red Star stars.

I knew that Toma was a better player than me and was secretly worried that he might be selected over me. But when we got there, there were about forty other boys who had also been invited to take part in the trials. It was not a regular training session; they first asked us about school, our families, and our lives in general. Only after a long conversation with each boy did they split us into teams. Once on the pitch, we all displayed keen fighting spirit; we had to play several matches before the coaches were able to select the best players among us.

On "D-Day," they read out twenty-one names. I did not hear Toma's name, but to my great amazement and delight, I did hear mine. I was not the best nor the worst of players, but I was the fastest. That had proved decisive. Twenty-one names became twenty-two with the late addition to the squad of Perica Radenković. Perica, whom everyone called the American, was a cousin of the club's equipment manager, Aca, who helped him get on the team. We soon became best friends and have remained so ever since.

* * *

Joining the Red Star apprentice team and meeting Dr. O, equipment manager Aca, and Perica American signaled the beginning of a new period in my life. I was to make new friends and assume new responsibilities. My parents did not object as long as I promised not to neglect school.

A small group of people took care of all the club's business in those days. There was Aca, whose job was to ensure the players and staff had all their equipment prepared and ready for training and match days. His pretty wife, Ankica, and her assistant, Mara, were responsible for cleaning the kits and soccer cleats. There were no washing machines, so they washed everything by hand and dried it on the outdoor line. Then there were Uncle Dule-Frog and his assistant, whose job was to maintain the grounds and take care of the pitch. They kept two large German shepherds who completed the support team and watched over all of us.

The apprentice team was coached by Coach Uncle Mitke. The club did not have much money in those days, so the equipment assigned to the apprentice team was in terrible condition (used uniforms and shoes from the first team players). We played with balls that were heavy and ragged, and we trained in soccer shoes that had studs which went right through the soles and dug into our feet. But we didn't mind. We were proper players of a proper soccer club, training on a real pitch and, to top it all, we had the privilege of watching the first team train and play. It was idyllic.

Apart from attending training sessions, we were also expected to do small chores around the club—clearing up the dressing room, gathering shoes and kits, and collecting balls when the first team trained or played matches at home. In truth, we were all assistants to the kit manager Aca, who took me under his wing, and with good reason—I was hard-working, dutiful, and considerate, someone he could rely on. However small, these tasks were important for the smooth running of the club and by extension, for the success of its first team.

That is probably why Aca put me in charge of the apprentice squad. When he announced it, only my friend Perica American was against it. He still maintains that I was chosen just because I was the eldest, forgetting that I was eight months younger than him.

As leader of the boys' team, I became close with the first team's head coach, Svetislav Glišović. But it was through my friendship with Aca that I found myself in a privileged position of learning the starting eleven ahead of anyone else, even before the players themselves.

To start in a game meant everything because the rules at the time did not allow substitutions; a team could only ever use eleven players in a match. If one of them got injured, the game would continue with the team down to ten men and so on.

Aca the equipment manager would be told the starting lineup several hours before each match, to give him time to prepare the players' kits. He would share the lineup with me, in strict confidence, of course. The players knew that and often pressed me to divulge the secret before the matches, but I never did. All they ever got out of me was a curt: "Rajko Mitić is the captain."

They knew that much themselves, because Rajko was irreplaceable. I once asked Rajko if he remembered the market and the watermelon affair and he said he did, adding in jest, "Good of you to remind me, from now on we better all mind our wallets!" But I had a sense that he grew fonder of me from that day on. For my part, I started dreaming of the number eight on my jersey and following in his footsteps.

During my time with Red Star Belgrade, the club won the Yugoslav National Cup three times in a row—in 1948 with Coach Glišović, and in the following two years under the tutelage of Aleksandar Tomašević. In 1951, we became champions of Yugoslavia for the first time under coach Ljubiša Broćić. Throughout this fantastic run, I kept my position as an assistant to Aca the equipment manager. I never slipped up. I had found my path in soccer and nothing was going to make me turn away from it now.

6

Don't Be Stupid

I made considerable income reselling movie tickets, but it came with a hefty dose of anxiety. I was afraid that if someone found out what I did in my spare time it might put an end to my soccer career, at a time when rumors were circulating about the clubs forming an official youth league. However, the constant dread I felt did not make me stop; I still had to earn my pocket money somehow. But then as the rumors were finally confirmed, my soccer career came under threat from something altogether different—my tonsils.

Following a routine checkup, the club doctor recommended surgery to take out my tonsils, concerned they might affect my physical development. I knew my mother would never agree to have her first-born go under the knife as a mere precaution. She believed that tonsils protected against tuberculosis. Desperate to resolve the situation, I persuaded two girls I knew from a dance class I had attended to forge my mother's signature on the letter of consent, which I took to the hospital. That afternoon the problem was resolved, and the obstacle to my soccer career was eliminated.

When my mother found out about it, she rushed over to the hospital in a fury, threatening and cursing. But there was nothing she could do about it, my tonsils were history.

I still felt suffocated by the environment I lived in. Rationing was still on and poverty pervasive, but much more frightening and claustrophobic was the closing of the minds I witnessed around me. The communist dogma, with its propensity to see "class enemies" in everything and everyone and its relentless repression of anyone who dared think differently, slowly saturated the minds of the people around me.

Politics and sport were as intertwined then as they are today, but the difference was that in Belgrade, at that time a sportsman wanting to progress had to be actively involved in political life. A club had to have strong party connections so at Red Star, center forward Tomašević, a goal-getter who played in the first team, acted as the club's Communist Party secretary, while reserve player Miljan Miljanić acted as secretary of the SKOJ (Yugoslav Communist Youth League).

One day, Miljanić passed around the forms for joining the Communist Youth League, instructing us to fill them in and sign on the dotted line, confirming that we were willing to become members. Perica American asked me what we should do. I didn't know myself, so I decided to ask my father for advice. When he saw the form, Father flew into a rage—he swore he would disown me if I signed that piece of paper, recounting once again all the injustices he had suffered at the hands of the Communists—his sham trial, the harsh sentence, and the loss of our property.

A few days later, Miljan collected the forms from a number of boys who seemed eager to join the Communist Youth League and never noticed that Perica American and I did not hand in ours.

* * *

When Red Star finally decided to create a proper youth team, Coach Uncle Mitke was entrusted with selecting eighteen most talented players out of twenty-two boys. For the first time in my life, I came face-to-face with bitter disappointment: Perica American and I were among the four apprentice players that Coach Uncle Mitke had decided to drop.

Neither Aca the equipment manager nor Dr. O agreed with his decision and as Perica American and the other two boys with heavy hearts departed the club, they told me to disregard the coach's decision and stay put. I did as I was told. For a short while I neither trained nor played, but despite the deselection, I remained at the club. Coach Uncle Mitke had the power to deselect me, but that did not mean he could get rid of me. In fact, I found myself on the pitch again soon after and trained and played in many matches.

Dr. O believed in my talent and, knowing that the youth league was about to be established, saw me as an important player in it. But seeing how assiduous I was in completing all my other tasks at the club, he worried this might subvert my soccer ambitions and limit my chances of fulfilling them. He decided the best thing was to distance me from my duties at the club for a while and kindly offered to send me to Montenegro for a year, to improve my game. So I ended up playing for Bokelj FC in the Montenegro Ligue.

My parents took the news of my transfer pretty well. They knew I would continue my education and were pleased that it was to be at a Naval College, no less. I liked the idea too—I imagined myself in a pristine white uniform at the helm of a ship, sailing to exotic ports across the seas. Such musings brought to the fore my long-held desire to travel and see the world but were frustratingly cut short when I found out that one could not become a captain of a ship unless one was a member of a navy family. Those whose forebears were in the navy had the advantage over everyone else.

As a result, this city boy ended up a machinist. Not for me the command bridge and endless horizons; the bowels of the ship and the noise of the motors were destined for continentals like me. Nevertheless, I unexpectedly found myself in Kotor, living by the sea and playing in the Montenegrin league while my friend Perica American joined Milicioner (the police soccer club).

I spent the entire season playing for a much smaller club than Red Star, in an inferior league, but at least I was given time on the pitch. I was able to progress much more quickly than I would have had I stayed in Belgrade, playing sporadically in friendly matches and spending most of my time collecting balls and cleaning shoes. But I don't have many fond memories of my year in Kotor.

Despite making friends at the college and at my new club, I felt strangely displaced. I was used to Belgrade winters—freezing cold and everything covered under a thick layer of snow. In Kotor, it rained for four months straight instead.

* * *

While I waited for the rain to stop, an under-eighteen squad was being assembled by the Belgrade soccer association for a competition in Belgium. A squad representing the city was to go to Antwerp in July that year for a tournament that was to include the hosts and the squads representing Brussels and Paris. When I finally returned at the beginning of summer, I found the squad already assembled. I had been away and did not figure in the plans.

I shared my disappointment with Dr. O, who believed in me and was determined to help me join the squad. He thought I was a better player than many of those selected to go and promised he would do everything he could to get my name added to the list. He also told me that there were three players in the squad who were over eighteen, which was not fair. He was very strict and said that I should not mention that to anybody.

My problem was that I was the son of Rubi, "the enemy of the people." This made me an unsuitable candidate for the trip, but Dr. O was a formidable man, whose opinion was held in very high esteem in soccer world. He was Red Star's best soccer scout, with an uncanny ability to spot talented players as they were just starting out or find them languishing in the lower-ranked teams, and he was rarely wrong. He often snatched players from under the noses of other teams; they retaliated by repeatedly reporting him to the Soccer Association of Yugoslavia. He gained the distinction of being "banned for life" three times in his career.

He was doing his utmost to make it possible for me to travel to Antwerp. The players selected were already fully prepared, with all the formalities completed, when he called me and said I should get two photographs for a passport ready just in case but warned me to keep quiet about it. He knew that one of the players was hiding an injury and might be forced to drop out at the last minute, allowing me to take his place.

He also instructed me to go to Aca the equipment manager and sign out a pair of soccer cleats in case I should need them.

I hastily arranged to have my picture taken and collected the shoes, and then went home and told my parents that there was a possibility I would be going to Belgium with the junior squad representing Belgrade. I warned them that nothing had been confirmed yet and asked them not to tell anyone. They were naturally excited at this news, as I was myself. They had never traveled that far from home, nor had they wished to—foreign countries provoked in them only fear and concern.

At that time in Yugoslavia, traveling abroad entailed long and complicated procedures and, most importantly, required authorization from the top of the political establishment. One had to be "politically suitable" to be allowed across the border. My father, who knew such an adventure was out of his reach, seemed pleased that I was going to see a different world, where people were free to live their lives, earn their living, and think as they liked. As for me, all I could think of was the prospect of finally seeing for myself the world I knew only from movie screens.

Mother, my brother Bora, and I had dinner together that evening and although we were all elated, I could sense a quiet sadness permeating the mood, as if we knew we would not see each other for a while. "You've just arrived, and you might be leaving," she said. "Be careful you'll be traveling in the foreign land."

Father was at the restaurant and came home around 9 P.M., bringing me a message from Dr. O to come to the railway station around ten. Dr. O said he would be waiting for me there. But he added that nothing would be certain until the very moment the train departed. I put on my only suit and packed my bag and cleats. As I expected, now that the time had come for me to leave, Lenka became distraught. She pulled some bills out of a drawer—one five-dollar bill and four one-dollar bills—and said: "That's all I have. You might find it useful." Then she turned away to hide her tears.

My father and brother walked me halfway to the train station before turning back. My father worried that if someone saw us together, it might ruin my chances of going. Our farewell was short, almost curt. We shook hands, embraced, and that was it.

When I reached the station, Dr. O was waiting for me at the entrance. He was not traveling with the team but had told everyone he would be there to see them off. It was only later that I understood why he insisted on coming in person. When he saw me, he patted me on the shoulder and drew me close. "Everything will be fine as long as you manage to cross the border," he whispered in my ear, careful not to be overheard. In my excitement, I did not comprehend the significance of what he was saying and hardly wondered what he meant by "everything will be fine."

"Thank God you are here"—I heard the voice of Coach Uncle Mitke behind me. He explained that two of the selected players had to drop out at the last minute. He appeared surprised at this, although he knew, as we all did, the real reason they had to cancel the trip. They were either considered politically unsuitable or injured.

I know now that one of the players could not travel because of his injury, but I never found out why the other player was prevented from going. Perhaps he was from a family similar to mine.

* * *

The team was to travel on a group passport with the photographs of all the players affixed to the front, which was entrusted to the commissar and closely guarded by him. The commissar was not from our club, nor did he have any connection to the sport—essentially, he was a police officer with instructions to keep an eye on the team and to report anything that could be construed as subversive or unbecoming of communist youth. At that time in Yugoslavia, every group traveling abroad was assigned one or two commissars, and that was a rule common to all communist countries.

One could always spot them by the way they dressed: They wore white shirts buttoned all the way up, no tie, dark blue stripy suits, black shoes, and leather overcoats. They were more influential than the coaches themselves and demanded absolute obedience from every single member of the traveling team. They pulled the strings; anyone who said the wrong thing or made a reckless move of any kind had to answer to the commissar.

Coach Uncle Mitke explained to the trip leader and commissar that I would be replacing one of the missing players. I handed over the photographs. The commissar looked down the list, found the injured player's name, pulled his photo and inserted my picture instead. It took a moment to realize that he had omitted to write my name next to the picture. That is how I ended up traveling under someone else's name. I would never have been allowed across the border under my own name. I was not a member of the Communist Youth, my father was a former convict, and he was not a member of the Communist Party.

There was no doubt that this had all been a part of Dr. O's plan. He employed his brilliant judgment of people and situations to help me get on that train. When he saw that the commissar had omitted to note down my name on the passport, he whispered in my ear, "You are a child of fortune."

I was confused. "But he didn't even ask for my name."

Dr. O gave me a stern look. "Shut up, don't be stupid."

There would be no evidence I had ever left Yugoslavia, as there would be none that I entered America a few years later. I set out into the world under someone else's name, then assumed yet another—my real name remained in my memories of childhood, with my parents and friends in my hometown of Belgrade, which still keeps the memory of Dobrivoje Tanasijević-Bata, a youth who left it hiding behind the name of an injured player who was not able to travel and continued his life as Dan Tana.

7

Journey Into the Unknown

Belgrade railway station was crowded on that hot summer night. I found myself in the swarm of people jostling on the platforms alongside the trains, their locomotives engulfed in steam, heading for mysterious destinations. Suitcases stood everywhere, along with piles of boxes tied with string and traveling bags bursting at the seams. Their owners made for an eclectic mix, dressed in overcoats and fashionable hats or peasant attire, in headscarves or caps with chickens and piglets in tow.

As I waited to board the train with the rest of the players, the commissar approached me and put his arm around me. My heart beat faster.

"Coach Uncle Mitke is very happy that you have joined the squad," he said in a surprisingly pleasant voice. "I didn't get a chance to meet your parents earlier. I need some details about you and your family, but we have time. It's a long way to the border." He patted me on the back and led the way onto the train. Dr. O's words boomed through my head, "Everything will be fine . . . once you cross the border."

Our squad was assigned an entire car with several compartments. The trip leader separated us into groups, deciding who was going to be seated where. As we noisily settled ourselves in, the piercing sound of the locomotive signaled that the train was about to leave.

We all rushed to the windows, waving and shouting goodbyes to those who'd come to see us off.

Following an old Serbian custom, they splashed water on the train and the tracks from bottles brought especially for that purpose. The tradition holds that sprinkling water after those departing helps their journey pass and washes away any difficulties on their arrival. I was waving too, although my parents were not at the station. However, I did not feel deserted. I knew why they were not there and just how difficult the decision to stay away had been for them.

In fact, I felt elated. When the train finally moved, I could not contain my tears. This was it! We were on our way!

* * *

One of the older crew members was assigned to each compartment and I was somewhat dismayed to see the commissar settling himself in ours. He looked ordinary, unremarkable, but the type who enjoyed his work and the power that came with it. It was easy to see he relished the dread his position elicited from others, but I noticed that at certain moments he looked confused, even frightened. I realized this must be his first trip abroad too.

Our team included twenty-one players and nine members of the supporting team. We called them *technical directors*. The commissar was at the top of the pecking order as a representative of the state, there to protect us from the influence of the wicked West. Then there were officials from the Soccer Association we all knew: The trip leader in charge of logistics and finances, who like the commissar, had no connection to soccer and probably got the job because he could speak a foreign language and the team physician, Dr. Polak.

The squad also naturally included Coach Uncle Mitke and his assistants: fitness coach, goalkeeping coach, physiotherapist, first equipment man, but also another man we'd never seen before. He was introduced to us as the second equipment man. He would later turn out to be anything but.

The players were from all over Belgrade, selected from different youth teams in the city. I knew only three of them well—Pop, Charlie, and Raka. Once on the train, I met the others: Gidra, Lefty, Dambo, Aca—nicknamed Baron Munchausen—Milos the Schnoz, Mile the Dumbo, and Misha-pig. Charlie got his nickname because he was imitating Charlie Chaplin, Pop got his name because his father was an orthodox priest, Schnoz had a big nose, Dumbo had a big ear, Baron Munchausen got his nickname because he liked to make up stories . . .

We got to know each other by these nicknames and that is how it stayed—few of us knew anyone's surname except, of course, the commissar, who knew everything. The commissar soon acquired his own nickname—Stooley, after his job. We even called him that openly in front of him, but he had no idea who we were talking about. The phrase "stool pigeon" wasn't in the vocabulary of people who hadn't seen Hollywood films.

Less than an hour into our journey all one could hear was the rustling of paper as everyone unwrapped various bags: cold meats, sausages, tomatoes, pickles, chicken slices, and the inevitable onions. Long journeys stimulated the appetite and made one peckish. Serbs were known to eat well when traveling, enduring the ordeal by munching their way through the mountain of food they brought along.

The train sped through the night. It was pitch black outside, with lights flickering only occasionally from a faraway town or flooding the compartment on those rare occasions when the train approached a station and stopped to collect passengers emerging from the shadows beyond a starkly lit platform. We were good kids, if a bit intimidated by the many warnings and instructions issued by our parents and coaches in the run-up to whatever awaited us in a new and very different country.

* * *

We were still in Yugoslav territory a few hours later when the commissar came back to our compartment, having completed a round of the whole car. He said in a quiet voice that he wanted a word. We stepped into the corridor and he went straight to the point.

"I told you at the station that I'd be needing some information from you. Tell me about your family . . . Who are they? What do they do?"

I knew there were things it was unwise to mention. My heart pounding, I made an effort to respond truthfully but carefully omitted certain key details. I did my best to appear nonchalant in recounting my story and was, judging by the commissar's demeanor, succeeding. He seemed pleased with my responses.

"Thank you for cooperating so fully. And now listen carefully. I've explained all this to your teammates already, but you were not at that meeting. You need to stay together at all times. Never venture anywhere alone because there are many defectors and political undesirables who might try to kidnap you."

He paused for effect, looking straight into my eyes and continued in a grave, conspiratorial tone. "If you hear anyone speaking Serbo-Croat who is not part of our group, ignore them, do not speak to them. And if you hear or see anything suspicious, inform me immediately." Satisfied that I understood the gravity of his message, his demeanor changed, and he added softly, "You seem to be a serious, dependable young man. Dr. O pointed you out to me. He said you were a brilliant youth leader in Red Star."

He gave me a wink and added gleefully, "You see, I know a bit about you after all. You know the rules of SKOJ, stick to them."

I returned to my seat, pondering the exchange. So this was what Dr. O meant when he urged me to lie low until I was across the border. He'd anticipated this interrogation and did what he could to prepare me for it.

The second equipment man joined the trip leader and the commissar in their rounds of the compartments, and a few times tried to join in the boys' conversations, but it soon became apparent that he didn't know much about sport. We thought that odd for an equipment man, but nobody paid him much attention—it was the other ones we were wary of.

We didn't talk much about what awaited us in Belgium. And what could we have said anyway? All we knew about the country was where it featured on the map.

Our main topic was the latest soccer season. Red Star had won the Yugoslav Championship for the first time in the club's history in 1951, due to the catastrophic collapse by Dinamo from Zagreb, who had a five-point lead in the last three rounds of the championship but squandered their advantage.

At one point, Dr. Polak butted into our conversation with a remark about former star Aca-Bus, complaining about how we at Red Star sent Aca-Bus to Arsenal and Herbert Chapman to teach the English how to play soccer. "In his prime, Aca was the best player in the world," the doctor said. "Had he stayed at Red Star, you would have won the championship much sooner!"

The truth was that Aca-Bus had simply disappeared five years earlier, when Red Star played in Trieste. He was one of the first players to defect from Yugoslavia; later there'd be many more. He was why the Communist authorities started assigning a commissar to every group going abroad to compete.

I spent most of my time with the three friends I'd known from before the trip: Pop, Charlie, and Raka. I told them about the characters who frequented my father's restaurant, famous basketball players (Borislav Stanković, Radomir Šaper, and Aleksandar Gec). At that time basketball wasn't that popular in Yugoslavia, and we naturally gravitated more toward soccer. I also told them about my school in the village and the American pilot who got stuck in the mulberry tree.

They found my stories amusing, but also a bit outlandish—they were city kids and could no more imagine life in the village than that of the country's top brass.

One of them asked about my friend, Perica American. I said I hadn't seen much of him in the past year, as I'd been in Montenegro. Pop also knew Perica American and was telling us about what he'd been up to in the interval when the commissar entered our compartment, looking alarmed. "The second equipment man told me that you were talking about some American policeman?"

I could not believe our conversation had reached him so quickly! I was taken into the corridor to "have a chat." I explained that we had been talking about Perica Radenković, a good friend since we met at Red Star as fourteen-year-olds, but whom I hadn't seen in a while. I assured him he was not American at all, and certainly not a policeman.

I said that his father was a renowned musician who had traveled to New York in 1939, just before the outbreak of World War II, to represent the Kingdom of Yugoslavia at the World Exhibition. The war erupted while they were still there, and they could not return home.

Perica American had been left at home in the care of his grandparents and hadn't seen his mom and dad for over thirteen years. He got the nickname because of the packages they kept sending him from New York after the war.

The commissar gave my explanation his full attention and every now and again jotted down something in his notebook. It was obvious he found my story suspicious. When I finished, he snapped the notebook shut and sent me back into the compartment, then called Pop over to ask him the same questions. Fortunately, Pop repeated the same tale.

It was a stroke of luck that Pop knew Perica's background and could corroborate my story because that bought me a bit of trust with the commissar. The commissar could have kicked me off the train because of Perica's nickname alone.

When we finally reached the border with Hungary I felt far from calm, but I willed myself to appear so. The Yugoslav border guards ordered us to disembark and line up for a roll call. One of them started calling out names. "Milan Petrović"—Gidra responded with "here." "Nikola Todorović"—Schnoz raised his hand. "Dragan Jovanović"—Gagi responded. "Milos Petrović"—nothing. Silence.

"Milos Petrović," the guard repeated, louder this time.

The commissar turned to me. "Bata, can't you hear?"

I suddenly realized that this was the name I was meant to respond to, so I quickly raised my hand and said "Here!" The guard looked at my face closely, then moved his gaze to the group passport in his hand and then back to my face again. After what felt like an eternity, he nodded and resumed the roll call. I felt a huge surge of relief. All was well.

We were ordered back on the train. Once safely back in my seat I muttered under my breath: "There you go Dr. O, I've done it."

* * *

I'd always imagined the border to be as high as the Great Wall of China, and going through it filled me with the kind of excitement that came from scoring goals and winning trophies. But what I had never experienced before was the magnificent sense of freedom this simple act gave me.

The conditions in Yugoslavia were so strict that even those in the top echelons of the Communist Party were unable to acquire passports or necessary permits to travel. Only the chosen few were trusted enough to have the privilege of free movement and could do what I had just done.

The Hungarian border guards seemed as crude and loutish as their Yugoslav counterparts, but this time I was ready and raised my hand the instant they called my assumed name. Everything went smoothly, and we were soon speeding through Hungary, which looked disappointingly like our own country. The towns and villages we passed through appeared run-down, with crumbling roads and dilapidated buildings swathed in flags and banners proclaiming communist achievements.

At the railway station in Budapest, a Hungarian officer boarded our train and then, without explanation or warning, the station staff separated our car from the rest and moved us to a different track. We were then pulled slowly out of the station, until the train jolted to a halt a few minutes later and we found ourselves surrounded by old, broken-down train carriages and bits of abandoned equipment. Nobody knew what was happening. Even the commissar looked nervous.

Our car remained stationary for the next couple of hours. We were not allowed off the train, so we sat and waited in apprehension. Left to our own devices, we quickly came up with a worst-case scenario: We were detained because of the quarrel between Tito and Stalin and the enmity between our two countries. We were now in a Russian satellite state and would be punished for being Yugoslav. Dr. Polak whispered: “Do not send Serbs to Siberia!”

Two hours later it transpired that we were simply waiting for the Vienna-bound train to turn up so that we could join it to continue our journey. All that panic for nothing!

We continued the journey in high spirits typical of the aftermath of a tense situation that had reached a satisfactory conclusion. Laughing and chatting, we sped toward Austria under the ever-watchful eye of Stooley.

Hungary may have been a bit of a disappointment, but Vienna proved a revelation! The train slowly pulled into an airy, clean, and orderly station, with not a piglet in sight. In fact, the moment we'd crossed the Austrian border the world outside looked transformed. Passengers getting on and off the train in small towns along the way looked extraordinary. Most of the men were in traditional Austrian costume, with odd-looking hats perched high on their heads, short pants, and thick knitted socks. Women resembled dolls in their flowery dresses with aprons and short, puffed sleeves. We found them beautiful, but also farcical. Townsfolk sported long coats, cravats or bow ties, and top hats. To us, they looked like circus ringmasters or film characters.

But we didn't mock anyone too harshly, however strange we found the garb—we knew that if they could have seen our own clothes, they'd probably have thought them pitiful. Coach Uncle Mitke was impressed by Austria and rumbled: "If they have lost the war, God please let us lose the next one."

The journey through Austria felt short. We remained glued to the windows, elbowing one another out of the way to get a better view of the wonderful landscape. The train sped through forests, valleys, and immaculate towns and villages, their wooden houses rimmed with baskets of flowers and beautiful, picket-fenced gardens.

Both the country and its inhabitants looked surreal, like a fairy tale. Which abruptly ended when we reached West Germany and it transpired that the second equipment man had disappeared from the train. There were thirty of us on the passenger list, but only twenty-nine people presented themselves at the border. In the confusion that ensued, the dubious second equipment man was outed as an undercover informant in the employ of the commissar. The commissar and the trip leader spent hours with the border guards explaining the discrepancy. We were finally allowed to pass.

The commissar must have raged at his right hand's defection, but I suppose he was even more concerned about the punishment he was certain to receive once back in Belgrade.

The green fields of Austria gave way to the uniform gray of West Germany. We saw ruined buildings roughly patched up for habitation everywhere, just like back home. Juxtaposed to the clean, precise perfection of Austria, this presented a sad picture of a country still ravaged by a war that had ended a few years earlier. At last we reached Aachen and crossed into Belgium.

8

Last Tango in Belgium

Belgium appeared completely untouched by war. The stark difference between Belgium and Yugoslavia lay in that slogan I remembered from childhood: "Better war than the pact!" Belgians let the Germans pass through their territory without resistance, so saved their people and their country. We did not and suffered the consequences.

We were met at the station by the host delegation, and I was delighted to spot Svetislav Glišović among them. Glisha was a former Red Star coach who had won the Yugoslav Cup with the team in 1948. We met while I was part of the apprentice team of the Red Star. I had no idea what he was doing in Antwerp, but seeing a familiar face made me feel safer somehow.

He must have felt a moment of closeness too because he greeted me warmly: "So, Bata, who are in the starting eleven today?"

We stayed at a student campus in Antwerp, which was almost empty due to the summer vacation. To our eyes, everything about Antwerp was new and compelling. We moved about in groups, as the commissar had instructed. All around us well-dressed people sat in cafés or strolled around the parks, while gleaming cars glided along wide streets.

Shop windows were heaped with goods and customers had no need of ration cards to obtain them. My friends had no money to spend, so faced no dilemma whether or not to buy anything. I, on the other hand, was in real difficulty. I had those nine dollars sewn into the lining of my coat pocket (my mother saw to it that they were secure), but I didn't want to show off in front of my broke friends and the commissar. I don't know who found it tougher, them or me; at that moment I decided never to spend the nine dollars and surprise my mother when we met again.

Our encounter with this new world was more enthralling than any film. We could feel we were in a country free of communism. On our first outing we came across a brothel unashamedly open in the middle of the day! Most of us knew nothing about sex, as sex before marriage was still a taboo in the conservative society we were brought up in. In Yugoslavia, Communist authorities had closed down all the brothels after the war in a move to erase bourgeois values.

During our stay in Belgium, our team came to realize we were a good soccer side but working in terrible conditions. We played better soccer than our competitors despite not having proper shoes and official jerseys like the other teams. We played in striped blue-and-white T-shirts that were too big for us; I don't know which club they'd been scrounged from, but nobody got the right size.

Before the official start to the competition we had several practice sessions, most of them attended by officials from the Yugoslav Embassy and groups of Yugoslav émigrés. During the breaks from training, former Red Star coach Glišović and Misha, the interpreter provided by the host organizers, told us about their life in Belgium. They explained there were enough Yugoslav émigrés for three Yugoslav restaurants to be run by expatriates to operate in Brussels.

Our first game was against Antwerp and we won 2–0. Around a hundred Yugoslav supporters cheered us on with genuine enthusiasm. Their number was few, but they made up for it by being loud.

Paris won against Brussels, and we ended up in the final against Paris. We lost 3–2 and finished in second place. There was no official award ceremony immediately after the final match like we see today; instead, the winners would be announced at a party organized in their honor later that evening.

Coach Glišović and Misha the interpreter came to congratulate the players and take the technical directors out to dinner. Coach Glišović asked me if I would like to join them, but Coach Uncle Mitke interjected with an emphatic, "NO! His place is here, with the players." So, I had dinner with the players and commissar.

* * *

All four squads attended the celebratory dinner, which took place in the sports hall of a student dorm in Brussels. We sat at tables, eating, drinking, and relishing our success. At the end of the hall a gramophone with a horn was playing classical music. We were all elated. For us, the second place we had won was golden. Even the commissar seemed pleased.

After dinner, a group of pretty girls swept into the hall in a flock, probably students from another part of the campus. Their presence raised the tone notably and soon the place was ringing with chatter and joyous laughter. The music changed, and the familiar sound of a waltz made me think of Brankica and Danica and the steps we endlessly rehearsed. The French and the Belgians were not shy, they sprung to their feet and boldly approached the girls as soon as the waltz started. The dance floor quickly filled with couples.

My friends, on the other hand, sat as if tied in knots, whispering to one another and watching the dancing couples with unconcealed astonishment. None of them knew how to waltz. Nor did they know that I had taken dance lessons back home. I sat there, deliberating what to do. I realized that I was just as good a dancer as those twirling in front of me, maybe even better.

It was the first dramatic notes of the tango that finally spurred me on. "The tango is not about the steps, it is about what happens between the steps." The dance teacher had taught me well. I chose the best dancer among the girls, not the prettiest girl, not the slimmest or best dressed, but the one with the best moves. I approached her and, like a true gentleman, bowed slightly and extended my hand in silent invitation, the only option as I couldn't speak her language.

She was definitely a better dancer than me, but only she and I knew that. The two of us performed as though professional partners with years of practice. She may not have been the prettiest, but she was a damned good dancer and with every move she became more beautiful to me. My heart soared, and I lost myself in delight.

I relished every move and didn't even notice that the podium had emptied and that the other couples had moved aside to watch us. When the dance ended, I bowed to thank my partner and, with the applause ringing in my ears, went back to my table.

* * *

My friends were still clapping and hooting when I came face-to-face with the enraged commissar. He didn't waste time but put me on the spot in front of everybody about where I'd learned "that bourgeois dance."

"In Belgrade!" I responded.

"You learned it in Belgrade? Then that is where you will answer to the authorities for bringing your parents, your club, and your country into disrepute! Shame on you!"

"You must be joking; how could I have brought anyone into disrepute by dancing with a girl?"

I could not understand his fury; how could a room full of people clapping bring shame on anybody? Playing soccer or dancing the tango, what was the difference? If you did it well, it was because you knew how and if you gave your best, it was because you loved doing it. What was so wrong with it? What harm could it possibly do to my country? How could it possibly subvert the system and shame us in front of the world? I did not know that dancing was considered a political provocation.

Only later did I learn perfection provokes just by being perfect. It grates the nerves of those unable to produce it, nor conceal their envy.

Raka, Pop, and Charlie sprung to my defense, telling the commissar, "That's not right. We should all be proud of Bata. Can't you hear everyone applauding? What is so wrong with it?"

"You too will have questions to answer when we get back to Belgrade, for speaking and thinking like that," he hissed. The commissar glared, but they would not be silenced. They continued to defend me, and the more they did, the more we fell into deeper trouble.

Finally, Charlie told him with surprising calm: "Sorry, but we are currently in a democracy. We are free men and you do not rule over us here, in liberty."

My friends were a bit older than me and they knew what I did not—that the commissar had no legal power over us outside Yugoslavia. The commissar seemed thrown by resistance he had not anticipated. He kept repeating that we would continue the discussion in Belgrade until one of the guys scoffed, "And what are you going to tell them about your partner who vanished from the train in Austria?"

Our commissar, primitive and uncouth in both dress and manner, now totally lost his temper. Unable to control us here, where the laws of fear and political oppression did not apply, he turned on his heel and marched out of the hall.

The rest of the squad, uninvolved in the argument, started making fun of us for the trouble we were in. Irritated by their behavior, Raka looked at Charlie and me and said, "Let's go outside for a walk and get some fresh air. This is not fun!" As we left the hall, the last thing I heard was, "She is nice, Bata, the fatty you were dancing with. Why not take her along? You'll need a witness in Belgrade and much more."

* * *

We walked out into the quiet evening. The people strolled about, talking and laughing. Unlike us, for a dark cloud loomed over us. Raka broke the silence by softly stating what we all knew. "If we go back, we shall never leave Yugoslavia again. The commissar's word is law there. He will report everything we said to the authorities."

"And much, much more," Charlie added.

I couldn't even consider this possibility; this was my first sweet taste of the free world, and I was not prepared to let it go. Not going back home had never been part of my plan, but it looked like Raka and Charlie had it in mind all along. My dancing and the altercation with the commissar had given them the courage to act. As fate would have it, we came across a parked police car. Without any warning, Raka ran toward it, yelling hysterically, and started kicking the car.

I was stunned. Before I understood what was happening, Charlie joined him, shouting: "NO Communism! NO Tito! NO Stalin!"

I watched this performance rooted to the spot, too shocked to react. Two police officers got out of the car, saying something in Belgian. They looked bewildered, as I was myself. I vaguely felt that I was about to take a momentous step, away from the border I had crossed by dancing the tango.

Realizing we were foreigners, the police officers tried speaking to us in other languages—French and what I thought must be Flemish—but we still could not understand them. "Yugoslavia . . . Tito . . ." they repeated after us, mystified by our behavior. Then one of them opened the back door of their car and calmly motioned us in. My friends jumped in without hesitation, while I stood on the pavement, still too astonished to move. Finally, I managed to utter, "What the hell are you doing . . . ?"

"We are not going back. You can go back and dance the tango in jail," they replied excitedly.

"I'm with you!" I heard myself shout, as I raced to the back of the police car and climbed in with them. "Fear is not a freedom."

I had no idea what had come over me. But one thing was clear in all this craziness: We were not going to make the train back to Belgrade.

Part Two

Salad

9

An Accidental Fugitive

Once in the police station, the officers motioned to the bench in the corner and instructed us to wait. As we sat there quietly, they brought us tea and potato chips with mustard. We stayed silent, glancing anxiously at each other at times. I had by now resolved to stay—there was no turning back. Raka broke the silence, suddenly grinning widely. "Just think, instead of us being interrogated, it's the commissar who's in the shit now. He will be held responsible for losing the three of us and his stooge, and who knows how many more will abscond on the journey back."

We all laughed. "Aca at the Red Star will kill me for not returning the cleats he loaned me!" I joked.

"Coach Uncle Mitke was right, your place is with the players." Charlie chuckled, and we joined in, but it was a nervous laughter. We did our best to cover our trepidation by joking.

I was in no way prepared for this step. I had not planned to defect, but I understood that the situation required presence of mind. I realized that the other two guys had planned to use Belgium as a springboard to travel further afield.

Sometime around midnight, Misha the interpreter arrived at the station. He had attended the official dinner with the ambassador and technical directors and had gone home to bed afterward but was woken up by the embassy staff hunting for the three missing players. They asked him to help.

Misha had lived in Belgium since childhood, and had contacts everywhere, including the police and the courts. He was a sworn translator and knew which number to dial and who to ask and soon found where we were. He didn't inform the embassy; he wanted to hear our side of the story first. When we saw him, we thought we'd been betrayed and would be sent back to Belgrade. Fortunately, when he heard what we had to say, he decided to help us, but not before warning us about the gravity of the situation.

"Nobody knows where you are, so if you want to return to the residence halls, I'll run you back and everything will be forgotten; but if you don't want that, we have to leave here immediately. Any minute now somebody from the embassy could show up here. The cops here are confused, they have no idea who you are or why you created that ruckus earlier. If you really want to stay, we need to get you out of here straight away, then we can work out what to do next."

He looked at each of us in turn and we all confirmed we wanted to stay. Misha went over to the officers and spoke to them briefly, explaining we were lost sheep he would return to the flock presently. Then he gave us a hard stare and nodded toward the door. We bolted out, quick as lightning.

Thrilled but bewildered by this turn of events, we moved quickly through quiet streets, away from the police station, the embassy staff, and the technical directors who might be searching for us.

We didn't slow the pace until we reached a boutique hotel with a barely discernible sign: RESTAURANT AND BAR BELGRADE. The heavy door was bolted shut but we could hear muffled voices inside. Misha knocked on the door and when nobody answered, knocked again. A curtain in the small window twitched and a man peered out. The door opened. We walked into a smoke-filled room with only a handful of tables. Pictures of anti-communists—Chetnik leader Draža Mihailović and King Peter II—decorated the walls. This did nothing to put us at our ease. At a table in the corner four men were playing poker using real money, while at another the waitress was taking an order from a woman and two men so drunk they could barely keep their eyes open. Misha introduced us to the owner, Pera, who joined us at an empty table.

"They are not going back, and they need somewhere to stay tonight," Misha said.

Pera shook his head and said he had no rooms available, but that we could sleep on the chairs in the bar. He offered us plum brandy, as was the custom, but we politely declined, so he brought us tea. Gruffly, he declared that he had seen all our games at the tournament and that, to be honest, he thought we played better than the rest, but that the referees were on their side.

"You are in good hands," Pera said and then he got up and left us alone with Misha, who was already plotting our next moves.

"You can sleep here tonight, but from tomorrow we'll have to work something out. I'll check with the Catholic nuns at the monastery, they might put you up for a while. They have helped émigrés before. For the moment, focus on getting through tonight. Your teammates are traveling back tomorrow, but until then, you risk being discovered by the cops and put on a train home."

He told us we were safe at Pera's but warned us to lay low and not discuss our situation with anyone. On his way out, he said, "I have to go now, I must be up early. I have obligation to escort your squad on their departure. Pera, please no word to anyone!"

Pera nodded. "Do not worry. They are my children now."

* * *

That night we slept uncomfortably on chairs in the bar. The air was full of tobacco smoke. After everything that had happened, I hardly slept a wink but did enjoy watching the foursome playing poker. For a while I sat next to one of them who had the most money in front of him. His name was Nikola.

The next afternoon Misha appeared to say that our squad had left and that, thanks to God, the nuns had agreed to help us. We had to respect their rules: times for breakfast, lunch, and dinner, 6 P.M. Mass, 10 P.M. curfew. He also asked us to hand over our passports and was surprised when we told him we didn't have any.

He took us to the monastery, and we faced the first problem. The nuns insisted that he must tell the police about us otherwise we wouldn't be able to stay. He took our full names and dates of birth and went to the police straight away. On his way back, he bought us the essentials: a change of underwear, toothbrushes, and such, as all we had were the clothes on our backs. He also brought a paper from the police. The nuns were satisfied, and they showed us our new rooms.

As we settled down, we sat around the table and Misha gravely explained. "You have been reported to the police as refugees. Soon we can sort out the paperwork. You have to declare yourself political exiles seeking asylum to UNHCR (the United Nations High Commissioner for Refugees). You must convince them that if you are returned to Yugoslavia, you will be imprisoned. The commissar's fury and bourgeois dancing will not cut it with them. We need more serious reasons."

"Do not worry, we have many, many!" we offered loudly.

I immediately mentioned that my father had been imprisoned a couple of times and Misha jumped at the opportunity this information provided.

We had no idea what UNHCR was. I was frightened; the adventure so far had been almost enjoyable, but now, as I listened to

Misha, it dawned on me that we were playing a serious game. To win this time, I had to play my best yet. "Their agents will ask you lots of questions," Misha continued. "You must say that you are against Communism and that you strongly believe in God and more—otherwise they'll send you back."

Over the next couple of days, Misha prepared us for the interview. He combed through our biographies and adapted them to fit the tales we were going to tell the UNHCR officers, making them as authentic as possible. This frank discussion with Misha exposed the fact that my friends had planned to defect all along. Raka disclosed that he had an uncle in Australia and pulled out a scrap of paper from a secret pocket in his pants with his uncle's address on it. Charlie said that he had a friend in Brazil. I had no one outside of Yugoslavia.

But what nobody considered at the time, and what became vital to our attempt to stay in Belgium, was that we were all underage. According to Belgian law, as minors we required guardians, sponsors who in cases like ours were usually chosen from the emigrants, Belgian residents who were financially stable. Misha explained that once we had sponsors, we could apply for official permission to stay.

Had Misha not turned up to help us, I have no doubt we would have ended up under guard on the train back to Belgrade. He also told us that besides the police, Pera the restaurant owner, Nikola the card player, and a soccer fan named Mate knew where we were staying.

On the following weekend Misha took us to visit the Serbian Orthodox church, where he introduced us to the priests and local Serbian community. They looked at us like we had fallen from the sky. Misha and Pera spread the word about our need for the guardians.

Then, out of nowhere came a visit from coach Svetislav Glišović. We talked for a couple of hours about Belgrade, soccer, our decision to stay, and his life in exile. Glišović had made the move long before us. A professional soccer player for years before the war, he was an attacking player for BSK, playing among the great stars of the Yugoslav national squad of the period. He originally came to Belgium intending to work as a coach, but BFA rules banned foreigners from working as pro coaches for two years.

Currently he was listed as a manager on the roster of the famous soccer agent Julius Ukraińczyk, who acted as a mediator between players, coaches, and clubs across Europe. At the time we met him in Brussels, Glišović was training an amateur team from Brussels while waiting for a coaching position to open for him in Greece. The team was competing in the amateur league. He suggested that the three of us could join the training sessions with the team, which we gladly accepted.

He knew FIFA's unfair regulations banned any player or coach who defected from the communist countries without a release from their home club and a permit from their National soccer association from playing professionally anywhere in the free world for two years. But he contended that this regulation might not apply to us as underage players without contracts.

Glišović was kind to us. He had a particularly soft spot for me, maybe because he knew me from before. We went back to his apartment several times, where I met his wife and teenage daughter.

The week passed by. Misha had a volunteer who was willing to sponsor me, but we were still missing two. The next weekend he took us to the Orthodox Church again. The two priests really wanted to help us, but they were bothered by the fact that we were staying with the Catholic nuns. Another priest, an older one, scolded them. "Shame on us. Catholic nuns welcomed them to their monastery, and we are having a problem finding them guardians." In the next few days we had more than two guardians.

Finally, we were able to go to the UNHCR offices with our guardians. The first question they asked was whether we were members of the Communist Party. Misha protested that we were too young. "Communist Youth?" I said that I was not a member. The other two had to admit they were. But my friends said they had signed up because they were forced to under the threat of punishment.

After a thorough interrogation over a couple of hours, we were free to go. We would be informed of the UNHCR's decision in due course.

* * *

Time passed, and Belgrade felt ever more distant. We were still in the monastery waiting for the paperwork to be done when Misha showed up with Mate Kirigen, another familiar face. Mate had attended our training sessions and matches in Antwerp and Brussels. During that visit, Misha was informed that the nuns needed the space that we were occupying. Mate immediately said that he could provide room and board and employ us at the mine in Liège (Seraing) that he was managing.

As the manager of the mine and an ex-soccer player, Mate welcomed us warmly, like his sons. He even found us an apartment to stay in close to the mine and paid for it. In exchange, we helped fill his shortage of miners. We spent two weeks in that hole in the ground as apprentice miners. We dug coal, loaded the carts, pushed them up and down the track, and knocked in supporting beams to secure the roof of the shaft.

It was extremely hard work. The stifling heat and dust made it difficult to breathe. At the end of every day, we were covered in soot, only our teeth gleaming white in our blackened faces. After two weeks, though, we received work certificates stating, "Professional Miner." We also had some money, enough to leave Liège and return to Brussels. By September we had the necessary documents confirming our refugee status and were in receipt of UNHCR aid.

My friends and I were stateless émigrés with no passports, but these temporary documents allowed us to stay or leave Belgium if we wished to. Only I stayed, albeit briefly. I saw my friends only a few more times, the last just a few days before they emigrated from Belgium. Raka set off for Australia as he had planned all along, and Charlie ventured to Brazil. I'll always be indebted to them for taking my life in a direction I never would have on my own, changing my destiny forever.

With my friends gone, I spent much of my time with Nikola, the card player I'd met our first night hiding out in Pera's bar. Nikola had been forced to flee Yugoslavia in 1945, after the country had been overtaken by Tito's Partisans and the Russian army. At our first meal he told me how much he missed home, how he had spent four years in the mountains and forests of Serbia fighting Germans and later Communists. He boasted he had been a boxer and wrestler. He had also spent five years in the Foreign Legion and had many stories from the African continent.

He was currently taking a two-year break but was planning to rejoin the Legion. He had a lovely apartment in Brussels and let me stay in one of his rooms. We spent hours together, talking about past times. I was captivated by his stories from the Legion. He also bragged how great a poker player he was and about his love life. He used to say, "If my mustache could talk, you would hear much more!"

I soaked up his every word. "Getting into the Foreign Legion is tough," he said. "The tests are grueling but quite apart from physical strength, you need mental stamina. You commit to keeping clean, learning French, and acting honorably. You can no longer steal or lie! You have to be a bit crazy to want to join. But once you get in, you cease to be what you were; you leave the past behind, along with all the burden you've accumulated in life. You are a soldier in the best army in the world."

Nikola took me twice a week to the training sessions of the amateur club that Glišović coached before he left for Greece. While watching, I worried that I was getting further and further away from soccer. I hung around émigré haunts in Brussels, listening to them recount their experiences of immigrant life. I learned there were different organizations through which it was possible to emigrate to Australia or Canada legally. Reaching America was much more difficult; they were very choosy about who they would admit.

To me all those options sounded farfetched, but I knew unless I sorted myself out soon, I would have to attempt one of them.

* * *

Then I learned that my old club Red Star was playing a friendly game against Anderlecht in Brussels. I told Nikola about it and he could see how keen I was to go. He warned me it could be dangerous; they might try to kidnap me and bring me home.

Once again, I found myself facing political manipulation of the sort I knew well. On the train, the commissar had warned us off associating with Yugoslav émigrés, claiming they might kidnap us, and here my guardian was saying the same about the people from my beloved club! He was right to worry, it was well known that secret police agents tagged along with all the clubs playing abroad.

But I was determined to see my team play. I loved the way they played the game and the desire to see them again outweighed the fear of being captured. I heard Nikola's warnings and saw the concern etched across his face, but in the end, there was no dissuading me. And seeing that, he decided to come too and even bought us tickets to the best seats in the stadium. He invited along Pera and two trusty friends, just in case there was trouble. It was something to see—me, walking to the stadium with a posse of four burly men.

Red Star played brilliantly. At the end of the first half, they were leading 5–0. We had seats right above the tunnel to the changing rooms. The stadium was buzzing; there was quite a crowd considering it was a friendly match. At halftime, as the players headed to the tunnel, Rajko Mitić looked up and saw me hanging from the terraces. He could not believe his eyes.

"I thought you were still in Montenegro?" he shouted, incredulous.

"NO! I live here now," I yelled back.

"I'll see you in the second half," he shouted.

In my excitement, I leaned so far out that Nikola had to put his arms around me to stop me from falling over. He held me, his eyes scanning the area, looking for Yugoslav agents. Tomašević, the Party secretary at Red Star, was behind Rajko and when he saw me, he shouted at him furiously: "What are you doing talking to that trouble? He is a traitor!"

He tried to pull Rajko away, but Rajko shook off his grip. Branko "Stane" Stanković (nickname Ambassador) and Dragan Džajić also stopped to say hello. Nikola and his friends were impressed when they saw me talking with superstar players who knew me by name and who were happy to see me there.

At the end of the game I briefly saw Rajko, Stane, and several other players. I told them about the tango and Rajko said that instead of dancing the tango I should've danced Russian kozachok. He was determined to help me.

"You'll get a call from the people at Anderlecht. I put in a word for you. Where can they contact you in Brussels?"

Nikola answered for me. "They had best come to the restaurant Belgrade and ask Pera the owner, he'll know where to find us."

Sure enough, a couple of days later, the management of Anderlecht got in touch, inviting me to their offices for a chat. I took part in a couple of training sessions and played in two practice matches, and to my great delight, I was offered a contract with Anderlecht by an associate of the famous sports agent, Julius Ukraińczyk, who ended up representing me from then on.

* * *

I signed a four-year contract with Anderlecht worth $4,000, plus wages and bonuses. They gave me $2,000 in Belgian currency straight away, and I would get the rest after I played in twenty league and Cup games.

We had a good team, the best in Belgium at the time, and the club was happy with my performances in the first six games (two in the Cup and four in the league). For a brief moment, it felt like my dream had come true. I had a contract, I had money, and I was playing soccer. But the devil never sleeps and a month or so later the Belgian Soccer Association informed Anderlecht that they were in breach of FIFA rules and would be penalized if they continued to play me.

Anderlecht had the right to sign me, but they were not supposed to let me play in competitive games for two years because I did not have permission from Red Star and the Yugoslav Soccer Association, which was authorized to issue permits only to those who had done national service and were over twenty-six years old.

I tried to explain that I was never offered a contract by Red Star because I was still a junior. People in Anderlecht took the view that I did not need a release from my former club because I was under eighteen and had no formal contract with them. They were overruled by FIFA.

My agent, Julius Ukraińczyk, offered Anderlecht three options to resolve my situation. The first was that I stay put and play only in friendly games for two years. The second option was for me to be loaned for eighteen months to Hanover 96, where I could play—they were in the British zone of occupied Germany and therefore outside FIFA jurisdiction. They were also looking for an attacking right-footed midfield player like me and prepared to pay the same wages as my contract with Anderlecht.

The third option was to play for the team put together by Julius Ukraińczyk. He had assembled a team of refugees from communist countries, all excellent players, who could not play legally for any other European club. The team took part in friendly games and practice matches in Italy, Spain, and France. It was mostly made up of older, more experienced players, many of whom had been stars in their own countries before going into exile.

Their games against Spanish, French, and Italian teams were routinely watched by thirty thousand to forty thousand spectators. Ukraińczyk had a special arrangement with the clubs and received a percentage of the gate receipts. He used these earnings to pay the players, so everyone was taken care of. Once the ban expired, many of them were snapped up by big European clubs like Roma, Barcelona, and Real Madrid.

Ukraińczyk was a remarkably capable soccer agent and had charisma to match—he spoke eleven languages fluently and looked handsome, tall, and immaculately dressed. He liked me and offered to take me on but he admitted that, considering my age, there was little chance of me getting a spot in a lineup full of such excellent, mature players.

He advised Anderlecht to keep me active, to keep me playing because I was still developing. He suggested Hanover 96 as his preferred option. "Soccer is not on the same level as in the other unoccupied European countries," he said, "but you'll get a chance to play and improve your game."

I knew this was one of the most important, decisive moments in my life. In my frustration at how things had turned out in Anderlecht, I even considered packing it all in and scurrying home. But I would be returning as a black sheep, with no profession and no career. Nikola suggested that I should go, and if I was not happy there, I could come back. Good advice.

I decided to go to Hanover, stay there for a season and a half while waiting for the ban to expire, then return to Anderlecht and continue where I left off. And so I took another leap into an unknown future.

10

Stateless

A few days before my departure, I was in my room when Nikola rushed in to tell me breathlessly that he was off to Marseilles. The Legion was calling, and he was to depart immediately.

I was surprised by this sudden turn of events, but before I could think through the implications, he was packed and at the door, ready to leave. We said our farewells fondly, like father and son. I thanked him for everything he had done for me and he promised he'd stay in touch to find out how I was doing in Hanover.

"Leave the key with Pera in Belgrade," he said before the door slammed shut and he was gone.

The day before my own departure, I went to the bank to draw some money for the journey. Pera came with me but when we arrived, I was in for a shock. My bank account was almost empty! Pera helped me explain to the bank clerk that my account should have quite a bit more in it than two hundred dollars, but the clerk just shrugged his shoulders and pointed to some papers he had in front of him.

I couldn't understand what had happened. As my guardian, Nikola was a countersignatory on my account and all withdrawals required both our signatures. I asked to see the check that was cashed, and when the clerk produced it and I saw that it had two signatures on it, I realized that my actual signature was on the check. He had forged my signature and I had been conned.

I could not even draw the tiny balance left in the account, as Nikola was not there to countersign my request. I was hurt but took it stoically. Why should anything be easy in life?

Julius had paid for my train ticket to Hanover, first class, so I resolved to go. Only Pera was there to see me off at the station. I gave him the key to Nikola's apartment and we said our goodbyes. One last time he tried to convince me to stay in Belgium. As he was taking his leave he said encouragingly, "Go, teach the Germans how to play soccer!" before disappearing in the crowd.

I was left standing on the concourse, holding my suitcase, feeling a bit lost. I had very little money in my pocket and was on my way to West Germany from where everyone else was trying to emigrate, including the Germans. I boarded the train and set out into the unknown.

It didn't take long for the train to reach the border with West Germany. I passed through the checkpoints at the Belgian side easily enough, but when I showed my UNHCR travel document at the West German side, I was met with shaking heads of officers exclaiming in unison, "*Nein! Nein! Passaporte! Passaporte!*" I must have looked confused, looking at them blankly, because they started mixing in a bit of French. "*Pas bon, pas bon . . .*"

To my dismay, I finally realized they were saying my papers were not valid and that I had to return to Brussels! There was apparently a train to take me back to Belgium in a couple of hours. Two officers escorted me to a room that looked more like a waiting room than an office and instructed me to wait there. I sat and waited. I was young, but I had by then become accustomed to the privations of life; not much could throw me off balance completely. Nevertheless, troubling thoughts filled my head. My journey looked like it was over before it had begun, a worrying prospect considering I had nowhere to return to.

As I sat there waiting, officers in different uniforms came and went, none of them paying any attention to me. After a while, I noted that the officers who had taken me off the train were no longer around. About two hours into my wait, I heard the whistle of a train and saw it pulling into the station in a cloud of white steam. It came to a stop on the same platform my train to Hanover had done earlier. Without really thinking about it, I took a deep breath, grabbed my suitcase, and without looking around, walked out of the room. Outside on the platform, I checked the departure board, which said that the train I was about to board was bound for Munich.

I hadn't the faintest idea where Munich was in respect to Hanover, but the train seemed to be heading in the right general direction. I closed my eyes and mumbled into my chest, "Come on, Bata, let's get you to Hanover."

* * *

The train was picking up speed as I made my way along the narrow corridor, looking for a free seat. Long army coats hanging from the coat rack in one of the compartments caught my eye and I saw it was occupied by four young men in uniform who seemed in a jolly mood. The two remaining seats were empty, so I walked in with a smile and nodded in greeting.

It wasn't long before my fellow travelers and I started a conversation of sorts, despite not having a language in common. It was not easy, but two of them were Polish and knew a bit of Russian, so we could understand each other relatively well. In the beginning they seemed baffled by my questions about where the train was heading and where Munich was in respect to Hanover and gesticulated wildly while explaining that the two cities were on the opposite sides of Germany.

But they said not to worry, that there would be a station coming up ahead where I could change trains and still make it to Hanover.

They were very friendly, one of them even offering me his seat by the window because it was closer to the heater. Like many times before, a mere mention of soccer and Red Star did its trick of breaking down barriers and we were soon engaged in a lively discussion. The Polish guys each bragged about their favorite team—one supported Legia FC from Warsaw and the other Visla FC from Krakow—and were curious about my soccer history.

I told them about playing for Anderlecht and my plan to go to Hanover. They seemed impressed with my sports exploits and connections, but I was more interested in them and their story.

I noticed a large letter "A" and other insignia on their uniforms. They confirmed it was the insignia of the American army volunteers. They too had emigrated to Germany from their home country to join the American army as volunteers. They were now paid like professional soldiers and what's more, after five years of service they had the choice of going to live in America or staying in the army until retirement. It was my turn to be impressed.

Once they realized I was a professional soccer player, they grew excited and shouted over each other to tell me about the American army soccer club in Munich, boasting that a former Legia FC player was in the team. I liked the sound of that! They suggested that instead of going to Hanover I continue with them to Munich and do as they had done, join the army, and luckily play for the US soccer team! They made it sound easy, even promising to take me to the army recruitment center, which, they insisted, was right opposite the Munich railway station.

"Forget Hanover, this is a much better deal."

They were fired up.

My interest was piqued when one of them said, no doubt referring to my love of Hollywood and my desire to live in America, "Getting a visa for America is hard. Army service is the quickest and the easiest way to get it."

This was really worth considering. I was seventeen years old; in five years I would be twenty-two. If I'd stayed in Yugoslavia, I would have been conscripted into the army for at least two years, or three in the navy, and would not be able to play soccer at all in all that time. Playing in Hanover now seemed like a waste of time, treading water instead of getting closer to my dreams.

That thought made up my mind. The prospect of legally living and working in America clinched it for me. On impulse, I decided that going to Munich and joining the American army was the best option after all—I could complete the army service, receive all the benefits my new friends mentioned, and best of all, I could play soccer while doing it. My American dream seemed to be inching closer.

* * *

Because I was sitting with the soldiers in the same car, the conductor never checked my ticket, which stated that I was on my way to Hanover. I could continue my journey further but there would be problems in Munich because on the exit they would notice that I'd arrived at the wrong place.

The soldiers offered to help.

As the train pulled into the station one of them took my suitcase and the other gave me his army coat and cap to put on. Then they placed my ticket in between theirs and gave them all to one of the soldiers to show at the exit point. The ticket collector looked tired and bored. He saw we were in a group and checked the number of tickets but did not look closer at each one. He assumed they were all for the same destination and let us through without a second look.

When we came out of the station, my new friends did as they promised and took me to the recruitment center, which was indeed opposite the station. We wished each other good luck and they left me to my fate.

At the recruitment center I was assigned a translator, a strictly officious Yugoslav woman who listened impassively as I explained my case. She had a look of someone who had heard it all before. She explained her role was to help me sort out the papers, but when I handed her my UNHCR permit she said she could do nothing with it, that the document was valid only in Belgium and was completely useless here in Germany.

More alarming, she also informed me that the American army was not accepting volunteers at that time.

But there was hope. The army would be recruiting again soon, in a month or so, and there was a list of those waiting to join. There were two Ukrainian guys who were in the same boat as me and they were going to Nuremberg, where they would be staying while waiting for the call from the recruiting center.

She advised me to go with them. I must have looked confused, because she added that there was a refugee center in Nuremberg called Valka Lager, where those without papers could live and eat free of charge while their cases were being processed.

"When you get there, tell them you have escaped Yugoslavia recently, hiding under a train. I've heard of cases like that. Forget that you've ever lived in Belgium—do not mention it. You'll stay at the camp for a month or two, until UNHCR issues you new papers. Keep your old document, but don't show it to anyone, even once you receive new papers. Americans know where you are, they have all your details and will find you as soon as the new round of recruitment starts."

She added with something resembling a sad face, "I wish you good luck, young man."

* * *

Another train, another chapter of my life unfolding. This time it was taking me across Germany to Nuremberg. I thought back to how I got here: the mad departure from Belgrade, my émigré life in Belgium, then the aborted trip to a country still under military rule and now, here I was on my way to a refugee camp.

I was grateful for the terminally boring Russian language lessons now—my basic Russian was of more use to me in my new surroundings than French I'd picked up in Belgium. Although we were seemingly in similar circumstances, my Ukrainian fellow travelers' lives and mine had different trajectories—they were in search of a better life, while all I wanted to do was play soccer.

Regardless of what fate had in store for us later, for the moment we were all on our way to the camp.

In Nuremberg, we were picked up by an American army jeep and driven to the camp. We drove at breakneck speed through a city that looked at once disheveled and glorious. There were imposing buildings in German brutalist style, but also charming cottages lining the canals in the old center. Then, as we left the city, the driver pointed out huge terraces from which he said Hitler had given speeches before the war.

The camp sprawled across a vast area on the outskirts of the city, with rows of wooden barracks stretching as far as the eye could see. The wire fence that once encircled the huge compound had been removed years before, but everything else was probably just as it had been during the war, when it operated as a prisoner-of-war camp. I found it fascinating to observe later that nobody left the camp perimeter, although there was nothing to stop them.

We were taken to the main camp building, where we were registered and assigned living quarters. Remembering the advice from the interpreter lady in Munich to avoid mentioning my stay in Belgium altogether, I hid my meager knowledge of French and asked for a Yugoslav interpreter. A short while later, a tall man appeared and said he was there to help me fill out the forms. He noted down my name, date and place of birth, and other particulars, but seemed particularly interested in my nationality and religion.

Interview done, they issued me a bag with a blanket and some sheets and sent me to find the designated barrack. I said goodbye to my Ukrainian friends and set out in search of my new "home."

The camp seemed to encompass the whole of Eastern Europe. There were people from all walks of life; émigrés, political defectors, and criminals of all shades, speaking different languages and following different customs. A single aim united them, however—to leave behind the camp and forget the communal cauldron as quickly as they could.

Each barrack in this makeshift city of barracks housed forty to sixty people, and the camp was divided into blocks arranged by nationality. There were Hungarian barracks, Croatian, Ukrainian, Polish, and so on. I was assigned to barrack no. 47, one of the two housing Serbs. Room no. 4 in barrack 47.

It took me a while to find the Serbian quarters in the maze of wooden dwellings, and when I finally located my room, I found it empty. It was a tiny space, no more than ten feet across, with a big window and two bunk beds on each side. All the beds were made except one on the right, which had a rolled-up mattress and some bedding piled on it. I assumed that was intended for me. The mattress was stained and smelled moldy, and the sheets I'd been given at the reception were threadbare and worn out, but at least they were clean. I made the bed and tucked my little suitcase under it, then sat down to gather my thoughts.

I slowly exhaled and counted to ten before taking another breath, as I had been taught to do before big games. Cutting through the chaos of thoughts, emotions, and recriminations swirling through my head, I had to come to terms with my new environment. But there was no denying I felt miserable. Looking around, I noticed inscriptions carved into the paneled surfaces around the bed and drawings on the walls: poems, hearts, and messages of love and loss.

Later I noticed them in all the other rooms and corridors in the camp; the whole place was full of the echoes of former prisoners of war. To this day, whenever I see graffiti on the walls of cities I am traveling through, I am reminded of the inscriptions on the walls of the Valka Lager camp in Nuremberg.

Misery soon turned to anger. I was annoyed at myself. I thought I had made a terrible mistake and more than anything, I longed to go back home. I wanted to see Belgrade again, taste my mother's cooking once more, and hear Rubi tell me how I should find a hot Hungarian or Romanian girl. I yearned for those carefree times when my biggest problem was Aca the equipment man scolding me for putting the cleats in the wrong place.

Still, as much as I was consumed by longing for home, I knew things could be worse.

I decided to face whatever was coming head-on and to get the best out of this awful situation. I started making a plan of how to get through the next few days, all the while imagining myself aboard a ship bound for America. I still think the most important thing in life is having a goal. Once one has that, things start being good or bad with respect to that goal. It provides direction, the ability to decide on the next steps. Regardless of the circumstances you find yourself in, as long as you are moving toward your goal, you are moving in the right direction.

The goal might even change along the way, but that is not important; the struggle to reach it is what it is all about. The struggle is constant and real and facing it head-on is the only sure path to success.

* * *

I shared the room with a Montenegrin and two Slovenian guys, who had been moved from the Croatian quarters after getting into some trouble there. Issues and conflicts were the norm in the high-strung atmosphere of the camp, but we lived together peacefully, without any problems. For many people there the war had never ended; it was still with them, contained in their hatred of "the other."

The four of us often took walks around the camp and during one such walk, I spotted a face in the distance that looked familiar. Nikola! But that was not possible. Nikola had gone to Marseilles to rejoin the Foreign Legion! I thought I might be going a bit loopy, seeing things that were not there, but when I looked closer at the silhouette in the distance, it really did look like him. Too stunned to shout, I rushed toward the man who was now standing with his back to me in deep conversation with a couple of women. I grabbed him from behind. "Nikola?!"

For a split second I wondered if I'd made an embarrassing mistake, but then he turned to face me and I saw it was indeed my friend and benefactor from Belgium who had, not incidental to this situation, absconded with all my money. He had a look of utter surprise on his face. He looked mortified. He uttered my name softly, as if he had seen a ghost. Then throwing his cigarette to the floor, he grabbed my hand and gave it a forceful squeeze.

"Do not say anything . . ." he whispered in my ear briskly and motioned toward the Serbian barracks.

I followed him in and as soon as he closed the door of his room, he grabbed me into a hug and kept me in his clinch for so long that I was struggling for breath by the time he let go.

"What brings you here, Bata?" His voice was full of genuine concern. We sat down and talked, like father and son. He found out what I was doing there, and I found out what had happened to my money.

"Bata, believe me, I was never going to steal from you, I only borrowed the money. I was embarrassed to ask you for a loan, but I always planned to return every last cent. I had a serious debt, double the money in your account, so I took a chance."

In the end, he admitted he'd lost the money at a gambling table in Baden. I cannot say I forgave him straight away. He swore he would pay back what he took from my account and my anger soon subsided. I understood then that he was a gambling addict and was not surprised later that addiction was considered a disease. I could see that the addiction had him in its hold, and that however much he tried, he could not break free.

Nikola convinced me that this place was more dangerous than Belgium, so I had to be very careful and not go anywhere without his knowledge.

Despite his obvious flaws, he was once again in a position to take me under his wing. People were wary of him in the camp, just as they had been in Brussels. Rowdy and bold, he kowtowed to nobody and had no qualms about beating up those who crossed him. These were perfect qualities for a guardian in the circumstances we were in. I knew how hard it was to be alone and in trouble in a foreign country and was soon thinking myself lucky for coming across him again.

He told me his story: It was his third stint in a camp, the second in Valka Lager. He had joined the Legion the first time from this place. He tried to reassure me by saying that the life in the camp wasn't all that bad. To prove it, he introduced me to his fellow Chetnik, a captain who had been in Valka Lager for almost six years and seemed perfectly happy with his lot.

At that moment there were around ten thousand refugees living in the camp, stateless people of different nationalities. Among them were many fugitives from the law who were hiding behind assumed identities. Just like I was, except I was not a criminal. No matter what Nikola said, it was a dangerous place. A few days after my arrival, several bodies were found dumped by the latrines, a grisly outcome of the war between different political and criminal groups active in the camp.

11

The Fenceless Camp

I found out there was a soccer league in operation in the camp, with different nationalities playing against each other. Games were tense affairs that often flared into clashes between players on the pitch and quickly spread among the supporters crowding the sidelines. Each game was attended by dozens of fervent supporters.

The Serbian club was called White Eagles. They found out I was a talented soccer player from Nikola. He bragged about my friendship with Rajko Mitić, Stane-Ambassador, and Bane-Capricorn. He said Mitić had, in fact, guided me to Anderlecht. So, the manager called me over and declared, "You have to play for White Eagles. It is a matter of national pride!"

I was dying to play soccer again but was also wary of getting injured. The playing ground had no markings. It was just a field with two goals on each end and it probably predated the war. It appeared to be in the same condition as it had been ten years earlier, when the captured officers played matches against their German adversaries. The pitch reminded me of when Perica American and I started playing as the kids at the Red Star, him playing midfield, and in one of the games both of his soccer shoes got stuck in the mud. Coach Uncle Mitke ordered him to play goalie. Perica American started crying but went to play in the new position, saved the penalty and played in goal until his retirement at age thirty-six.

The grass was patchy in the extreme, a sea of dried mud and gravel with a green island here and there. When it rained, it was a mud bath. There were no bleachers to speak of, with supporters packed close to the sidelines, which gave them the opportunity to trip enemy players. It seemed reckless, but there was no getting out of it—the White Eagles manager was insistent. In the end I agreed to play, but only in goal.

Camp inmates received one dollar of spending money a month. At the time that was worth four or five German marks. This financial help was provided by the American Red Cross, and it was mainly intended for things like soap, toothpaste, and other personal hygiene essentials. Food was prepared in the main kitchens, and we took turns bringing meals to the barracks each mealtime. Whole families, mostly from Eastern Europe, were living in the camp.

We even had an American living among us, an African American who had served his time in the army but then refused to go back to segregated America. He was well connected and could obtain contraband from American soldiers he'd kept in touch with—all he had to do in return was fix them up with a couple of girls and that was payment enough. He was the first person I met who was scathing about America and the life there.

We all knew what life was like in the countries we'd left behind. Many of us had been convinced that everything was better elsewhere, especially the West. We were running from what we knew toward the unknown. Some were also hoping to return home.

A tense, depressive atmosphere pervaded the fenceless camp born of futility and frustration. None of us could leave, because we had nowhere to go. Hunger and disease were rife, particularly the extremely contagious tuberculosis. I recalled my mother's warnings that tonsils protected from this horrible illness and wished I had heeded her advice not to take them out, but it was too late. Still, I was young and strong, a healthy sportsman, and had every reason to hope illness would pass me by.

Those who got sick had just two options: try to return home or stay put without hope of recovery. People died waiting to get better, as only the healthy were allowed to emigrate. I heard stories of married couples divorcing if one of them fell ill, to give the other at least a chance of escaping the camp. When it became known that different church organizations from Canada, South America, and Australia offered their members help with arranging visas, many rushed to avail themselves of the opportunity without the slightest qualms about changing their religion.

There was a limited number of ways one could make money in the camp. The craftier among us meddled in dubious deals and scraped a living that way. Prostitution and gambling were chief among them, as well as the black market in commodities like food, cigarettes, and clothes obtained from American soldiers. Montgomery coats were highly prized.

In the postwar years there was an acute shortage of metals of all kinds, so many inmates made clandestine night visits to what had been an underground ammunition factory, now closed and guarded by German police, to rummage for scraps of copper, lead, and other metals they could sell on the black market. Desperate times called for desperate measures.

Those of us who had been glued to the Voice of America or BBC News at home never thought something like this could befall us on our arrival in the West. None of us had ever heard anything like this mentioned on the radio or portrayed in films. Most of us had set out in search of a better life, and now we found ourselves as far as it was possible to be from the promised land. Everyone in the camp thought they were a step away from a better world, but all we got was illness and death.

I played soccer and that brought benefits in terms of food and accommodation, so I managed somehow, but most of the people there were destitute.

* * *

Nikola did his best, but he could not protect me from everything. One night, a group of Serbs who were known to be running prostitutes brought a young East German girl to our barrack. I saw them take her to the room at the end of the corridor and heard the sounds as men took turns going in. I remained in my bunk, pretending to be writing a letter home. After a while, a couple of guys from the Serbian gang came over and said, "It is your turn now."

It was only then I fully comprehended what was going on. I was horrified. To me love was sacred and happened between two people in the grip of sweet passion, not in a filthy room with a helpless girl who was forced to endure this ordeal because men somewhere owed other men money. But I had no choice. I knew that to them, a refusal would be a mortal insult, like rejecting a present or a favor.

It was cold, but the room was very warm, with the fire roaring in the furnace in the corner. The wretched girl was in a terrible state, lying naked on the bed. Next to it, there was a bucket of dirty water. I was overwhelmed by the heat and the stench of unwashed bodies, sweat, and misery permeating the room. That was the worst thing I had ever seen or felt in my life. I could not find words to comfort her, so I sat on the bed and took her hand in mine gently.

She winced, but when she realized I was not going to hurt her, she clasped my hand tightly, repeating pitifully, "*Danke, danke . . .*"

I held her hand and waited for her sobs to subside, doing my best to soothe her. But soon the others were banging on the door, shouting for me to hurry up and finish. She begged me to stay and I did, as long as I could, but in the end, I had to go out, pretending

I had "done the deed." I felt miserable beyond words. Fortunately, a couple of women realized what was happening and reported them to the camp authorities. The police came surprisingly swiftly and took the girl away, still naked.

This sorry episode would stay with me for life.

Each group in the camp had its natural enemy, so the Serbs were separated from the Croats, the Polish from the Russians, while Ukrainians had to deal with animosity from both the Russians and the Polish. The rest, Hungarians, Czechs, Slovaks, Bulgarians, and Romanians were similarly wary of one another. It was strictly prohibited for the groups to mix, particularly in the context of young boys and girls meeting and, God forbid, falling in love.

It was unthinkable for a Serbian boy to walk out with a Croatian girl, or a Russian boy with a Polish girl. On one occasion, I asked out a pretty girl I'd met at one of the games, when she'd stood close to the goal during the entire match, flirting with me, smiling shyly, and giggling with her girlfriends. I did not know who she was or where she was from, but I found out which barrack she lived in, so I decided to go there and hang around for a while.

Soon enough, I spotted her going out for a walk. I asked if I could accompany her, and she smiled, so we walked on together in the direction of the small makeshift market, where one could get a flat soda or a cup of fake coffee for a cent. I discovered she was Ukrainian and that her name was Lara. She had a beautiful smile and I liked her timidness—it seemed such a contrast to everything around us. We took a couple of turns around the common part of the compound and for once, I forgot the ugliness and the horror of camp life.

We spent a carefree afternoon together, chatting in our bad Russian, laughing, teasing one another, all without so much as touching. At sunset, I walked her back and as we said our goodbyes I felt a strong urge to take her in my arms and kiss her. But I knew that would not be a right move there, among her people, so I reined in my desire as best I could. We lingered for a long while in front of her barrack and parted knowing we would seek each other out again.

But the next day, a group of Ukrainians came over to our barrack, and asked to speak to the captain. They left a message for me: If I wanted to live, I would forget charming Lara. My one attempt at romance in the camp thus met with a sorry end. I shuddered to think what might have happened had I tried to kiss her.

Nikola always hovered close by, watching who I was hanging around with and where I went, making sure I stayed out of trouble. He knew what life in the camp was really like. Despite its obvious drawbacks, Nikola maintained that it wasn't all that bad, that one at least had free room and board. He had a room to himself. I don't know how he managed that but thought it must have come about as a result of his friendship with the captain. He was doing his best to help me, I could see, but I no longer trusted him blindly, like before.

I told him how I found myself in the camp, but I kept from him my plan to join the American army as a volunteer. I was probing around, even dropping a hint that I was thinking of joining the Legion, like he had done, but he became furious when he heard that. He said my place was not in the army but on a soccer pitch and pressed me to promise I would never forget that.

He said army life was for different types of people, "those like me, without roots or talent, without fear of death, and not a little crazy. And, Bata, you are not that type!"

* * *

A month passed, and the time came to receive the one dollar we were all due. The day we received the money, a meeting of the Serbian barracks was called and we all trooped into barrack 48. The captain, who had called the meeting, was the first to speak, declaring in firm, army tones, "My Serbian brothers and sisters! I called you here because I have a suggestion to put to you. I think it would be a great idea if we collected all the dollar bills we received and sent them to our King Peter II in London."

We all stood in silence. A few of those present nodded their heads, but most lowered their gaze to the ground in evident disappointment. Still, nobody dared speak up to contradict the captain. He scanned those present with steely determination and, as each man in turn lowered his gaze and the silence deepened, he knew he had succeeded. Now, certain nobody would protest, he added, almost as an afterthought, "So, brother and sister Serbs, you agree, then?"

I was standing at the back of the room in the crowd of downcast people. On an impulse, I raised my hand and in my most charming voice quipped, "Dear captain, I have an even better idea. Why don't we collect all the money, give it to the women to go to the market, buy groceries, and prepare for us a proper Serbian feast; we can always send a Christmas postcard to the king with greetings from Valka Lager."

Even before I finished, I saw that my comment had infuriated the captain. He was livid. My words were drowned out by his thunderous voice swearing at me, cursing my "Communist mother" and calling me "dirty Commie" and "Tito's stooge who'd been sent here to spy."

I was taken aback by his rage. Still seething, he collected the money from everyone but refused my dollar bill, although I offered it. "Get out of here!" he said dismissively when I tried to hand him the buck. I went back to our dorm and told my roommates what had happened. They warned me he was a very dangerous man.

A couple of hours later Nikola came in looking visibly perturbed, which was very unusual; he rarely looked concerned about anything.

He called me to his room and, as soon as I entered, said in a quiet voice, "I told you not to go anywhere without my knowledge. I tried my best to calm the captain down, but he is very stubborn and very angry, and I don't need to remind you that he is dangerous at the best of times. Even if he does nothing himself, he has a swarm of hangers-on who suck up to him the whole time; they may take matters in their own hands and decide you deserve to be punished. Tonight, after the lights out, sneak out of your room and come over to mine. I'll sleep in your bed. But don't forget to lock the door!"

That evening I fell asleep in my bed, forgetting what he'd instructed me to do. A couple of hours after lights out, I woke to find Nikola standing above me, shaking me and whispering urgently, ordering me to go to his room. Still half-asleep, I gathered my things and without another word stumbled out, leaving him to slip into my bed.

Sometime before dawn I was woken by a commotion in the hallway. Someone was running through the corridor toward the exit. Confused and fearful, people were milling out of their rooms. In the chaos that ensued I heard one of my roommates calling my name. I unlocked the door and made my way through the crowded corridor toward my room.

I shall never forget the sight that greeted me when I finally reached my quarters: Nikola sitting on my bed, in a pool of blood, with a knife sticking out of his back. He was still calm and composed, as if nothing had happened. He had the situation under control. He told us not to take the knife out, as this might cause him to bleed to death, and was telling those around him how to transfer him safely to the hospital with it still lodged in his back.

It was raining outside, there was mud everywhere, and with the hospital at the other end of the compound, it took a good half an hour to get him there. The medical staff later said that he'd been extremely lucky—the knife went straight through his back but did not touch any of the vital organs. He took it like a man, never once betraying how much pain he was in.

Rather than go back to the barrack, I stayed with Nikola in the hospital. He knew how Serbian gangs in the camp operated and what would happen once I was labeled a "dirty Commie." He was afraid one of them would decide to take revenge and the only way he could stop them was to put himself in harm's way and try to calm things down. He insisted that we should get in touch with the club in Hanover.

"That's the best way to protect you," he said.

I finally told him about my plans to volunteer in the American army.

"You are an idiot. What army? You are a soccer player. You must play soccer. You are not fit to be a soldier. We must get in touch with Hanover. I'll take care of that."

Three days later the man from the Hanover soccer club came to collect me and I said goodbye to Nikola. I never saw him again. To this day, whenever I remember Valka Lager, I wonder where that huge, rough-faced man with a soul of gold ended up. Despite stealing the first proper money I'd ever earned playing soccer, the legionnaire Nikola Popović proved that he was indeed my guardian and protector.

12

No Looking Back

Leaving Valka Lager behind, I did not look back. I wanted to forget the misery and deprivation I encountered there—the broken, lost dreams; the empty, useless hope. I could not even remember how those Polish guys on the train talked me into going to Munich with them. I still believed deep inside that one day I would find my way to America, but now it was clear that was not going to happen by joining the American army as a volunteer.

Another train took me to Hanover. Germany was still devastated from the war and along the way one could see women and children clearing the ruins, here and there accompanied by a man, usually older. It made me think of Belgrade in ruins. I thought of my mother, Rubi, and my little brother. I sent them a card from time to time, never lying, but never disclosing the dire straits I'd found myself in.

All they knew was that I was somewhere in Germany and that I was well. I didn't mention the camp in my letters. What would have been the point of worrying them with the truth when they could do nothing to help me?

I was given a warm welcome in the club in Hanover. I lived in a small, comfortable hotel, with two Polish guys and a Hungarian who also played for the club. We played soccer for the same club, but now for the money. Not for love, like we did when we were teenagers back home.

I started training straight away. I played for half a season quite successfully. The club paid for my room and board, transport, and gave me a salary of 100 marks per week (around twenty dollars at that time), which was considered excellent. I also earned bonuses: forty marks each time we beat our opponents, and twenty for a draw, conditions similar to those in Belgium.

Club Hanover 96 at that time played in Oberliga Nord, and this was their fifth season in a row in that league. The team manager was Helmunt Crosbain. They had quite a good team at the time, with the majority of players recruited from the pool of foreigners who could not obtain permission to play in European clubs from their home clubs, just like me. Foreign players in the club were generally a bit older, while the Germans on the team were my age or younger.

We were like soccer legionnaires, with no country and no roots, with the beautiful game as our homeland. When we were winning, everyone was happy, and when we were losing, the supporters complained, "It's those fucking foreigners' fault."

Five months after I arrived in Hanover, something strange happened. After a match against Hamburg, during which I scored one goal and assisted on two more, the club's secretary and two gentlemen were waiting for me at the hotel. The two men were elegantly dressed. One of them was wearing a hat, and the other an unusual cap, which I learned was a Jewish yarmulke.

He introduced himself as Joe Schwartz and explained that he was the co-owner of the soccer club Montréal Hakoah in Canada. The other guy said he was an agent who worked for manager Ukraińczyk.

I was surprised when they asked me if I was interested in playing soccer for his club in Canada. They were looking for two young offensive players and they thought that I would fit in that position, especially after they saw me play against Hamburg. I explained that I had another twelve months left in Hanover, then I had to return to Anderlecht. But the agent accompanying Mr. Schwartz said I didn't have to worry about returning, that he would take care of it.

At the end of our conversation, they said that they would leave the offer with the Hamburg general secretary, who informed them that I would be playing in a friendly match for Braunschweig in four days. They said they would love to attend the match and see me in action again.

* * *

From time to time, the foreign players were loaned to other clubs to strengthen them in friendly games against teams from abroad. Germans were eager to win, particularly when playing foreign teams, and would supplement their teams with guest players like me. To be victorious was an imperative for the Germans, in life as well as in sport. On this occasion two Polish players and I were invited by Braunschweig FC to boost their team against a Czechoslovakian club, they said.

We arrived the day before the match to give us a chance to train with the Braunschweig team. That evening after dinner I decided to linger with my Polish teammates in the hotel's bar. I usually never drank, but that night I relaxed in their company, one schnapps led to another followed by a beer, and I got properly drunk for the first time in my life.

The next day I woke up with an indescribable headache. I could barely stand. I hardly managed a couple of mouthfuls at breakfast, nothing for lunch, and still felt ghastly when the car came to take us to the stadium for that afternoon's match. The Polish guys laughed at my feebleness but said not to worry, that the trick was to run as much as I could in the first ten minutes of the match to sweat out the alcohol and that I would be okay after that.

We arrived at the stadium around two hours before the game. Supporters were already trickling into the terraces as we made our way to the dugout, where we waited for the opposing team. Once they arrived, we were supposed to go to the dressing rooms to change for the game. The Polish guys and I had just our cleats with us; the Braunschweig team was going to supply us with their kit.

Looking around idly, I noticed a Yugoslav flag flying on a pole next to the German one. This took me by surprise. What was the Yugoslav flag doing there? Apprehension flooded through me. My first instinct was to run away from the stadium, this looked like a setup.

"Take it easy, the Germans made a mistake," one of my teammates said.

"The Czech flag is also tricolored with a red star, relax," another added.

I didn't buy it.

"This is the Yugoslav flag for sure," I said.

The visiting team bus finally arrived, and the heavy door clunked open, and who should come out first, but Red Star center half, Djura-Peacock! I immediately said to the Polish guys, "This is Red Star!" I felt excitement swell inside me, as if I'd returned to Belgrade. Djura was followed by an even bigger surprise: My dear friend Perica American Radenković! I could not believe my eyes. Behind Perica American the other players trooped out, and I realized I knew most of them, although I realized this was not Red Star, but BSK from Belgrade!

In an instant the tiredness evaporated, and I forgot about the hangover. I sprung to my feet and ran over to Perica American and Djura and the other players, shouting greetings and hugging them each in turn. It was their turn to be astonished.

"What are you doing here?" they all shouted in one voice.

"These two Polish guys and I are on loan from Hanover 96, here to help your opponents."

As I said that I realized I was not going to be able to play against a team from my hometown. It just did not feel right. I informed the manager of Braunschweig of my decision not to play and he was understood. He agreed that I could not play against my home boys. Perica American was very excited because the coach told him that he would start the match, for the first time, as the number 1 goalkeeper for BSK. Since I was not going to play, he asked me to stay near the goal and help by telling him what I knew about German players. I think what he really needed was a moral support, but I agreed and settled myself behind the goal, next to a goalpost.

There were twenty-one shots and Perica American defended nineteen of them, conceding only two goals. By the seventieth minute, he was so tired that he asked to be substituted and the substitute who came on after him conceded another two goals in the last twenty minutes of the game. The final score was 4–1 for Braunschweig. The Germans were happy; they even paid me the bonus although I didn't play and apologized for having wrongly told me the game was against a team from Czechoslovakia.

As the Belgrade team was leaving, both Perica American and Djura-Peacock hugged me and promised that once they returned home, they would tell my parents that their Bata was alive and well. I mentioned my Canadian offer to them.

"Going to play hockey?" Djura-Peacock joked.

"You'll get by, I know you," Perica American said with a smile.

The club secretary and the Canadians wanted to know why I had not played and what I was doing behind the goal. After hearing my explanation, they laughed all the way back to Hanover. There, the club secretary informed me about the offer from Canada: six hundred dollars per month plus bonuses for games the team won and a four-year contract. The terms were amazing—the money was seven times more than what I was earning in Germany. I imagined all that money waiting for me across the ocean.

Beyond that, it felt as if my Hollywood dream was inching closer, too. There would be just a single border separating me from the life I dreamed about. Needless to say, I didn't deliberate too much before accepting the offer.

* * *

I did my best to keep in touch with my family in Belgrade. Communication channels were not what they are today, and that was especially true of occupied Germany. A telephone call from abroad had to be arranged with the local post office, then one had to come at an appointed time and wait. I booked a call, and my entire family dressed in their Sunday best for their trip to the post office to speak with me.

"Dad, Dad, can you hear me?" I asked.

They all started talking at the same time, calling my name, and I, excited and delighted to hear their voices, continued pratting away at my end. All that mattered to me was convincing them that they had no reason to worry about me. I told them I was well, living in Germany and doing what I loved, playing well and making good money. I told them about the offer to go to Canada and how much I hoped that it would come to pass. I mentioned the trouble with the passport but said I had faith in the Germans I played for, who had told me to leave the passport issues to them.

"If I make it to Canada, I'll bring you all over."

"Bata, can you hear me?" I heard the sweet voice of my mother, and I knew she was holding back tears, and failing. "Come back, Bata. We are all waiting for you here. We spoke to Aunt Lola and she said you will not get much, maximum six months in jail, and you may even evade that because you left the country legally and then stayed on. We must be together again. I live for that moment."

Now it was my turn to hold back tears. "I am well, Mother, I am eating well, all healthy food, but nothing compares to your cooking. I won't be coming back for a little while yet. Take care of yourself."

An agent from Ukraińczyk's agency appeared to help me sort out the transfer papers and I signed the pre-contract to play in Montréal. The average age of the players on my new team was twenty-nine and they wanted younger players, so at eighteen, I fit in perfectly. Without a proper passport, I should have hit a stone wall, but strings were pulled and I became a proud owner of a German travel document. It was temporary, but in my real name, Dobrivoje Tanasijević, with my real birthday, May 26, 1935.

I could only use it to leave Germany; it would not be valid for reentering the country once I left for Canada. I applied for a visa in the British consulate. The person helping me there checked my new travel document, and while everything seemed in order at first, a problem arose. I could not enter Canada until I was legally an adult, and for that I had to be twenty-one! My visa request was denied.

I was heartbroken. During this entire process, I was playing soccer for Hanover, but my head was already in Montréal, and I had no idea how all of this was going to end. I was heartbroken as I sat in the Hanover club offices after receiving the news about my visa request. The club secretary looked equally glum. Then he did something I could not believe. He took a pen and, without any reservations or so much as a look in my direction, masterfully turned the five in my year of birth to one.

In an instant, I was four years older, no longer born in 1935 but in 1931! And just like that, I was legally adult.

But that created another problem, this one personal. Although I qualified for a visa now, I knew that this change would affect my soccer career, that being four years older would shorten my playing career on the transfer market. The club secretary calmed my concerns by saying Mr. Schwartz knew this and would correct my birthdate when I signed the contract with Hakoah in Montréal.

The deal was done, and I was issued a Canadian visa on June 12, 1953. It was valid until July 31, 1953. Only the Atlantic Ocean separated me from my new destination, Montréal. On July 2, 1953, in Bremerhaven I boarded a ship named the *Laura*, which was scheduled to depart at sunset. Nine hours later, shortly after midnight, it finally left the port to huge applause from the passengers.

I had a first-class cabin paid for by the club. Still, it was a small room, and my movements were limited to the deck, the restaurant, and the narrow gangways between them. After a couple of days at sea, I received an invitation from the captain to dine at his table. It was a huge honor and I was quite surprised by the invitation. I figured it must be a mistake. Then I found out the captain was a passionate soccer supporter. His team was Bremen FC, and when he heard there was a soccer player from Hanover 96 among the passengers, he was quick to extend an invite.

Dinner was formal with around a dozen people present, all of them invited by the captain. The conversation was varied, but it centered mostly on soccer. I took the opportunity to tell the captain that I had attended a navy college. He laughed and said I could visit the bridge and show off my navigation skills. He added that it would give me a chance to see what I had been missing in my life. He was a proper sea wolf who obviously adored his job, the sea, and sailing.

There were two young German girls in the company around the captain's table that night, Gertrude and Sophia. Gertrude was the prettier of the two, more eloquent and engaging, even if she was more interested in ice hockey than soccer.

The next day I went to see the captain on the bridge and found that Gertrude had beaten me to it. When he saw me, the captain took his cap off and placed it on my head. "Wow, what a handsome young captain!" Gertrude exclaimed with a laugh. When we finished with the Captain, I saw Gertrude back to her cabin. She complained that the captain was making passes at her and that she was looking for a way to refuse his advances without hurting his pride.

At that point Sophia joined us and suggested a solution: Gertrude and I should pretend to be lovers. With a cheeky smile, she added that we could leave the captain to her. And that is what we did. The two of us started playing lovers, and I had to admit I liked the game. Gertrude was always beautifully dressed, and she smelled divine. I had one nice dinner suit for special occasions, and I wore it all the time. We promenaded across the deck hand in hand, the wind in our hair, looking at each other longingly. We even went through a storm together, which wasn't pleasant at all. The huge ship heaved in the enormous waves. Most of the passengers were seasick. I was surprised that I had no problem.

I detected a new and unfamiliar feeling taking hold inside me. Gertrude and I were both émigrés, albeit with different histories, but with common goals. We spent hours talking about our pasts—I'd learned a lot about life in East Germany, which reminded me of home, and that is probably what brought us closer. When I told her that I didn't have any contacts in Montréal other than the phone number of the Montréal Hakoah, she offered a coy smile and gave me the address and phone number of her apartment.

"There, now you have another number—mine."

* * *

As we approached the port, I could not hide my excitement. Gertrude and Sophia teased me about the tears they claimed they could see in my eyes. The truth is, I was close to tears. Finally, I was about to set foot on a new continent, and I felt elated. I had no idea what awaited me in Canada. I didn't even know if anyone would be there to greet me. All I had was the club's phone number.

Once we disembarked, in the mass of people crowding the dock, I saw two men in suits who were waving a blue soccer jersey and scanning those coming off the ship. When I came a bit closer, I noticed that one of the men had a cap emblazoned with the team's logo on his head. It was Mr. Schwartz. The other was the team's coach, Coach Michael. I was relieved to see them as I hadn't given much thought as to how I would reach Montréal.

They were surprised to see me in the company of two charming women. Sophia said goodbye to us at that point, promising to see me at some point later in Montréal, while the rest of us found a coffee bar in the port to have a drink. At the time, my linguistic abilities were as follows: a bit of Russian (what I remembered from school), a bit more of French, with my German still way ahead. I had zero English, though. I changed countries too frequently to learn any of the languages well.

Luckily, Gertrude was there, and apart from Russian, she was fluent in all the languages I mentioned. She asked them what plans they had for me and they said they would put me up in a hotel in Montréal for two weeks to get used to the new environment while they found me an apartment.

"Well, I have a large apartment in the center of Montréal. Bata could stay with me for a couple of weeks, and I can help him acclimatize," she said to them before turning slightly and giving me a provocative wink.

Coach Michael agreed that was a good plan. The season had started six weeks ago, he explained, but Hakoah had already been relegated from the Québec and Dominion Cup. Mr. Schwartz handed me an envelope. I thanked him and was going to put it in my pocket when he stopped me and said, "Money is for counting." He insisted I open the envelope and check its contents. I counted thirty twenty-Canadian-dollar bills. I thought that must be my first monthly wage and was delighted. I got paid before even touching the ball! I was loving life in Canada already.

The club officials gave us a lift to Montréal and during the journey they bragged about Hakoah being in second place in the league. They said that because they were out of both cups, now they would be focusing on winning the league. They described the city stadium where they played, which they shared with three other Montréal clubs: Italy FC, Ukraine FC, and Algiers FC. Its capacity was fifteen thousand. The four Montréal clubs were competing in the Québec Province Ligue, alongside eight other clubs. They also mentioned several first-class players from Yugoslavia who were playing in the Ligue.

My head was spinning by the time we arrived in Montréal, and it spun even faster while I waited for Gertrude to unlock the door to her apartment. All I wanted was to take her in my arms and kiss her. But she beat me to it. As soon as the door closed behind us, the refined Gertrude threw her arms around me and started kissing me passionately and tearing my clothes off.

Twenty-dollar bills flew around us as she breathlessly repeated, "Captain, my captain, we are finally alone!" We made love in the entrance hall among the suitcases, bags, and our discarded clothes. Canada welcomed me with open arms indeed.

* * *

Gertrude gave me a couple of shelves in her closet and watched as I unpacked my worn-out and unstylish clothes. Her voice betrayed her frustration as she said firmly, "Bata, we are going shopping. You are going to kiss those European rags goodbye. You are going to spend those dollars from the floor in the hall." I did in fact put the better part of the wages toward a completely new wardrobe, from socks to overcoat, but I kept Lenka's nine dollars that had spent all this time sewn in the pocket of my now-discarded jacket from Belgrade.

Ever since leaving Belgrade I had nobody to take care of me. I had to do everything myself—get food, cook, wash, and press my clothes. But now that all changed. I had the use of a beautiful apartment in the center of the city and a lovely girlfriend to share it with. Her pampering and attention felt good; she really knew how to spoil me and I was slowly but surely falling in love with her.

I stayed with Gertrude for a couple of weeks, until the club found me a furnished apartment. It was a nice, spacious apartment, in a nice part of town, and my rent was fifty dollars per month. Gertrude and I continued to see each other after I moved away, although not every day. I was quite busy with practice sessions and games but made sure I saw her at least three or four times per week. She also came to all my games and was one of my most ardent supporters.

None of the players from my own country played for Hakoah, but we met each other almost instantly. I became fast friends with the brothers Mladenović, and Dragan (aka Gidra), and Bosko (aka Bole). There was also a group of Yugoslav boys who came to all our games—Marko the Hat, Boki the Bank, Laza, and Nesha. They lived the high life, piling into VIP lounges in nightclubs and executive boxes at hockey matches. Gertrude didn't like them and did not approve of my socializing with them. She thought they were shady characters. I disagreed. They were fun and knew lots of girls, most of them dancers or waitresses in the nightclubs.

Marko was called "the Hat" because he wore one at all times. Upon entering a nightclub, he would take it off and throw it like a frisbee to the cloakroom girl. If she caught it, she'd get a nice five-dollar tip. Gidra was playing for Ukraine and was engaged to a stunning Ukrainian girl whose parents ran a restaurant in Montréal with home cooking, which would become our favorite hangout.

My Canadian life had a perfect start. This was the first time since leaving Belgrade that I could relax and breathe freely. I could finally stop looking over my shoulder. I no longer had to be worried about being killed or kidnapped. As time went by, I felt more and more like a free man. I even opened a bank account with only my signature.

13

Let the Ball Do the Running

Gidra suggested to the Ukrainians to ask Hakoah to loan me for the Québec cup game and since they were already out, they agreed. So, my first game in Canada was for a Ukrainian team. I played well, but sadly, we lost. Still, they paid me the promised fifty dollars. For my second game I was loaned to the Italian team for the Dominion cup and that is where I met the legendary Aca-Bus, who was now the star player on the Italian team and the Québec league.

At the training the day before the game, as we were warming up, Aca-Bus was juggling the ball by the sideline and watching us as we went through the exercises. As we started a practice game he joined us. In one of the breaks in the game, he came over and put his enormous arm around my shoulders and gave me advice I would never forget: "Son, you run too much. Learn to let the ball do the running and your career will be longer and better."

Aca was powerful and agile; taking the ball off him was impossible. All one could do was foul him, but even that was not easy. He was stable on his feet and sturdy like a double-decker bus (hence his nickname). Aca-Bus controlled the ball as few other players could. But he had that Balkan streak running through him. He liked to be the center of attention, and he liked to show off. He played soccer effortlessly, as if it was the easiest thing in the world.

I finally debuted for Hakoah and immediately after the game, I received my second pay packet. But this time, there was only three hundred Canadian dollars in the envelope. That surprised me, as the deal with the club was to pay me six hundred Canadian dollars per month. I asked the club secretary why my wages were lower than what was agreed.

"No worries, I'll explain how it works, but in private."

Later, he explained the rules stipulated that professional players could get up to three hundred dollars

CAD in wages, plus bonuses. The other half, it turned out, had to be "earned." The club management would stay within the rules by finding additional "jobs" for players in their subsidiary companies or partner businesses.

A few days later, Mr. Schwartz introduced me to a mechanic who was working for one of his businesses and said I should go with him. The man spoke good German and first took me to a specialized equipment store where he bought me overalls and a large toolbox full of mechanic's tools. Then he took me to a huge Mercedes-Benz garage. I was confused, but I figured they had to know what they were doing.

Still, I was slightly bemused and did wonder how I had found myself there, surrounded by gleaming cars I knew nothing about and tools I didn't know the names of or how to use. I couldn't even drive!

It turned out that they mistook my machinist schooling for mechanic schooling, so they found me a job in the mother of all mechanic shops!

The manager showed me how to punch my timecard in and out and explained that I had to spend only one week at the job and after that I only needed to show up on the first of each month to collect my paycheck. The manager would punch my card in and out for the rest of the month. The mechanic took me to the locker room where workers stored their possessions and tools. Most of the lockers were gray, but two in the corner were painted light blue. I was given one of those. My name was already written on it.

The following Monday I put on my overalls and a cap and went to "work." The garage manager was there when I arrived, and he informed me that I would be working with the mechanic on fixing brakes. The mechanic was aware that I knew nothing about cars, so he gave me an easy manual task. While he was fixing the brakes of a huge Mercedes, I was supposed to work the foot pump to keep the pressure up. When pumping became hard, I was to stop while the mechanic moved to the next wheel. I did that for the next three days.

While we worked, the mechanic told me a bit about cars and driving. He showed me how to turn the ignition on and how to change gears, but it was all theory, I never actually drove a car. On my fourth day at work, the mechanic I'd been working alongside never turned up, so they assigned me to another mechanic for the day. I was disappointed to see that we were working on brakes again. I was sick of all that pumping! But the new mechanic gave me a different instruction.

"Bring that car inside, please," he said casually and motioned toward a huge Mercedes parked outside the large gaping entrance to the shop.

He said it pleasantly enough, but it was an order nevertheless. I thought he knew what he was doing and went over to the car and got in. I tried my best to remember what the other mechanic had taught me about starting a car and running it over the previous few days. Ignition, clutch, first gear . . . I went through the motions as I remembered them and the car moved. I slowly maneuvered the mammoth engine through the garage door and would have made it inside had it not been for a wall which suddenly materialized out of nowhere in front of me.

I panicked, and, trying to desperately avoid the looming wall ahead the gleaming hood, I pressed my foot on the gas pedal instead of hitting the brakes; everything accelerated at an unbelievable speed. The wall was now hurtling toward me so I swerved left, then right, and in the end, I hit a brand-new Mercedes that was at that moment exiting the garage. There was a loud bang and moments later the mechanics swarmed around the car, totally astonished, trying to assess the damage. I was too stunned to find words in any language to apologize for my mistake, so I stood there silently while the mechanics clamored around the damaged cars, completely incredulous. Nobody had ever heard of a mechanic at a flagship Mercedes-Benz garage who could not drive!

At that point, my career as a mechanic literally crashed to an end. The club continued paying me the rest of my wages, nonetheless. They were extremely fair and honored all the promises they made while I was with the club.

* * *

Club Hakoah in Montréal was officially a Jewish club. Players wore the star of David on their light blue jerseys, but only three out of nineteen of us were Jewish—and unfortunately, at most games they were reserve players. The rest were English, Hungarian, Polish, Scots, or French. The symbol on my jersey was identical to the one Jews were forced to wear on their sleeves in Belgrade under German occupation. Then, the star meant almost-certain death, while here, in the free world, people wore them with pride.

Our supporters were brilliant: We had seven thousand to ten thousand of them at each game. The whole league was put together as a competition between twelve national clubs although the players themselves were rarely from the nation they were supposedly representing. What was important to each club was to keep the name and the supporters who chose who to support according to their own nationality.

Soccer fields had a certain extra-territoriality, like battlefields. They often reverberated with chants that would be considered totally unacceptable outside the stadium. The different nations still fought their long-lost wars; nobody knew anymore how their quarrels had begun or why. There is a saying I heard years later which perfectly illustrates the atmosphere of the soccer games of that time—and maybe still: "When they banned public hangings, the English invented soccer."

* * *

Gertrude enjoyed cooking, and her table was always beautifully set. There were always two fresh white roses in a vase in the middle of the table. We had been seeing each other for several months when one night she invited me over for dinner and told me she wanted to introduce me to someone very close to her. I went to her apartment straight from training. She appeared happy to see me but seemed somewhat reserved. I noticed the table was set for three and in the vase were three white roses.

I thought that Sophia or another one of her friends was joining us, but I soon realized that was not the case. A tall, handsome Black man came out of the bedroom. I was startled for a second, but he smiled broadly and approached me, his hand outstretched, speaking perfect German.

"Thank you for keeping my wife company on the ship, and particularly for protecting her from the captain's advances. She told me all about it and speaks very highly of you."

I noticed Gertrude blushed slightly as she quickly interceded, "This is Dr. Paul, my husband, whom I mentioned often during the passage."

Of course, I did not say that she had never mentioned him at all. Dr. Paul was a charming man, open, warm, and highly intelligent. Over dinner I learned he had been a doctor in the American army hospital in Germany, where he met Gertrude, who was working as a nurse in the same hospital. They fell in love and married. But he didn't want to return to his native hometown, Buffalo because of the racial prejudice, which was then, at the end of the '50s, at its height.

A marriage between an African American man and a white woman was unconscionable in Buffalo—and illegal in much of the US until 1967 (while legal in New York, it was socially unacceptable). The Québec region was much more tolerant in that respect, and a large city like Montréal was even more so. Up to then, I had never thought about racism at all, but talking to Paul, I realized for the first time that the story of racism was not black and white but had many shades in between. I saw that even more clearly for myself when I moved to America.

I grew up in the Balkans, where there were no Black people. The only Black people I ever saw were characters in films, if one doesn't count the former soldier I met in Valka Lager. I simply had not realized that the hatred was so entrenched among the races. Canada was much more tolerant; so many people came from all over the world in an attempt to escape from racism. Consequently, they showed more tolerance and understanding of others in their new homeland.

Paul told me that Montréal was, for him, the best city on the American continent, comparing it with Paris for its openness and culture. I was sure that Paul was completely unaware of my relationship with Gertrude, but I did not let my guard down. I told him my dream was going to Hollywood and that I saw Canada as a stepping-stone to achieve that goal.

Paul's arrival into our lives hit me hard, but I accepted the situation and remained on friendly terms with both of them. They came to all my games, and we saw each other socially too. Gertrude and I never revisited the wonderful period we had spent together and never mentioned what went on between us.

* * *

I finished my first playing season with a broken nose. I headed a ball in a game against Ukraine and scored, but Gidra, who was in goal for the Ukrainian team, tried to defend with his fist, missed the ball and hit me instead. I was unconscious as the ambulance took me to the hospital.

When I woke up, I saw the team's doctor together with the doctor who was treating me. The team doctor put his hand on my shoulder and said, "Do not worry, we will make sure that you will be better looking."

Winter started in Canada and it became unbelievably cold. I had never experienced such low temperatures in my life. Winters in Yugoslavia were sometimes harsh, but not like this. I spent a lot of time with Gidra, his brother, and the other Yugoslav players.

With the arrival of spring, life in Canada resumed its normal pace. I stopped seeing Gertrude as much as before, but I became very good friends with Dr. Paul, who often took me to hockey games. He had season tickets for the Montréal Canadiens, although he was a passionate supporter of the Buffalo Sabres.

The soccer summer season started, and I kept back some tickets for my pals—Marko the Hat, Boki the Bank, and the others—but they never showed up. I was puzzled by their absence until one day Gertrude called me and said I should look at the daily newspaper.

She said I'd see what had happened to my friends. Their faces were staring from the front pages of all the local newspapers.

I discovered that my so-called friends were a criminal gang which operated in and around Montréal. I had to admit that Gertrude had been right all along when she claimed they were shady characters. Gidra and I paid them several visits and brought them cigarettes and magazines while they awaited trial. They were gentlemen-thieves who never used weapons.

They each got three to four years in prison or could choose deportation to Yugoslavia. All opted to go back rather than serve a prison sentence in Canada.

The time came when my two-year FIFA ban expired and I briefly considered going back to Anderlecht, now that I could actually play professionally for them. European soccer was much better quality, but I would not have exchanged the freedom and the life I had in Canada for anything. Also, I was not going to go backward. I firmly believed that life had new adventures in store for me.

I didn't know where or what that might be, but as Aca-Bus had told me, I let the ball do the running.

* * *

Another Canadian winter was approaching. The soccer season ended with an exhibition game in Vancouver organized by the British Columbia soccer association, and they invited Québec all-stars. Hakoah's coach was instructed to select eighteen players for the Québec squad. Aca-Bus, Gidra, and I were among those he chose. Including the four members of the coaching staff, we were a group that had ten different nationalities and spoke eleven different languages, yet we all wore the same uniforms with the big Québec coat of arms. We could have been called the United Nations squad.

We traveled by train, and I noted how much more comfortable and speedier the Canadian trains were than those in Europe. I never dreamed that this would be a start of yet another life adventure for me, nor that this would be my last train journey ever.

We settled in the hotel and soon we learned that everybody spoke only English. That surprised us; we thought that all of Canada spoke French. Before we could adjust, we were visited by Yugoslav soccer fans. One of them, Luka, originally from Montenegro, got glued to us. When I told him about playing for Bokelj from Montenegro he hugged me like a long-lost friend. He offered to take three of us around Vancouver to show us the sites and introduce us to his father.

Luka and I got on really well, so well that he suggested I should stay in Vancouver for a while after the game. Why not? The soccer season was about to be over, and it wouldn't restart until spring, so why rush back to Montréal after the game? We played the game on Saturday and won 6–0. Aca-Bus was the star of the match.

On Sunday, Luka's father prepared an incredible lunch for the three of us and the team's coaching staff at his hostel. Speaking in Serbo-Croatian, he offered the three of us—and two of the coaches—room and board in his hotel free of charge if we decided to stay longer. Luka did everything possible to talk me into staying few more days. It sounded like a good idea, so I asked Coach Michael, and he agreed.

"You know your arrangement with Hakoah. Be back by March 1," he said, adding with a joker's glint in his eye, "In fact, it is better you stay here. It is safer for the cars in the Mercedes garage!"

I decided to stay a week in Vancouver with Luka and his friends. They were young and we had a lot in common. Ever since leaving home, I had mostly kept company with older people, and I almost forgot what people my age were like. I particularly fancied one girl, Vesna, who was very pretty and smart.

Luka's father's hotel catered to miners who would spend nine months in Yukon but come back to Vancouver during the wintertime. He also ran an illegal gambling den from a secret room at the back of the inn that doubled as a dance club on the weekends. This was a familiar scene to me. I first came in contact with poker as a teenager in a secret room in my father's inn, where I acted as a dealer to Rubi's customers. That's where I learned to play European poker, with thirty-two cards, and later improved my game watching Nikola and his buddies in Belgium.

In other words, I was good. Luka and his friends didn't stand a chance against me when we played for small stakes to quell the boredom of hanging out. Seeing that I played well, Luka came to me with a business proposition. He explained that students played poker for fun and for small stakes, but the miners who were just returning from Yukon would be gambling for very high stakes.

When the miners hit town, most of them spent vast amounts of money eating, drinking, and indulging their senses in the company of prostitutes who would materialize out of thin air as soon as the first miner arrived. Some of them liked gambling above everything else. I had enough to live on and had no need to gamble, but Luka, a law student still living with his parents, saw in my card skills a chance to get his hands on some money.

He talked me into chipping in a hundred dollars to enter the game. (The minimum entry was two hundred dollars so we would go in as partners.) He was right about one thing: The miners from the Yukon were crazy about gambling. And they were mediocre players. The first evening, we won five hundred dollars. The second night they demanded the buy-in be five hundred dollars. We won $1,500. The third night they increased buy-in to $1,000. We won again, $2,200.

They asked for a rematch, but I said no. After three consecutive nights playing eight hours per night, Luka and I had won over

$4,000 CAD. I was exhausted. The smoky room and the strange musty smell hanging over the gold miners, whose hygiene left a lot to be desired, disagreed with me.

I was considering going back to Montréal, but Vesna, the girl I fancied, invited me to a weekend picnic in the woods and also whispered that her parents would be out of town. Luka and his gang were invited to the same party, along with a few others, mostly Yugoslavs along with a few Canadians.

The clean air suited me much better than the foul-smelling gambling room. It was a perfect Indian summer Sunday. We roasted a whole lamb and a piglet on spits. The mood was relaxed and convivial with everyone a bit high on beers that were cooling in huge buckets to the side. Someone mentioned San Francisco, enthusing about what a beautiful city it was and all the fun one could have there.

In high spirits from the booze he'd imbibed, one of Luka's closest friends, Srba, who was soon to be married, put his hands up to silence everyone and declared, "That sounds like a perfect place for my stag night!" Without hesitation, Luka offered to cover the expenses of the trip, safe, he thought, in the knowledge that it would all come to nothing as he knew we needed visas to cross into America. I jumped on the same bandwagon and offered to split the costs of the trip with Luka.

And so, the idea of going to San Francisco was born. One gambling story turned into another. To me, it all had an unreal quality; I thought that it was all just booze talking, that they were all just spinning yarns. All my life I'd been hearing that attempting to enter America without a valid visa was a fool's errand. But the groom-to-be and his best man, Mike, seemed intent on going nevertheless. They were adamant that crossing the border from Canada to the USA was strictly a formality, nothing more.

"The Canadians will let us pass there and back with no problems, and the Americans won't stop us either."

"But if they do?"

"If we do get stopped at the American border, we will abandon the trip and return to Vancouver together."

"People do it all the time."

"There won't be any issues."

Everyone chimed in enthusiastically, and as I thought about the risks and rewards, I knew I could not resist another adventure, especially if it included the promise of fulfilling my boyhood dream and finally setting foot on American soil.

14

To the City of Angels

It took around twenty hours by car to reach San Francisco. We stopped only for gas and arrived late at night. Finding a room was not easy at that time in the busy city, but we managed it somehow. Exhausted from the long drive, all four of us dropped off to sleep as soon as we hit our beds. The next day we woke up refreshed and ready for new adventures, so we asked the man at the front desk for suggestions for places to go to and sights to visit.

He wanted to know where we were from, probably confused by the different passports and papers we had presented at registration. When we said we were all originally from Yugoslavia, he said that a lot of Yugoslavs lived in the city. Even the hotel's manager was Yugoslav. He mentioned that Tadich Grill was owned and run by a Yugoslav couple and a favorite hangout of the expatriate community.

He also recommended baseball star Joe DiMaggio's restaurant, Grotto, on Fisherman's Wharf. Other highlights included the famous Golden Gate Bridge and Alcatraz, a museum today, but at that time a functioning prison from which, as legend had it, nobody had ever managed to escape.

"You can also just ride the trams up and down the steep hills of the city. That is a treat in itself."

And so we four musketeers set out to conquer this city and live our hearts in San Francisco. To my mind, Montréal in 1954 seemed bursting with life, with different sports and entertainment events happening regularly, but it was too timid perhaps. Vancouver was a handsome city, but quiet. San Francisco seemed a perfect blend of beautiful terrain, European refinement and culture, and American vitality. At the age of twenty I had reached the promised land, and it was love at first sight.

I felt a strange and significant alignment between my dreams of America and what I was experiencing around me in San Francisco.

On our third day in the city, the groom-to-be called his fiancée to tell her what a great time he was having for his stag party, forgetting that he hadn't mentioned it was taking place in San Francisco! When she found out where we were, she was livid. "Who are you there with? If you do not come back this instant, the wedding is off!" She slammed the phone down on the crestfallen fellow.

He had no choice but to go back. His best man also advised him to return rather than stoke problems for himself before even getting married. I agreed too, but I was far from happy about this change of plans. My feelings were irrelevant, though—they had the car. Luka, on the other hand, seemed very angry about this development. I'd never seen him so riled. But then his face brightened, along with his mood.

"You go," he said, throwing his arm around me. "Bata and I will stay the weekend as planned and have a great time. Oh, we are not chipping in for your trip back."

They left and we spent the weekend in San Francisco, but when the time came for us to leave too, Luka had another idea.

"Bata, I have no pressing business back in Vancouver, and neither do you. Let's go to Los Angeles, it's not that far."

A realization hit me. "If we went, could we stop off in Hollywood?"

He laughed. "Bata, Hollywood is in Los Angeles! We'll go to Hollywood for sure."

That was it. We took a bus south instead of north, and I was bristling with anticipation as it hurled toward the city of my dreams. For the most part we traveled along the edge of the ocean, so my first impressions were of the exquisite sea views and stunning nature we passed through. If San Francisco was that interesting and California this beautiful, I wondered what Hollywood must be like!

The bus brought us to the main bus depot in downtown LA, on Main Street. I could not imagine finding my way alone in that vast maze of streets that bustled with life. It was bewildering and I was grateful for Luka, who knew his way around. He was a very able young man, and we soon found a nice little hotel downtown. It wasn't luxurious, but it was clean and perfectly suited to our needs. We unpacked, showered, and immediately hit the town, with Luka leading the way.

We wandered around downtown LA for a couple of days and finally ended up at the ocean promenade. It was mid-October, but there were hundreds of people sunbathing and some were even swimming in the Pacific. I thought of frozen Montréal and my mind was made up; I was staying in this heaven of a place. Luka felt the same. We quickly talked one another into staying for a while.

The climate was divine, the ocean was alluring, and there were scantily clad girls everywhere. We had money, so why not stay?

* * *

We took a studio apartment near the USC campus in a boarding house run by a middle-aged Polish woman and her husband. Initially she didn't have any vacancy but as we talked, she mentioned that a couple of students from Cuba who had paid in advance hadn't shown up for several weeks and she gave us their place with the understanding we had to vacate if they did appear. We paid fifty dollars as a deposit and another fifty dollars for the month and we were all set.

The weather was gorgeous. Snow-covered Canada seemed distant and unreal, like a motif on a Christmas card. California was heavenly—clear sea air with no hint of smog, no traffic jams. We took a tram to the beach each morning and sunbathed and swam in the ocean until sunset.

Luka was not a typical Montenegrin. Where they are usually tall and dark, he was short and dark and looked more like a Mexican than a European. With my youthful physique and European looks, I did better with the girls, but I could not speak the language, so it was usually Luka who did all the talking, while I hung in the background, doing my best with the hundred words or so of English I'd picked up by then.

Days passed, and I was itching to fulfill my ultimate dream to see Hollywood, but Luka kept putting it off. He fell in love with the beach, the hot dogs, and the scantily clad girls. He had much more fun than me because he could actually flirt with them, while I stuttered and stammered in my practically nonexistent English. We lived like the students around us except instead of studying, we worked on our tans.

We kept our money hidden in the mattress, thinking it safer than carrying it around with us. One day Luka suggested that we convert it into American dollars and start a bank account so that we could pay for things by check instead of cash, which we agreed was the safest option. He went to the bank on the Friday, instructing me to have coffee in a corner coffee shop while he sorted out the formalities.

Before too long, Luka came to the coffee shop carrying a bag. The image is still vivid in my memory. "All done," he said. "I opened a savings account instead of checking, but I kept two hundred dollars for our pocket money! And the reward for opening one is . . . twenty-four eggs and a frying pan!" He opened the bag to show me. I must have looked surprised, because Luka laughed and explained that was what they were offering to all new customers. We would eat the eggs and later make a gift of the pan to the nice Polish landlady.

The following Sunday Luka suggested that we go to a Serbian church on the outskirts of LA, in Alhambra, so I could hear familiar language and partake of the lunch they served afterward, which included *sarma*, a dish of cabbage leaves with mince and rice filling. He knew I was frustrated from not being able to understand so many of the conversations around me. He was also tired of listening to me trying in vain to communicate.

We missed our intended bus by seconds, learning firsthand that in the US buses did not wait for anyone. We had an hour and a half to kill before the next bus. Luka spotted some shops down one of the nearby streets. He saw a pair of shoes in one of them and a glint appeared in his dark eyes.

"Let me check to see if they have my size," he said.

Two Black teenagers had a shoeshine stand in front of the store and were working really hard, one busy with a customer sitting in the highchair, engrossed in his newspaper, and the other with about a dozen pairs of shoes which people had left to be cleaned.

"At least clean your shoes while I pop into the store," Luka said. "Look how scruffy your shoes are!"

He tossed a few coins to the boys and went in. I waited for a couple of minutes for the boy to finish with the customer before climbing up on the chair and fixing my feet to the shiny rail. It was my first shoeshine experience ever, and I watched in amazement as the boy's practiced hands did their dance around my dusty shoes. Soon they'd be back to full shine.

A few minutes later Luka came out of the shop, looking pleased with his new shoes. He carried his old pair in a bag. I was just marveling at the finishing touches on my now-gleaming shoes when Luka walked past us and casually said, "See you back here in a few minutes. I'll just take a turn in my new shoes, to get them going." He grinned. "Look how beautiful they are. I asked, they have your size too."

I watched him from my highchair as he walked down the sidewalk. He hadn't gone far when a dark green car pulled up behind him and two men in identical suits came out, their dark ties in perfect contrast to their crisp white shirts, which seemed to shine in the bright California sun. They approached Luka from behind and said something to him—I was too far to make out what they were saying—and even if I could hear them, I could not understand them.

After they exchanged a couple of words, one of the men opened the back door of the car and to my astonishment, Luka got into the back seat. I wanted to shout, to call him, but something held me back. I didn't really understand what was going on, but I had a strong sense of foreboding when I saw Luka calmly enter the strangers' car.

I slowly climbed down from the shoeshine stand, all the while watching the car. The only reasonable explanation I could think of was that Luka had forgotten to bring his passport along and that the men were immigration agents who were now taking him back to the apartment to check his papers. What alarmed me was that Luka never once even glanced in my direction. That was the most confusing part and an indication that something far more serious than a forgotten document was at hand.

I hung back and watched as the other man climbed in the front and the car sped away. I stood there in my sparkling clean shoes, too astonished to think. What had just happened?! What was I to do now?

I couldn't think of anything other than to cross the street again and go back to the bus depot, hoping Luka would meet me there in time for our bus, which was leaving in a few minutes. All I had on me was the fifty-cent bus ticket, ten dollars in cash, and my German travel document. What should I do? Wait for him to come back or go to the church and ask someone there for help? Or perhaps I should try to find my way back to the flat? Maybe Luka was really taken there to collect his passport. Then I thought if I did that, and he was actually coming back to catch the bus, we might miss each other. All sorts of things were going through my mind.

The bus arrived and Luka was nowhere to be seen. I gave up on going to the church and decided to go back to the flat to look for him. My heart jumped when I spotted the dark green car parked in front of the house. Something was seriously wrong. I was suddenly petrified that I was in America illegally and that I might get deported not to Canada, or even Belgium, but home to Belgrade! Back to square one.

I decided to hide behind a huge palm tree across the street from the house and watch to see if the two men in suits would come out. On high alert now, I thought it safer to wait until they were gone before going in and confronting Luka for abandoning me like that. After a few minutes all three of them came out together. One of the men was carrying our bags, which he unceremoniously dumped in the trunk, while the other unlocked the car and opened the door for Luka.

My friend appeared relaxed, not at all like someone in bad straits. Before he entered the car, he turned around a couple of times, looking for me or perhaps taking a final look at this California dream of ours. I almost left my hiding place away behind the palm. Luckily, I did not. I watched once again as the dark green car sped away. That was the last time I ever saw Luka.

I waited awhile longer before going in. The apartment was cleared out, the drawers and the wardrobe empty. The only things I found were a couple of eggs that were left over from our prize for opening the bank account. Panicking, I checked under the mattress, where we had kept our money, hoping to find a dollar or two, but there was nothing. It dawned on me that I'd been abandoned yet again, penniless, in a foreign country whose language I could not speak.

15

Lost and Found in Paradise

I focused on getting myself back to safety again. I did not have much choice—my only hope now was the deposit that we left with the Polish landlady. I was relieved when I remembered that she spoke a bit of Russian, so it would not be impossible to speak to her about it. I rang her door and found her alone. She seemed flustered when I explained my predicament.

In her mixture of Russian, Polish, and English she explained that Luka and the men had just left, adding they were looking for me and had asked her to let them know when I arrived. She gave me a number they had left for me. As she handed me the note, it confirmed my feeling that everything had gone wrong. She seemed to realize something had gone wrong too.

I asked if she could give me back the deposit we had left with her, but although she seemed willing to help me, on hearing my request, she just shook her head. "If I had the money, I would give it to you. My husband has it." Before I could say anything, she added, "It is Sunday too, so I cannot draw your money from the bank." She suggested I could come back that evening when her husband returned, but I knew the apartment was no longer safe for me.

I went back to the bus depot in the vain hope that Luka might be waiting for me there, but he was nowhere to be seen. The only reasonable thing left for me to do was to go to the church and see if I could find him there. I spotted a bus with the destination HOLLYWOOD inscribed across the front and, without thinking twice, I bought another ticket and made it on board at the last minute.

As the bus rumbled toward Hollywood, my mind raced. Nothing made sense—and the cold sense of foreboding would not abate. My train of thought was interrupted by the voice of the driver announcing, "Last stop, Hollywood and Vine." The bus came to a halt and I got off, feeling completely lost. I had no idea what to do or where to go from there. All I had on my arrival to my dream city was $9.50, two bus tickets, and my lucky charm hidden in the lining of my wallet—the nine dollars my mother had given me when I was leaving home.

I didn't count on that as spending money, though. I wanted to hang on to that, for luck. So it was just $9.50.

I stood at the corner of Vine Street and Hollywood Boulevard, deliberating whether to go east, south, west, or north. I felt like a lost sheep. Following my intuition, I turned right and walked down Hollywood Boulevard, from Vine Street toward La Brea Avenue. I came across an enormous, illuminated advertisement for the Knickerbocker Hotel. It said, "SINGLE ROOMS $5 TO $7 PER NIGHT" in huge letters. At least I had enough money to pay for a bed for one night; then if I ventured back to my apartment and somehow the Polish man gave me the deposit back, I'd have enough money to go back to Canada.

That was the one sensible plan I could come up with. I was thinking more clearly now but was still stunned by what had taken place over the previous six hours.

Walking aimlessly down the busy boulevard, I was both petrified and excited—this was, after all, the realization of my boyhood dream, albeit under slightly different circumstances than I'd imagined. In front of one of the restaurants, I came across a throng of people, excitedly shouting and waving. I could hear the pop of cameras and realized the crowd was probably there for someone famous, an actor or an actress. I was in Hollywood after all! It was in front of the Musso & Frank restaurant and just as I was passing, a gorgeous blond came out and the crowd went crazy.

"Doris! Doris!" they all shouted and waved frantically. I thought for a moment that she could be Yugoslav with a name like that.

Soon after I reached the Grauman's Chinese Theatre and came across another huge crowd of tourists gathered in front. They were all looking down, examining the pavement. That really intrigued me. I was surprised to see feet and hands imprints of Hollywood names I knew in the asphalt, along with their signatures. One could hear laughter and chatting and the almost-constant pop of the cameras from the crowds of tourists.

Huge placards and posters announcing new movies were all over the place. I realized I hadn't set foot in a cinema in over two years.

I crossed the road to go back downtown and found myself facing the Hotel Roosevelt, where the first Academy awards were staged. This time, walking along the other side of the Hollywood Boulevard, I passed a couple of cinemas (Paramount, Hollywood, Egyptian). About halfway to the bus stop I came across Las Palmas Street, which intersected with the boulevard. There was a newsstand at the corner offering local and foreign newspapers from around the world, all alphabetically arranged. I almost screamed with delight when I spotted *Politika*, the main daily in Yugoslavia, and *Tempo*, the sports magazine. I hung around the newsstand for a long while, hoping someone from my distant homeland might come to get the paper.

* * *

Around 6 P.M., I realized I was waiting in vain, and a chill went through me. I was really lost. Quite a few people had crowded the stand, but nobody picked up anything in the languages I could understand. I had to admit that my plan had come to nothing. Now I was angry with myself for not heading to the church that morning—at least I could be sure there would be people speaking my language there, someone I could ask for advice or help.

I started to panic a bit. I had been a successful soccer player with a promising career, and now I was lost in the film paradise from my childhood dreams. I contemplated asking the police for help, but was worried I'd be deported and forever banned from entering America.

Across the street from the newsstand was the Las Palmas Theatre and next to it, Miceli's Pizza House. A group of people stood in front of the pizzeria, loudly applauding every now and then. I crossed the road to see what was happening. Through the window of the pizzeria, I saw two chefs in tall white hats spinning pieces of dough above their heads like acrobats in a circus. They threw the flattened dough onto a large wooden board in front of them, with powdery flour flying all over the place.

With practiced movements, they hurled the pieces of dough to one another, exchanging the flying discs with acrobatic precision—they worked really well together, like partners in some intricate dance with each dancer perfectly executing his moves. At the end of each number they would wave and bow to the gathered crowd, inviting them to come in for a pizza.

They hooked me. I was ravenously hungry anyway. In all the commotion of the day, I had completely forgotten to eat. I was thirsty too, so I decided to go in. The pizzeria was crowded as I entered. There were many waiting to be seated, but when I told the host I was by myself, he quickly found me an empty seat at the corner of the counter. I ordered a small pepperoni pizza and a Coca-Cola.

Once seated and with the delicious smell of food crowding my senses, I started feeling the exertions of that day. My legs hurt from all the walking I had done and my body ached. I rested my head on my hands, suddenly overwhelmed. It was dusk, and with the darkening of the skies, I felt my courage desert me. What should I do? Where could I go?

Was there anyone to call? I knew absolutely no one in this entire country. Maybe I should call the number that the landlady had given me, and see what happened? My dark mood was such a sharp contrast to the happy customers eating their pizzas and chatting to one another without a care in the world.

Then, in the cacophony of sounds, I thought I heard a voice saying something in a familiar language. I listened for it and it took a few seconds to discern it again. The voice was indeed saying words I could understand.

"Bata, what on earth are you doing here?!"

I raised my head up, toward the voice. I thought I must be hallucinating. Out of the corner of my eye, I saw the taller of the pizza acrobats leave his post and duck behind the door that led to a kitchen and disappear in a part of the restaurant I could not see. My pizza and Coca-Cola arrived, and I dived in. Although famished, I forced myself to eat slowly. Waiters and waitresses sang Italian songs as they served the guests. My hunger appeased and I felt a bit better.

The pizza acrobat reappeared at his post in the window through the same door he had disappeared into earlier. He resumed his post with his back to me, but I noticed he threw glances in my direction every now and then. After another stint on his stage, he left his post again and came toward me. He weaved his way to where I was sitting and stood directly in front of me.

"Sorry, but you are Bata Tanasijević, aren't you?" he asked in perfect Serbian. "What brings you here?"

Shocked, I barely managed to respond. "I came to see Hollywood!"

I was so thrilled to finally hear my own language spoken I could hardly think. Finally, someone from Yugoslavia. Still bewildered, I asked where he knew me from. He responded casually, "I am Bogdan Sharich, but I go by Bogie. We met a year ago while you were playing for Montréal Hakoah. Sorry, I have to run; it is the busiest time. If you can, come back at ten o'clock. That's when I finish work."

He started weaving his way back to his post.

"And what should I do until then?" I called after him.

"Go to the cinema. But be back before ten."

* * *

I stepped out of the pizzeria and found myself back on the busy boulevard. I recalled walking past several large cinemas on Hollywood Boulevard earlier but stopped at the theater closest to the pizzeria, thinking that must be the one Bogie had told me to go to. I was tired and relieved that I'd found it. I bought a ticket for fifty cents. They were showing two B-movies, which were repeated throughout the day. The cinema was packed when I entered, and I stumbled through the darkness to an empty seat.

The air was filled with cigarette smoke and the smell of hot dogs, popcorn, and Coca-Cola. When my eyes adjusted sufficiently to make out the people around me, I saw that they were mostly couples who seemed to have found better things to do than watch a film. Others were sound asleep; some were even snoring loudly. This was my first encounter with a twenty-four-hour cinema, and I found the whole concept strange and compelling.

Soon, as both the film and time dragged on, the inevitable happened and I fell into a deep sleep. I was woken by a shrill cry of the grief-stricken female character on the screen and for a moment I didn't know where I was, in the cinema or up there on the screen beside her, playing the lead in the movie of my life. When I looked at the watch, it was 10:20 P.M. I was late!

I jumped up as if on fire and bolted out of the cinema. I ran toward the pizzeria faster than I'd ever run before. Out of breath and sweating profusely, I burst through the door of the pizza place and scanned the smoke-filled room, looking for Bogie. A wave of relief washed over me when I spotted him sitting at the same counter that I sat earlier, with a bottle of Corona in his hand.

His face lit up when he saw me. "Here you are at last! I was just about to leave." He finished his beer and stood up. "Come on—let's go to Café Aldo's. It's quieter and more comfortable there. Or perhaps you have somewhere else to be?"

It took a moment for me to realize he was joking.

"I have, and I haven't, to tell you the truth."

We both laughed, and I could feel the tension in my head dissipate.

Aldo's was within walking distance, and as I followed Bogie there, he recounted euphorically his side of the story from earlier in the day. While I'd been standing fascinated in front of the window looking at them spinning pizzas in the air, he thought he'd spotted a familiar face in the crowd of onlookers but couldn't place it. His partner in spinning pizza dough, Aldo, a grumpy Sicilian, told him: "Do not bug me, go out and have a look." But just as Bogie decided to do so, he realized I'd disappeared.

"Had I not gone out for a cigarette break ten minutes later, we wouldn't be walking here together now." He chuckled.

We reached Aldo's shortly, found a table, and ordered coffees when Bogie suddenly stood up and said, "Wait here, I'll be back in a couple of minutes."

Five minutes went by, then ten. His coffee was getting cold and I was getting nervous. Was I being abandoned for the second time in the same day? Some twenty minutes later, though, he came in and, before he sat down, threw something at me. A jacket.

"Put that on. I can see you're freezing!"

Then, out of breath and with an incredulous look on his face, he told me what had kept him that long. "You won't believe what happened. I was going to my apartment to get you a jacket, and when I got there, I saw a couple in dining attire walking up the stairs that lead to my apartment. I thought this was strange as I did not expect anybody. As I stood surprised on the sidewalk, the manager and a waiter from Villa Capri, the restaurant below my place, came out.

"They bumped into me at the entrance and asked if I'd seen a couple getting into their car in the last few minutes. I said, 'No, but I saw strange couple going up my stairs.' We went up the stairs and found them cowering in front of my door. Could you believe it, the bastards looked like they had money, yet they ate and drank their fill and then tried to leave without paying the bill!"

I put on the jacket he gave me. It was warm and light blue, a color I wore as a Hakoah player.

"There, you can stop shaking now. And that color really shows off your tan!" He seemed pleased. "Even your nose looks okay."

"What? My nose?"

"I was at the game when Gidra broke your nose, but it's looking good. It healed straight. Remember, you went on to score regardless and stopped Ukraine FC from winning the league championship? We supporters were very angry, and I hated you at that moment." His coffee was refilled and he sipped the hot beverage. "So when exactly did you arrive in sunny California?" He went on before I could say anything, "I never dreamed sunshine mattered so much. I've learned to appreciate it, especially after my stints in Canada and New York."

* * *

I quickly relaxed in Bogie's company. He was the one person I'd found in this country full of strangers whom I could ask for advice and who seemed willing to help me. At the same time, I was cautious. Life had taught me not to trust people just because I liked them.

To be fair, I knew much less about him than he did about me. He was adamant we had met the year before in Canada, but I couldn't remember him. He explained that while he lived in Montréal, he supported Ukraine FC and went to all their matches. He seemed to know the same people in Montréal I did. Despite my initial reservations, I soon found myself telling him about my crazy weekend and finished the story with Luka's sudden disappearance that morning. I also told him that I was planning to return to Montréal as soon as possible.

Bogie was incredulous. "That Montenegrin is a swindler! How could you be so naïve, Bata?! That whole scenario is extremely dodgy. He disappears within minutes of getting his hands on your money, in a green car that appeared from nowhere . . . and they even stopped to take your stuff?!" His eyes flashed with anger. "You were duped, Bata. It was all a plan. You did not go into the bank, you did not see the money deposited. How gullible can you get?!"

I had to admit he had a point. He was just articulating the fears I'd been desperately pushing away throughout that long, fretful day.

"The only thing that confuses me is the note with the phone number they left you." Bogie grew serious. "Under no circumstances should you go back to that apartment." Seeing I was getting alarmed, he lowered his voice and said calmly, "You can stay at my place tonight. Then in the morning, you can decide what to do. Tomorrow is a new day. C'mon, let's go, they are closing here."

* * *

Bogie lived in a nice apartment, right above the restaurant he'd mentioned, Villa Capri. The apartment had a small kitchen but a spacious dining room, which was dominated by a heavy wooden table with a lacquered top. A chessboard sat open on its shiny surface, with pieces already lined up and ready for battle. I was finally able to relax completely, but to my surprise I found the fatigue completely gone. If anything, I now felt elated.

We had some pine nuts, opened a few beers (the only thing that he had in his fridge), and talked until dawn. He chain-smoked while we reminisced about our distant homeland, Belgrade, and our lives there. It was simply unbelievable that we had never met before as it turned out that we were from the same part of town, went to the same school, and had many friends in common. All that without our paths ever crossing.

He wanted to know about the people we both knew in Canada. I told him about Gidra and Aca-Bus and the story of my friendship with the Montréal "contractors," and he told me how he'd ended up in California. After leaving Belgrade he lived in Canada for a few years, and while in Montréal, he was seeing a girl named Lydia, a waitress in the restaurant owned by the parents of Gidra's fiancé.

She was Ukrainian and had two brothers, burly guys who worked as security guards in nightclubs around Montréal. One day she announced she was pregnant, and the brothers issued Bogie "friendly" advice to marry her without delay. But he was not ready to be a father and took off, walking across a frozen lake and into America, illegally of course. He managed to get to New York where he stopped for a while, but in the end, he came to California in search of sunshine and an easier life.

"I will never leave America," he said with intense fervor. "Not while I'm still alive at any rate."

I found his story baffling. I couldn't understand how he'd been able to live so casually and work openly without a valid visa or the work permit. How on earth had he managed that? I thought back to Valka Lager and all the complications I had across Europe because of the damned papers. In the end, it was the papers (or rather, the lack of them) that had brought me to Canada in the first place.

"It is all very simple, Bata. I tell you what, I'll show you tomorrow and you'll see for yourself just how easy it is. You have a passport, don't you?"

I showed him my German travel document.

"Great! All we need to do is pop over to the post office, and go to the federal window, fill out a form, show them your passport, and you'll get a Social Security number. It is that easy! Then you can work without having to worry about anything. It is not exactly going to make you legal, but if you keep out of trouble, nobody will bother you. Americans have to do just two things in life: pay taxes and die. It is a promised land, I'm telling you. Forget Canada. God created Canada for Eskimos, it is not for the likes of us."

As soon as soccer was mentioned, he offered to take me to the Church of St. Stephen—the same church I had intended to visit that morning with Luka—the following weekend, if I decided to stay a bit longer. He said that church was the sponsor of White Eagles FC, the Serbian amateur team he played for. Among the other Serbs playing for White Eagles was Mike Flush, the brother of a famous soccer player from FC Vojvodina. Mike got the nickname Flush because of his love of poker.

"White Eagles are amateurs, we play for fun, to keep in shape and because we love soccer, but there is a semi-professional side in San Pedro. They go under the name San Pedro Yugo-Americans. With your skills, I am sure they'd offer you a contract as soon as they see you play. It is a good club, one of the few to have their own stadium, and most importantly, they are loaded.

"But if you'd rather play for foreign teams, you have a choice: There are Scottish, English, Danish, German, and Mexican clubs around here. Even Jews have a great club, the Los Angeles Maccabees. They all play in the Greater Los Angeles Soccer League. It's one of the oldest leagues in the country. Each weekend there are at least two or three matches played at a city stadium, Rancho La Cienega, or Daniels Stadium in San Pedro. We can go to a game next weekend if you like. You'll see the level of football played here and can compare it to the game in Canada."

Bogie did his best to talk me out of returning to Canada, or even thinking about it, despite my contract with the Montréal Hakoah. Given all that had happened, I was confused and frightened, dazed from the whirlwind of events, and in no position to make any decisions.

Dawn was breaking when we finally went to sleep, back-to-back on the double bed, with pillows between us instead of under our heads. As Bogie snored next to me, I found that, incredibly, I still could not sleep. My body was exhausted, but my mind was reeling as I thought about where I was. I had dreamed of Hollywood my entire life. I finally got here, not through meticulous planning and hard work as I'd always imagined, but through a series of mishaps and coincidences.

The previous day I had been a tourist on my way to the church to eat sarma and flirt with Serbian girls, and there I was, ending that same day in a Hollywood apartment, sharing a bed with an unlikely companion—Bogie, the man who would alter the course of my life.

16

Here, There, Football Everywhere

As soon as we had breakfasted the next day, Bogie took me shopping for essentials like underwear, toothbrush, and a sweatshirt as all I had were the clothes on my back, just like in Belgium when the sisters took me in. This time though, there was one crucial difference—I had a travel document. He also purchased two more pillows.

Next, we went to the Hollywood post office. The line was moving slowly, so Bogie filled out the Social Security form for me while I kept our spot in the line. Halfway through, he came up to me, frowning. "We may have a problem. It says here that your travel document is valid until April 1955, and that's just six months from now. They may refuse to accept it as it expires so soon. We'll see. And what should I put down as your profession?"

"Professional soccer player," I said confidently.

"I am not sure how to spell that. Anyway, with your name, it is probably better to put you down as an actor, recently arrived from Europe." He shrugged. "We are in Hollywood, after all."

I signed the form and handed it to the young clerk at the counter, along with my travel document. She looked at my travel document, which was written in two languages, German and French. I doubt that she spoke either one. Regardless, she issued me a Social Security number and handed me the card. I could not believe it. I had in my hands the means to work and live normally in America, to pursue my American dream, and it was simply handed to me on a plate. That meant everything!

Outside, Bogie was positively glowing. "See how easy that was!"

Back at the apartment, he gave me the only key and said he had to go to work. But about an hour later, Bogie was banging on the door. He looked worried.

"We have a big problem. One of our busboys got lucky in Las Vegas and decided to stay longer. We are in the shit. We have loads of reservations and no busboy tonight. Could you help us out? The restaurant manager and I would appreciate it very much."

He looked really stressed and I wanted to help, but I wasn't sure I was capable of doing what he asked.

"Bogie, I have never worked in a kitchen, I wouldn't know what to do."

"There is nothing to it, Bata! You don't need special knowledge to be a busboy. The dishwasher does the washing. All you need to do is load and unload it. I'll show you how it's done. You'll get one dollar per hour, cash, and a free meal."

I could see this was important to him and I could not refuse someone who had been so good to me in my hour of need. And that is how I got my first job in America.

As the days passed, the idea of staying in America for good grew on me. I was working and eating. I saw plenty of HELP WANTED signs in other restaurants along Hollywood Boulevard. I knew I would not go hungry in America. With the Social Security card in my pocket, I felt I could make a go of it. And Bogie was doing everything he could to talk me out of returning to the "Eskimo land." He introduced me to his friends, expatriate Yugoslavs who hung out at Aldo's on weekends so regularly that they had a table reserved for them in perpetuity there.

On Saturday, Bogie and Mike Flush took me to a game at the Rancho La Cienega city stadium. We were there all day and saw three games in a row. I finally felt at home, surrounded by Europeans and South Americans who loved the game of soccer. All the Yugoslavs I met through Bogie that weekend, and later, lived the American dream. Mike Flush worked two jobs—two nights a week as a waiter, and the rest of the time as a cab driver. He was married to Eva, a German girl who was a respected film editor known for her skills creating montages. She earned a good living, and they lived in a beautiful house with a swimming pool in the Hollywood hills, but he bragged he could support himself in style even if he wasn't married to Eva, by playing poker.

Lala's was a different story, an altogether sadder one. He had hurt his back badly at work and had sued the company through a pro-bono lawyer. The deal was that they would split the money fifty-fifty. The factory's insurance company offered them $100,000 to settle out of court, but the solicitor insisted they should ask for at least double of that. When I met him, Lala, bent over his walking stick and in constant pain, had been waiting for the settlement for over a year.

The only one in Bogie's circle with a university degree was Milan. He was in a serious relationship with a beautiful American divorced girl whom he was planning to marry. He worked as an engineer in the Douglas airplane factory and was very proud of his position in such a large and important company. He made what I would then call serious money. He took pride in the fact that most of the managers in the factory were children of Serbian immigrants who were born and educated in America.

There were a few others. They all conversed in our language when together, of course, albeit with English words and phrases peppering the conversation. They were a jolly, interesting bunch. We spent hours hanging out, talking about soccer. The great debate centered on the issue of Germany winning the 1954 World Cup in Switzerland. How could a nation that had experienced so many losses in both infrastructure and population muster up the strength to become champion of the world in soccer, just a few years after total defeat?

Mike's wife Eva said something that I still believe to this day: "Soccer has always provided a strong motivation to people. It has the power to unite and give them strength to prevail and even win."

* * *

On Sunday, I finally made it to St. Stephen's Church in Alhambra. Bogie was now convinced that the best course of action for me would be to stay in America, join White Eagles FC, and keep living and working with him in the restaurant. If I did that and still wanted to return to Montréal, he argued, I would be in better physical shape than the other players, who would have spent months in winter hibernation. That made sense—and I had no plans to go anywhere.

I continued working in Miceli's Pizza House for the next three weeks first as a busboy until the previous employee came back broke from Las Vegas. The manager took a liking to me and created a job for me as a waiter on the counter that had ten chairs.

I worked most of my shifts together with Bogie. The owner of the pizzeria was Carmen Miceli, a Sicilian with little grace and none of the famous Italian charm. He was a great fan of three things: drink, women, and horse racing, and he thought he excelled at all three. He was dark-featured and short and wore a permanent scowl. He seemed to resent Bogie and me for our Balkan genes; we were both tall and towered over him.

With my new position on the counter, I got out of the kitchen and met the boss, who looked me up and down and proceeded to give me a warning: "You can serve here at the counter. But if I ever catch you picking up girls, you'll be sacked on the spot!"

I nodded. Bogie translated and possibly even softened the Sicilian's warning, but I got the gist from his tone and gesticulation.

I made close to two hundred dollars in the three weeks I worked there. It covered the living expenses. I could have earned much more, were it not for a bad tooth. One day I got a terrible toothache and ended up clocking in for work with my face swollen like a football. By the end of the shift, I was a wreck, pale and exhausted. Two attractive girls that I waited on noticed my swollen face and asked the manager what was wrong with me. He told them about my toothache and, feeling sorry for me, they said they would wait for me to finish my shift and then drive me to the all-night pharmacy to get something for it.

Right about then Carmen arrived at the restaurant with a couple of friends and sat next to them. They were a little tipsy and he was in a foul mood, as usual. He saw the girls and brightened up. He immediately invited them to a party he was heading to later. They declined the invitation politely, saying breezily. "No thanks, we are going with Bata, we are waiting for him to finish work."

I was in the kitchen behind a heavy door, but I could hear shouting and screaming outside. I ran out to see what was happening and was taken aback when I saw it was the boss. He was enraged. When he saw me, his red face went redder still and the veins on his neck bulged dangerously. I thought he was having a heart attack! He pointed his finger at me and shrieked, "You!! You are fired!"

I was shocked, but I'd also had enough. My tooth was throbbing, and I was exhausted by the constant pain. I could not stand being screamed at for nothing on top of it all. Without a word, I took off the apron, threw it on the floor, and marched out of the door, with the stunned girls in tow. And that is how I got my first and only firing in America. Within ten years or so, Carmen Miceli would become one of my closest friends and would remain so until his death.

I was now jobless, but Bogie wasn't giving up on me. I'd already enrolled in evening classes at the nearby Hollywood High, on the corner of Sunset Boulevard and Highland Avenue, and taken some English classes, per Bogie's suggestion. The classes were free and there were different levels available to immigrants. I took his advice and soon my English improved considerably, helped by the hours I spent in front of the TV.

Bogie was pleased with my progress but thought I could do much better. "You are not an actor, nor a kitchen porter, nor a food server. You are a soccer player. We are going to San Pedro," he insisted.

* * *

We traveled to San Pedro the week after I lost my job at the pizzeria. It was an hour's ride from Hollywood, south along the Pacific coast, and Mike Flush offered to drive us there. He hadn't seen me play and, although he trusted Bogie, he wanted to see my skills for himself.

Despite my progress in speaking English, I was relieved the meeting with the management of the San Pedro club was in Serbo-Croat. I spoke to them quite openly from the start. "I saw your team play last weekend in LA. I am playing professionally in Montréal, and I am on winter break from my club until the end of February. I am willing to help you, but I am not sure that will be enough to improve your play and get better results. You need better players to achieve better results."

The president of San Pedro Yugo-Americans, Andy Mardesich, explained that an Irishman named Johnny Best was the president of the league, but that a certain Mexican, Tony Marian, was actually in charge of running it. He oversaw every last detail related to the league. He ran the whole operation with the help of his wife from an office in their house on the outskirts of LA.

The league had twelve teams. The players were semiprofessionals between sixteen and forty years old. The referees were mostly recruited from the ranks of retired referees from Europe and South America. Many of them were in their fifties and no longer qualified to referee in their own country's Premier Ligue matches, so they emigrated to America where those rules were more relaxed.

They suggested a trial game and said that, if they were happy with my performance, they would offer me a package equivalent to what I was getting from Hakoah FC. The game was played the next day against the amateur club, Croatia FC. I played well, and we won 6–3. I scored a hat trick and had a hand in the other three goals. I realized that they needed more than just me. Their game was not up to the standards of the league they were playing in, and the management knew it.

After the game, we went to the Yugoslav Club and I gave them the details of my deal with Hakoah. Bogie and Mike advised me to ask for double the money I was getting in Montréal, but I decided to be straight with them and stick with what I'd promised. The one possible problem I could see was registration, but they assured me that nobody needed to know of our arrangement and that they would register me as an amateur, complete with a job in the StarKist tuna factory.

The deal was done. I promised to stick around for three months. I still urged the team's president to get reinforcements other than me but was willing to do my best to help them in the meantime. Andy said that they had the money and that they were prepared to spend it getting some new players. It didn't make sense to build up the team with just players from Yugoslavia, as there simply weren't enough of them, so Bogie and Mike suggested recruiting new players from the Danish club, which was amateur but came at the top of their league every year.

The Danish team was sponsored by Ken Hanson, who owned Scandia, a Sunset Strip bastion of fine gourmet dining and one of the most popular restaurants in LA. The Danish team had the opportunity to move into the Greater LA league but had decided against it because they would rather be the top of the amateur league than fighting to survive in the semiprofessional league.

I thought the Yugoslav Club should consider a couple of Croatian players, and singled out a certain Dinko Bilić, who had also scored a hat trick in our trial game, and who I noticed was an exceptionally talented left-footed player. But Bogie and Mike were adamant that no player from Croatia FC would agree to play for a Yugoslav team.

The team's president, Andy Mardesich, just shrugged. "Bilić's father works in my factory. Maybe we have some leverage there. We'll see!"

That's when I knew he was serious about building a better and stronger team. That reassured me, and I was ready to do my bit to help.

17

The Villa Capri

The Yugo-American club trained twice a week, on Tuesdays and Thursdays, and played matches on weekends. The club sent a driver to take me to and from the training and the games. San Pedro was at the time home to over 200,000 Yugoslavs, most of them from the coastal region of Dalmatia, and there were just as many Italians. The majority of them were seamen and professional fishermen who had come to America in the period between the two world wars.

The management of the Yugo-American club included several factory managers and owners of other small or in some cases, large businesses. One of them, the vice president of the club, had a barbershop in the city, where players could get a free shave and a haircut. The club's other vice president owned a restaurant where players and their dates were welcome to eat on the house—but only if we won the game.

Home games at the Rancho La Cienega city stadium normally drew three thousand to five thousand supporters—a decent number in view of where American soccer stood at that time in popularity. As in Canada, some players got half their pay in cash and the other half through fictional employment. I fell into that category and was paid as a StarKist employee although I never set foot in a factory.

Soon after I finalized my agreement with the club, Bogie was invited to Villa Capri for dinner to thank him for helping to apprehend the thieves who had dined and dashed up the stairs to his apartment above the restaurant. Bogie took me along and we had dinner with the owner of the restaurant, Patsy D'Amore. Bogie introduced me as a professional soccer player, knowing that Patsy, a passionate Napoli FC supporter and a lover of European football, would be impressed by the fact.

Patsy, a smiling, charming Neapolitan in his midfifties, was indeed interested, especially after Bogie told him about the game that had taken place exactly a year before in Montréal, when the Italia FC team won the Québec championship thanks to the goal I scored in the ninetieth minute of the game for the Hakoah FC against Ukraine FC, depriving Ukraine FC of winning that season championship.

Patsy found it hard to pronounce my name, Dobrivoje, so he shortened it to Daniello. Soon everyone would know me as Dany.

Patsy seemed truly grateful to Bogie for resolving the mystery of the disappearing customers, repeating a couple of times during the evening that he didn't mind feeding them if they were hungry, but he did mind very much of them guzzling his best wine and cognac, too! We spent a lovely evening in his company and ate in the traditional Italian manner, five courses of delicious pastas, meats, salads, and sweets, and finished with delicious Italian cappuccino Capri.

The following day Bogie went to work in the pizza place as usual. When he got there, he was told that his colleague—the other pizza chef, Aldo—had called in sick, so Bogie had to cover the shift by himself. He changed into his uniform and started doing the dough-magic at his post in the window, then filling the huge oven with pizzas he'd just made.

By pure chance, Carmen Miceli's brother, Tony, happened to be in Hollywood Bar, nearby the pizzeria; he and his mates were on a bit of a bender, and he decided to play a prank on Bogie. He knew

Bogie was in America illegally and thought it would be funny if he called the pizzeria from the phone in Hollywood Bar and asked to speak to him while pretending to be an immigration officer. Tony was shaking with laughter as he asked to speak to Bogie.

When Bogie picked up the receiver, Tony lowered his voice and made it sound official. "This is an immigration officer on the line. We know you are an illegal alien and we are coming to get you! We have men on all the exits, so there is no use trying to escape." Hearing this, Bogie panicked and left the phone off the hook, took off his apron, and ran out of the back door, abandoning his belongings and the oven full of half-baked pizzas. "Bogie! Bogie!" Tony yelled, ready to reveal the joke.

Too late. All he heard on the telephone was the noise of the customers. Now in a panic of his own, Tony ran over to see what was happening with Bogie. When he arrived at the pizzeria, the place was in chaos, full of thick smoke, distressed customers, and the smell of burning pizzas. Although he hadn't worked alongside that great beast of the pizza oven for many years by then, Tony realized that, to save his brother's business, he would have to roll up his sleeves, as Bogie was not coming back.

His prank had backfired, and instead of partying with his friends, he spent the rest of the evening making pizzas in the shop window.

While Tony was left remembering his youth spent making pizzas in the family business, Bogie, having fallen completely for his ruse, came running home. He found me at the bar in Villa Capri, chatting with the bartender. Surprised to see Bogie at that time of the evening, in his chef's whites and looking bewildered, we waited for him to catch his breath and tell us what had happened.

Just then the manager of Villa Capri, Bill Karan, approached us and, equally surprised to see Bogie in that state and at that time, asked why he wasn't at work and why he was walking around dressed like that. Bogie went from frantic to angry in a split second and replied brusquely that he was finished with the pizzeria and was looking for a new job.

"Great!" Bill cried out, delighted, "I have a job for you! Can you manage pastas and salads as well as pizzas?"

Of course, he could. It was an easier job that paid better than the one he had just left at Miceli's, and it was just down the stairs from our apartment.

The following morning, Bogie went to the pizzeria to hand in his notice and collect his things. The manager pleaded with him to forgive Tony's stupid prank and even offered him a raise, but Bogie was not to be swayed. He was extremely upset. A joke was one thing, but one's immigration status was not to be messed with under any circumstance.

* * *

Bogie smoked three packs of cigarettes a day, drank, and never lacked for female companionship. It still baffled me that we could have lived in similar places and run in the same circles without meeting until that auspicious night at Miceli's. How quickly life can turn! Bogie was someone who marched to his own drumbeat, and that drumbeat had taken him from Montréal to New York City, where he found work in an Italian restaurant.

He had a passion for chess and was quite proficient. He spent nearly every Sunday when he was in New York playing chess in Washington Square Park. The competition there, dating back to the 1940s when tables were first installed, was a magnet for world champions, hustlers, and skilled hobbyists like Bogie. Bogie and I played fairly regularly as we watched the horse races or the fights on his small black-and-white television.

He would spot me his queen and a rook, and we would play for a pack of cigarettes. I didn't smoke, but I never had much of a chance at winning either. I was making good money playing soccer so I didn't mind losing, plus all the help Bogie had given me took the sting out of it. And over time, my game improved to the point where he only spotted me a queen.

Bogie had held his own against some great players. Maybe a day or two after he had arrived in New York City in 1953 or '54, he found his way to Washington Square Park. He had ten dollars in his pocket, all the money he had in the world. He sat down at a board where a fourteen-year-old kid was playing five people simultaneously for five dollars a game. Bogie lost two games relatively quickly. The kid's mother was behind him, collecting the money. The kid's name? Bobby Fischer—the same Bobby Fischer who would become the World Chess Champion by defeating the Soviet Union's Boris Spassky in 1972.

Bogie laughed as he told the story. He had lost all the money he had in his possession but that was secondary to his fascination with the prodigy who had won each game before he had time to light a second cigarette. He knew he could always make money working in a restaurant. He could do anything—cook, bartend, pantry, dishwasher, waiter, maître d'. "I'll never be hungry," he said. "You can walk down the street and see HELP WANTED signs in ten restaurants."

He slipped seamlessly into the kitchen at Villa Capri, where he was already a fixture of sorts from living above the restaurant. He knew everyone, and soon I was familiar with the same people, both the staff and the clientele. Villa Capri was a beautiful restaurant, small, with only twelve tables and a bar, and decorated with ornaments and lights that gave the place an unusual, authentic, and intimate atmosphere.

Because of its lack of size, and because its regulars were a Who's Who of Hollywood, Villa Capri was more like a private dinner club than a restaurant. The Italian food was exceptional and the cocktails were strong, but the star attraction was the restaurant's charismatic owner, Patsy D'Amore. We became fast friends after that first dinner we had together, and he came to see me play whenever he could.

We enjoyed heated discussions afterward. Despite my halting English and his Neapolitan chatter delivered in English with heavy doses of Italian thrown in, we understood each other perfectly. His mixture of Italian and English sounded quite melodic, romantic even, but also funny at times. The Italian words and phrases Patsy used frequently remain with me to this day.

He had emigrated from Italy with his brother Franklin during the lull between the two great wars. Before coming to America, Franklin had been a famous acrobat, traveling with grand circuses all over Europe. They arrived in California in 1939 with an idea to introduce Neapolitan cuisine to the West Coast of America, along with proper Italian pizza. They opened Casa Di Amore in downtown LA. It was one of the first Italian restaurants in LA and quickly became famous for its Italian delicacies and convivial atmosphere.

Although they were doing well, the brothers decided to go their separate ways after ten years together. Franklin kept the restaurant, while Patsy opened Patsy's, a takeout pizzeria in the Los Angeles Farmers' Market. In a tiny space squeezed between two stalls heaped with fruit and vegetables he had a fold-up stove, a small cooler, and a table. But his pizzas started selling like hotcakes, and his business and profits grew.

After a year of business, he noticed that the produce vendors around him would lower their prices at the end of each trading day, practically giving away the vegetables and fruits they couldn't sell.

He realized that through these new contacts, he could have access to the best-quality products at competitive prices, and they were right there on his doorstep. He decided to start a restaurant again, and in 1950, he opened Villa Capri in Hollywood but made sure that Patsy's Pizza at the farmers market stayed in the family. Today, it is still run by his daughter, Filomena D'Amore.

* * *

Villa Capri was an instant success, attracting Hollywood's biggest celebrities and most powerful studio bosses. The location was partly responsible. Villa Capri was secreted on tiny McCadden Place north of Hollywood Boulevard, within easy walking distance from several large movie theatres (Grauman's Chinese Theatre, Paramount, Egyptian), making it a perfect hangout for the people in the industry after movie premieres. In this golden age of Hollywood, there were over a hundred movies made each year, so there was a new film opening almost every weekend.

But Patsy had a secret ingredient that could not be replicated by anyone else in town. His closest friend was none other than Frank Sinatra, and Sinatra spent more time at Villa Capri than Patsy himself. Patsy normally made an appearance early in the evening, but he was never happier than when in the company of produce market traders. The buzz and the lively atmosphere of a street market reminded him of his childhood in Napoli. Still, a table was permanently reserved for his friends regardless of whether he was there or not.

There were two entrances—the main entrance on McCadden Place, and the back door which led through the kitchen to the parking lot behind the restaurant. This was the entrance used by Patsy, the staff, and Sinatra and other esteemed guests wanting to avoid the paparazzi hanging out front. But only regulars like Sinatra and

James Dean dared to utter a hello or *buonasera* to Chef Carmelo, whose fiery Italian demeanor left no doubt who was in charge of the kitchen.

As you walked in through the main entrance, the long bar straddled the room to your left, at which toiled the permanently busy bartender, Baron. He was a handsome Dutchman who was in his early sixties and still better looking than many of the aspiring young actors hanging around the restaurant. His deep voice would greet you as soon as you stepped through the door. "Good evening, do you have a reservation?"

Baron cultivated a snobbish, imperious demeanor. He was an expert in making cocktails and a great connoisseur of whiskeys. He had a special talent for screening customers, and it was he who decided whether someone would get a chance to dine side-by-side with the Hollywood elites or not. He and the manager had a special code they used to communicate. If Baron mentioned the words "Pasadena" or "eighty-six," it signaled the people in question didn't fit in with the restaurant's ambiance and their request for a table should be declined.

Whether or not there were empty tables, they heard disappointing news. "Sorry, but the restaurant is fully booked the whole evening."

VIP guests would be escorted to their table by the manager, Bill Karan or Nico Romano. Bill Karan was originally from Chicago and was a gambling addict who had gone through recovery several times, but never really recovered. He met Sinatra in Sands Casino in Las Vegas. They became friends, but Sinatra soon realized that Bill was an addict who needed help, so he got him out of Vegas and brought him to Hollywood, where he found him a job in Patsy's restaurant.

Despite his addiction, he was hard-working and did his utmost to ensure that things were running smoothly in the restaurant. He was constantly flitting between the kitchen, the bar, and the restaurant floor, checking that everything was in order. Although he was always well presented and had impeccable manners, he never mingled with the patrons. He left that to Nico Romano.

Nico was an old friend of Patsy's and had been with him from when the restaurant first opened its doors. Nico Romano was his stage name. At that time, he was married to a woman who was thirty years his junior, a former dancer from New York. As a young man, Nico had worked in theaters and had traveled the world with circuses. He was a natural-born entertainer—not an actor, but an entertainer. He was flamboyant and a master at creating the convivial atmosphere that Villa Capri became famous for.

He would often chat to people waiting at the bar or would simply plonk himself at one of the tables and start dipping into his rich repertoire of jokes and stories. The guests adored him. He was there because he wanted to be. He was well-off, living in a lovely house with a garden, pool, and a guesthouse on the hills in Encino, so he refused to go on the payroll and consequently did not have working hours. He was free to come and go as he pleased.

The restaurant walls were painted in deep shades of red and orange, like the desert sunset, with a canopy of netting full of sea ornaments. Rows of empty Chianti bottles strung up with rough rope hung from the ceiling and from the large hooks on the walls. There were no windows and the beautifully shaded lamps gave out just enough light to bathe everyone in a soft pink glow, obscuring any imperfections and rendering everyone beautiful. Soft classical music played in the background.

The five waiters were dressed in white shirts, black trousers, black bowties, and red jackets. Everyone assumed they were professional waiters, but the truth was, they were a bunch of earnest young men from all over the place who had come to Hollywood following their dreams of making it big there.

From the start, Patsy introduced a rule whereby those who'd been there the longest would get the best tables. At that time, tips were not divided equally between staff, so having the best tables meant getting the best money. Johnny Parma, an Italian waiter with the longest experience at the restaurant, did well out of this arrangement. He worked at the restaurant five nights per week; on the other two, his section was given to another Italian, Tony Riggio, who'd also been at the restaurant from the start. But the other staff complained that this was unfair.

The loudest among them was Jean Leon, a talented singer who had come to America from Spain, hoping to make it in the music business. He had a beautiful voice with a timeless quality to it and at one point, was even offered a deal with Capitol Records, but he suffered from terrible stage fright and was as dead as a doornail when put in front of an audience. After getting married and having a pregnant wife, he said goodbye to his music career and got a day job driving a cab while working at Villa Capri in the evenings.

Then there was Matteo, who Sinatra had brought over from Vegas together with Bill. Matty had grown up across the street from the famous singer in Hoboken, New Jersey. Sinatra's midwife mother, Dorothy, had, in fact, delivered Matty. He spent years as a truck driver, crisscrossing America and developing a deep admiration for union leader Jimmy Hoffa, who he praised at every opportunity. Tired of the peripatetic life behind the wheel, he ended up in Vegas, working as a croupier in the same casino as Bill Karan.

Like Bill, Matty was an addict and despite Sinatra's attempts to get them straightened out, neither of them ever stopped gambling. Both continued spending every penny they earned at the horse races.

Bogie was the same way; he couldn't resist a game of dice or a good horse race. The only staff member I knew before setting foot in Villa Capri was Bogie's friend Mike "Flush" Rajkov, who I'd met that first weekend upon my arrival to America. He worked as a part-time waiter at the restaurant for two nights a week and the rest of the time drove a yellow cab, like many of my new friends.

In the kitchen, Chef Carmelo and his sous-chef, Pasquale, were responsible for the delicious Southern Italian cuisine. Their menu was not extensive by any means but followed the Italian tradition of offering five-course meals. At least one special of the day was always offered.

The kitchen was also where you would find Bogie, busboy Danny, and a dishwasher named Frank. Frank was an enigma—the only member of Villa Capri staff with a university degree yet he was working at the lowest-ranking job in the restaurant. From what I saw, they were a collection of disparate, dysfunctional, fiercely independent, and flawed characters, in many ways like a great soccer team; whether hungover, broken, or nearly broken, they showed up at the restaurant to work, and they worked hard, and it created a bond. They were a family.

* * *

I would frequently sit alone at the bar, chatting with the master cocktail mixer Baron, but after that initial dinner with Bogie, Patsy took to inviting me to sit with him and sometimes him and Sinatra and whoever else was part of Frank's group. Sinatra's inner circle in those days included Dean Martin; Sammy Davis Jr.; the agent Irving "Swifty" Lazar; actor Brad Dexter, who was of Serbian extraction and born Veljko Sosa before changing his name; and Prince Michael Romanoff, a self-proclaimed Russian royal who owned the eponymous Beverly Hills restaurant Romanoff's, one of the few successful places west of La Cienega at the time.

Patsy and I would lose ourselves in discussions about soccer regardless of who else was there. The others, in fact, usually looked at us as if we'd gone mad: They just did not get the passion we displayed for this completely incomprehensible sport. Those times when Patsy excused himself from the table to go home so he could get up early the next day to go to the market, I often found myself in the company of two guys I knew as Jimmy and Sammy, who were usually engrossed in a discussion about something I couldn't quite understand.

Every now and again, they'd pick up pieces of cutlery and start clinking them on glasses, ashtrays, or half-empty bottles littering the table, singing together in low, hushed tones, stopping and correcting each other, then finishing the tune in unison. Sometimes Sinatra popped in and joined them.

I wasn't quite sure what they were doing; I thought they were just fooling around, but it was entertaining, and the tunes were lovely, even if performed on half-filled glasses and empty bottles. It was only later that I realized that some of Sinatra's greatest hits had been written right there at that table by the legendary songwriting team of composer Jimmy Van Heusen and lyricist Sammy Cahn.

The staff in Villa Capri enjoyed spinning tales about those who sat at Sinatra's table, so they were baffled by my sudden promotion to this illustrious group. I was young, and nobody knew me; they were intrigued how I had wormed my way into this exalted company. They would whisper to one another that I was Daniello, an actor brought over from Italy to become the next Charles Boyer. I did not dispute it.

Many other notable figures from the film industry frequented the restaurant—studio heads and stars including Nat King Cole, Jackie Gleason, Cary Grant, Bob Hope, Kirk Douglas, Lauren Bacall, Marilyn Monroe, and Alec Guinness. Among the movie directors and producers who particularly liked to hang out at Villa Capri were Elia Kazan, George Stevens, the two Johns, Ford and Huston, Billy

Wilder, and a very young Stanley Kubrick, who was at the time still trying to find a financier for his first movie.

I thought I was dreaming when one evening I found Paul Newman sitting at the table with Patsy and was casually introduced to him. He was possibly the most handsome man I had ever seen, with a palpable charisma and none of the vanity associated with stardom.

The actors were a tight-knit group. They all knew each other socially and hung out together. Grace Kelly was dating Bing Crosby, and they could often be seen dining at the restaurant together. James Farentino and Montgomery Clift popped in together, as did Ava Gardner and Sinatra. Ava also occasionally came in with Lana Turner. It has been speculated that Sinatra ended his marriage to Ava Gardner after catching her and Lana Turner in bed together. I think that story has been dispelled over the years, but I heard it from Patsy's best friend at the time.

* * *

Sinatra was very active in Vegas, both as an entertainer and an investor, so he brought many of his business associates to the restaurant. One of the regular visitors on Tuesdays and Wednesdays was Joe Booker, a fixer for the notorious gangster Mickey Cohen. He took care of Mickey's betting business; he would take the bets by phone during the week and then come to Villa Capri on Tuesdays to collect the money from those who had lost. They would either wait for Joe in the restaurant or leave the envelopes with the money for him at the bar.

On Wednesdays, Joe came to pay out the winnings to those who had won, so there would often be a number of people waiting around to receive their prizes. This happened week in, week out. There were no unpleasant situations at the restaurant, but it wasn't uncommon for those owing money to fail to show up, and when that happened, we all knew we might not be seeing them for a long time.

Sinatra had his own routine. After walking into the restaurant, he often went over to the till where there would always be five ten-dollar bills waiting for him. He would give one to Baron first, then move through to the dining hall and pop one in the jacket pockets of his usual waiter and Danny the busboy, and then continue to the kitchen, where he would hand a bill to Chef Carmelo and finally to Frank the dishwasher.

Sinatra would whiz through this tipping ritual quickly, stopping only for a chat with Frank. They would shake hands, and Sinatra would ask him about his grand plan. Frank the dishwasher had a serious but a somewhat farfetched ambition to become the president of the United States. The two of them exchanged the same conversation every time they met:

Sinatra: "Hey, Frank, what do you think of Eisenhower?

Frank: "I have not made up my mind yet! But I will never forgive Truman for what he did."

Sinatra: "So, Frank, when are you going to make a move?"

Frank: "It is not the right moment, but it's close. I am getting ready and you will be the first to know!"

Sinatra (handing him a ten-dollar bill): "Here, take this tonight and when you start a proper campaign, I will make sure that the serious funds will support you. Remind me again, what's the first thing you will change once you become the president?"

Frank: "I'll abolish taxes. Nobody will pay taxes under my government! When America was founded, there were no taxes. But greedy, corrupt politicians introduced them, so they could rob people. Taxes have to go. They cheated us, saying they would take just a little bit, but then they wanted more, and more again! If we don't stop them, we'll drown in taxes!"

Sinatra: "You are right, Frank! Taxes! Taxes! That's why you have my support."

18

A Big Decision

It was February, and I had to make a big decision. I was supposed to report to the club in Montréal at the end of the month. I had plenty of money for the trip back to Vancouver, from where I still had a one-way ticket back to Montréal. I also had a friend staying in my apartment there. Either I was going to go back, or I was going to stay in Los Angeles. The club in San Pedro wanted me to stay and were ready to sign me to a longer contract for the next couple of seasons.

Every time I raised the question with Bogie, he looked at me like I was crazy for even considering it, then grumbled about wasting his time by asking for his opinion. I knew in my heart what I wanted to do, I just needed to hear other people say it. I called Gertrude. She laughed.

"Are you wearing a winter coat right now?" she asked.

"No."

"Have you been to the beach recently?"

"Maybe a week or two ago."

"It is twenty-seven degrees here in Montréal. There is snow all over the ground. It is freezing. I will tell you what you already know: Live in California!"

A phone call home to get my parents' blessing sealed the decision. But I don't want to make too much of it. There was no celebration, no change in my routine, no change in anything. I knew I was right where I belonged. Within days, Natalie Wood suggested that I improve my English. Natalie was one of a trio of young actresses who took classes from Tomi Schneider, an acting coach who worked out of a little house next door to Villa Capri. The other two in her group were Kim Novak and Angie Dickinson.

Natalie, who was still attending Van Nuys High School in the Valley, was the youngest of the three. They came in every Wednesday and Friday night after their class. Sometimes they brought friends, but the three of them were usually together. If each of them hadn't been more beautiful than the next, they probably would not have been as welcomed by Baron and Nico, but even then, they were always seated at the same table off the bar, in the area of the restaurant known as Siberia.

The reason was simple economics. All three were struggling actors. Kim had a contract with Columbia but still did not have any money. They would come in after their class, sit down, and order one pizza and a cup of coffee. They shared the pizza and the coffee refills. A good tip from them was ten cents, but more often than not it was a measly nickel—nothing that was going to excite a waiter.

Baron was the instigator of my friendship with those girls. One night he poured a glass of champagne and told me to take it and sit next to Natalie. She was too young to drink, but it was "my" champagne. She started talking to me, asked where I was from, and when I said I was from Slavia, "I'm a football player," they were all impressed. Another night I was sitting at the bar and Bogie nodded over my shoulder.

"Those kids are here again," he said.

I turned around from my perch and smiled at the girls.

"I am going to make a pizza, cut it in small, bite-size pieces, and you take it over to them," he said. "I'll tell Carmen it is for the bar."

We did this several times and occasionally I also got up and refilled their coffee, saving the waiter a task for which there was no reward. My generosity impressed Natalie, who wondered if I was auditioning to become a waiter. "No," I explained with a friendly laugh, I was just a customer. That night, as I recall, I was waiting for Bogie to get off work so we could go upstairs and play chess. I was telling Natalie about my childhood during the war and my family's struggles when she suddenly changed the subject.

"I think you should come to acting class with us," she said. "It will help you learn English, and the class is in the house right next door to Villa Capri."

The next week I started taking acting classes. I was fairly attractive, and, being an athlete, I was also accustomed to playing in front of thousands of people every week, I possessed a certain amount of natural confidence performing in front of other people. Acting did not seem that different. During my first class, the teacher brought me up in front to do an improvisation with two other students. It was one scene, and I felt I held my own. Apparently, the teacher approved.

"You have a great voice," she said afterward. "You're handsome. You have a spark, charisma. Learn English. You should be in this business."

I did not need any more encouragement than that to continue attending her classes. Whether I had talent was beside the point. The class was full of gorgeous young girls. I was only twenty years old, so the pursuit of sex and romance was of primary interest. I chased Kim Novak and Angie chased me, but none of us got each other. In fact, Angie warned me that going after Kim was a losing proposition since she was under contract to Columbia and would lose her contract if she was caught playing around with someone the studio didn't approve of.

There was no reason to be deterred. At the time, there was a party at someone's house every night. It was all potluck. Someone brought a bottle of wine, another person brought salami sandwiches, some of the women brought cookies, and at the end of the night everyone left with someone if they wanted to. You could get laid every night, and I did—or I tried to. I was at one party and saw the girl that I'd had sex with two nights before. She did not even look at me. Not out of scorn but for lack of interest. She was already with someone else. One night later on one of the girls I knew asked, "Do you score every time?"

"No," I said. "I score maybe 50 percent of the time."

She winked at me. "I score 100 percent."

* * *

Some of the regulars knew about the apartment Bogie and I shared above Villa Capri and periodically took advantage of it. One night Bob Hope and Milton Berle had both placed bets on a boxing match. Realizing the fight was on TV but they had no place to watch, they asked Villa Capri's manager, Bill Karan, if he had a TV in the back where they could watch. He said, "No, but Bogie does." From then on, it was not unusual to find one or both watching the fights in our place.

Our place was convenient for reasons other than watching sports. It was February 1955, not long after I had decided to stay in Los Angeles, and I was sitting with a group of people at Patsy's table, among them Frank Sinatra and Brad Dexter, who Sinatra constantly referred to as "the Serb." I had wondered about his nickname and one night I said, "I am Serb. Are you?" He said yes, he was, then he looked at me as if he were trying to focus his eyes and said, "I always thought you were Italian."

That evening, Bob Hope was dining with Marilyn Monroe and his publicist Frank Lieberman at another table nearby. Marilyn was either divorcing or had recently divorced Joe DiMaggio. After an hour or so, Marilyn got up to use the bathroom and she stopped at our table to hug Frank and say hello to Brad, who worked with her in the movie *The Asphalt Jungle*. Once she was gone, Frank waited until about the count of ten and excused himself from the table. He did not give a reason, and we did not ask.

"Stay here and finish up with the Serb."

Meanwhile, Bill Karan had gone back into the kitchen and told Bogie that he needed the keys to our apartment.

"For what?" Bogie asked. "We did not make the bed or straighten up anything else."

"Don't worry about it," Bill said. "We'll make the bed. Just don't go up there. And after you're finished tonight, find something to do."

Frank never came back to the table and Brad Dexter and I finished dinner. Bogie let me know not to go up to the apartment and the two of us spent the night playing cards at the Normandie Club in Gardena. We returned around 6 A.M., just as the sun was rising and turning the dusky sky into ribbons of pink and purple. We opened the door and saw that the bed was stripped of sheets and the place had been straightened up. Nico's wife had the job of cleaning up for us once or twice a week and she had been up there earlier. Her vacuum was still in the corner.

"Look at this," Bogie called to me.

He was beside our table, pointing at his chess set. The pieces were all set up as if ready for a new game except the black king and the white queen had been moved to the center of the board, where they stood side by side with two crisp one-hundred-dollar bills sandwiched between them.

"This is fantastic!" he exclaimed. "We have enough money here to pay the rent for the next four months!"

Later that day, Bill Karan found us and asked if either of us had found a pair of earrings in our apartment. He made up a silly story about his wife leaving them there, but Bogie and I knew they belonged to Marilyn. Eventually it came out that Nico's friend Pat, who had been helping Nico's wife straighten up, took the earrings and after that Nico was no longer welcome at Villa Capri.

* * *

Everyone knew that you did not want to be on Sinatra's bad side. He really only had one side. He either liked you or you did not exist. I realized that I was treading on dangerous territory the day Frank's ex-wife Nancy asked me for a favor.

Sinatra had married Nancy Barbato in 1939 and had three children with her, Tina, Nancy, and Frank Jr., before they divorced in 1951. She occasionally came into Villa Capri with her friends or brought her children for dinner and knew me from there as a nice young man who was friendly with everyone. One night in June she told Bill Karan that she had a problem I could help solve. Her and Sinatra's daughter, Nancy, was turning fifteen, but she'd had a fight with her boyfriend and was very upset.

She didn't have anyone to celebrate with her on this special occasion. The last thing she would have wanted was to go out with her mother, especially when she was nursing a broken heart. She thought I looked like a nice young man who was friendly with everyone and close enough to her daughter's age. Bill gave me a look as he explained the situation that basically said I had no choice in the matter other than to be on my best behavior. Then he handed me a twenty-dollar bill to cover the tab.

"It's going to be positioned as a blind date," he said.

"When?"

"You'll meet her tomorrow night for an early dinner."

I had one request. I didn't want to sit in the area behind the bar known as Siberia, and so we had a nice table, where we were enjoying ourselves, talking, and having a good time, when Patsy came in from the market with an armful of the produce he had just bought from vendors at end-of-the-day prices. He saw me sitting with Sinatra's teenage daughter and freaked out. I thought he was going to drop everything there in the dining room—or worse, throw them at me.

He didn't say anything, but he went home and called Bill Karan, who was not at the restaurant yet. He tried the bartender, Baron, and gave him hell. I don't know exactly what he said, but when I asked for the check, I was told it was taken care of. There was no charge—only a handwritten note the waiter slipped me that said, "Let this be the first time and the LAST time I see you with my daughter."

* * *

When James Dean wasn't in Texas shooting the movie *Giant* with Elizabeth Taylor and Rock Hudson, he was in town filming interiors at the Warner Brothers Studio in Burbank, and during whatever free time he had he was at Villa Capri, quite often playing chess with Bogie. He spent as much time in our place as he did in the restaurant.

At the time, he was dating Pier Angeli, an Italian actress whose bewitching dark beauty brought its own curse—various engagements, marriages, and ultimately a lonely death from a drug overdose at age thirty-nine. His best friend, Lew Bracker—a sometime writer and tennis pro who sold insurance to support his wife and two daughters—was another Villa Capri regular. The two of them were always together except when Jimmy was playing chess up at our place. I liked Lew, who was as steady and affable as Jimmy was flighty and strange.

I liked Jimmy as an actor but had trouble connecting with him one-on-one. Bogie had no such problem. He and Jimmy forged a deep connection over the chessboard when they would share stories about their painful pasts. Bogie, one of nine children, told Jimmy about growing up during the war and ending up in a concentration camp in Croatia at age eleven. Jimmy listened with a look on his face that led me to believe he was picturing himself in those same harrowing situations. In turn, he opened up to Bogie about his own childhood with an abusive, alcoholic father.

Jimmy was also close with Villa Capri waiter Jean Leon. Jean had emigrated from Spain, touched down in New York City, and put down roots in Los Angeles after gaining citizenship by serving in the Korean War. He was ready to move on from Villa Capri and Jimmy promised to bankroll his dream of opening a French restaurant with the money he made from his next movie. I believe it would have happened the way they planned if he hadn't been addicted to fast cars and the thrill of high speeds.

It was the end of September, one of the best seasons in Southern California. Days were warm and the nights were cool and filled with the sweet fragrance of night-blooming jasmine. Jimmy and his friend Lew were all wrapped up in the new Porsches they had acquired. Earlier that month Jimmy had traded his six-month-old Porsche 356 Speedster for a new Porsche 550 Spyder. Now, on the last day of September, I was among those admiring his car in front of Villa Capri. The silver Spyder had been customized with his racing number 130. On the rear it said, "Little Bastard."

It was late morning. Villa Capri opened at five, but Jimmy was supposed to meet Lew there before he drove up to Salinas, where he was competing in a race the next day. But Lew hadn't shown up. He had a stuntman pal following him in a Ford Country Squire station wagon, itself a wood-paneled beauty, with a trailer for the car.

"Anyone hear from Lew?" Jimmy asked.

"No."

Jimmy gestured at Patsy.

"Come on, Patsy, get in. Let me take you for a ride."

Patsy took a step backward and shook his head. "What are you doing in that tub? It's not a car. It's tub on wheels."

Jimmy looked at Bogie, but Bogie was already in his uniform doing prep as that night's salad man.

"Dan, you want to go for a ride?"

"No, no, no, thanks," I said.

Just then Bogie hopped in the passenger seat. He did not want to disappoint one of his favorite people. "I go around with Jimmy." They roared off down Hollywood Boulevard, then Highland and onto wherever street until they reappeared a few minutes later in front of the restaurant. Lew still had not arrived. As Jimmy checked his watch, Patsy walked around to the driver's side and said, "Jimmy, you have a great career. You're a big star. You have got to get rid of this racing. You are going to get yourself killed."

Jimmy waved him off. "I'll never get killed at the races. I might get killed on my way to them. But not when I'm on the track."

About six hours later, Jimmy was killed in a fatal car wreck outside of Paso Robles. He had told all of us that he was headed to his German mechanic's garage. He gave us Rolf Wütherich's name and phone number and instructed us to have Lew call him there. Lew never showed up. It turned out that he had taken his daughter to a college football game at the Rose Bowl. Tickets had suddenly come his way, and he had promised her they would go if he was able to get a couple of seats. Jimmy and Rolf set out up north without Lew, followed by his stuntman pal and a photographer.

I was upstairs watching television when Bogie came in crying. He sat at the table and put his head in his hands. I had never seen him so broken up. Finally, he looked up at me with a ghostly emptiness in his face that scared me.

"James Dean is dead," he said.

"What?" I could not fathom this shocking news. I had been talking to him earlier that day.

"He's dead."

Within hours the news spread, and Villa Capri regulars and friends of Jimmy's began showing up at the restaurant looking for answers and support. *Giant* director George Stevens, Elizabeth Taylor, and Natalie were among those who arrived wearing stunned expressions. They lit candles and shared stories about the charismatic young actor, who was only twenty-four years old. Around 11 P.M., Lew finally walked into Villa Capri. He saw everyone, the dozens of flickering candles, and turned to Baron at the bar.

"What's going on?"

"James is dead."

Lew turned white as a ghost and began to shake. Someone caught him before he fell and guided him into a chair. That event also marked the end of Villa Capri as I knew it. Some invisible bond was broken that night. I went to sleep very late, just before sunrise, with my head full of questions I couldn't answer. But I knew one thing. Luck played an important role in living a good life, and I knew I was lucky.

Part Three

Pasta

19

Movies, Marriage, and a Twist

The change happened right in front of me. Jean Leon quit the following Monday to open his own restaurant, though his path to independence was not an immediate one. Bogie packed up his things and moved to San Francisco, essentially vanishing into the fog-shrouded city without a forwarding address or phone number. I wouldn't see my friend and savior for another four or five years. And Patsy, with backing from Sinatra and some of his Las Vegas pals, made plans to move the restaurant from its original location on McCadden to a larger site one block away, on Yucca Street, just up the street from Tinseltown's temple to Tiki drinks, Don the Beachcomber.

I was on the move, too. Through Natalie Wood, I began studying acting with Jeff Corey, one of Hollywood's most respected acting coaches. Jeff had been a busy actor until he was blacklisted for refusing to give up the names of fellow Communists in front of Senator Joe McCarthy and the House Un-American Activities Committee in 1951. He turned to teaching and held his classes in a garage he had converted into a studio behind the little home he and his wife shared in Hollywood.

Natalie told Jeff about me—a young guy who ran away from the Commies and was in her other acting class and friendly with everyone at Villa Capri—and she returned with an invitation from him to visit his class. At the first class I attended, he gave me a warm welcome and told me to observe the other students. All the work was improvisational, with a focus on the psychological makeup of the character. A true artist and intellectual, Jeff pushed his students to understand what was going on deep inside their characters, at a subconscious level. "I teach people, not things," he often said.

"You can come to my classes," he told me afterward. "But you will just sit for a while. You won't have to do anything. Just listen. Then, gradually, you can start participating little by little."

That began a friendship lasting decades. With Bogie gone and Villa Capri in limbo, I needed a new place to live. Through George and Robert Swink—two prominent Serbs in the film industry who I knew through Brad Dexter—I heard about a studio apartment on Hollywood and Orange. It was in a new building with a swimming pool for sixty dollars a month. The Swink brothers' secretary was living there but needed to move out. She was raising a little boy, eight or nine months old, and the man she had been living with was drafted and killed in Korea.

It was a great apartment, and I was eager to take it. I happened to be wearing a suit and tie that day because Jeff had arranged for me to go to NBC and audition for one of the *Matinee Theater* productions that the network aired daily in the afternoons. I was nervous, so much was happening, and this was all in addition to my full-time job on the soccer field. As I walked out of the apartment, I saw the woman's baby had fallen into the pool. She had ducked into the kitchen while we were saying goodbye in the doorway and in that split second the baby had crawled into the pool.

I immediately jumped in the water and saved the baby. Many years later I received a letter from George Swink's wife, Shirley, letting me know that George had passed away. She added that the baby I had saved was George's son from an affair he'd had with his secretary. George and Shirley had been childless themselves. Now that baby was all grown up and married with four sons of his own.

As a result of that little drama, though, I missed my interview at NBC. This was typical of my life, I thought. Something seems like a great opportunity only to be derailed by something else unforeseen. Disappointed, I relayed the incident to Jeff, who made a phone call and arranged for my audition to be rescheduled the next day. I showed up on time, in more casual clothes since my suit was not completely dry yet, ready to prove I was the right actor for whatever part they had in mind. But there was no need. The casting director stood up and shook my hand.

"We don't need an audition," he said. "We heard about what you did yesterday, saving that baby. You have the job."

A week later, I had my first role as a professional actor. *Matinee Theater* was in its second season. The shows were broadcast live, shot on an enormous soundstage, and I worked all the time, typecast as a handsome young toughie. I played Germans, Mafia hit men, thugs, soldiers, and various other characters with rough exteriors. In over fifty shows, I was shot in nearly all of them and never once got to kiss the girl—at least on camera. Off camera the storyline was different.

It was a dream life, like the fantasy I had of Hollywood when I was a kid sitting in the cinema. I had a part all the time. I was playing football. I was making money. I was living like a king.

* * *

The story goes that Jean Leon left Villa Capri to open his own restaurant right after James Dean died, fulfilling the dream they had shared of Jean having a place of his own. That's true, but there's more to it. Jean's departure wasn't entirely voluntary—he had clashed with Sinatra.

One night, Sinatra stopped in on his way to a premiere with Zsá Zsá, Eva Gabor, and Mike Romanoff. He ordered linguine with clams and asked for finocchi—fennel—to clear his breath of garlic afterward. "No problem," Jean assured him. But when Sinatra was ready, Jean discovered that Bogie, the pantryman on duty, had already given away the last two pieces. Jean apologized, but it was no use. Sinatra erupted, stormed out with his guests, and vowed never to return as long as Jean worked there. Patsy, the owner, gave Jean a few days off to let tempers cool, but the message was clear: It was time for him to find another job.

Jean went to work as a waiter at Joe's Little Italy on Cahuenga Boulevard. A while later, Joe opened La Scala in Beverly Hills, and in April 1956 Jean bought him out. At last, his dream became reality—a restaurant of his own that would define Los Angeles dining for decades. Sinatra never set foot in La Scala, but both men fared just fine without each other.

Jean modeled La Scala after Villa Capri. The dining room had just nineteen tables—three by the bar in "Siberia," ten in the main room with booths along the front wall, and six more tucked into a back alcove. A staircase led up to the bathrooms and Jean's office. He recruited trusted veterans from Villa Capri, including Pasquale, the Argentinian cook who had been Chef Carmelo's second, and Matty "Matteo" Jordan as the maître d'. Jean printed his motto on the menu: *Good music. Good food. Good liquors.*

And good deal. La Scala was an instant hit. With Villa Capri closed, Hollywood's royalty needed a new clubhouse, and they flocked to this tiny outpost of fine Mediterranean cuisine on Little Santa Monica Boulevard. Kirk Douglas, Marilyn Monroe, Marlon Brando, Peter Lawford, the Gabor sisters—Zsá Zsá, Eva, and Magda—and Robert Wagner and his bride-to-be Natalie Wood were

Dan Tana, then Dobrivoje "Bata" Tanasijevic, as a young child with his mother, Lenka. Belgrade, Yugoslavia, 1939.

Source: Family estate

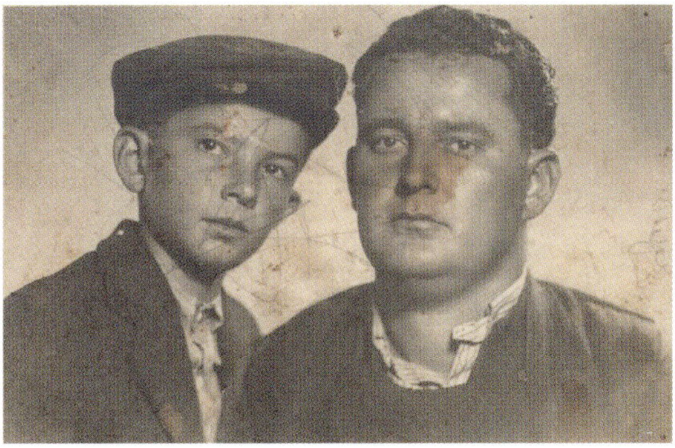

Dan with his father, Radojko "Ruby" Tanasijevic. Belgrade, Yugoslavia, 1953.

Source: Family estate

Lenka Milosevic Tanasijevic's family prior to marriage. (Lenka is second from the right in the back row holding a picture.)

Source: Family estate

Dan playing for Yugolsav American team. Los Angeles, California, 1956.

Source: Family estate

Clarence Dan Martin, Dan Tana, and Dan Reeves. Los Angeles, California, 1963.

Source: Family estate

Dan as chairman with Brentford F.C. celebrating promotion to the 3rd Division in the 1977–78 season. Brentford, London, England.

Source: Family estate

Dan Tana actor headshots. Los Angeles, California, 1960.

Source: Family estate

Dan posing behind the Peppermint West Club, on Stanley Kubrick's motorcycle. Hollywood, California, 1962.

Source: Family estate

Dan and Andrea at the dinner for President Tito. Los Angeles, CA, October 1971.

Source: Family estate

Dan and Jean Leon. Los Angeles, California, 1963.

Source: Family estate

Dan's father, Radojko, and Giovanni in the kitchen at Dan Tana's. Los Angeles, California, 1967.

Source: Family estate

Dan Tana as a young boy (with his hands together, two people to the right of the man with the trophy). At the microphone on the far right is his Red Star football hero Rajko Mitić.

Source: Family estate

Dan helping clean up the debris and fire damage at Tana's in August. Los Angeles, California, 1980.

Source: Family estate

Dan with Wilt Chamberlain, Harry Dean Stanton, Paul Stewart, Eric Braeden, and Guido. Los Angeles, California, 1975.

Source: Family estate

Adam Sandler, Chris Rock, Ben Stiller, Jim Carrey, and Dan at Dan Tana's, gathering after the charity event for 9/11 victims. 2001.

Source: Suzette Van Bylevelt

Dan, Katerina, and Gabrielle Tana. Los Angeles, California, 1964.

Source: Family estate

Dan and Bebe and their beloved Dash. Belgrade, Serbia, 2023

Source: Matija Koković/SVIJET

among the regulars Jean escorted to the prime booths he reserved for his celebrity clientele every night.

Matty was brilliant working the front. Just like he did at Villa Capri, he visited each table, usually complaining about how much money he had lost at the horse races, cursing jockeys like Willie Shoemaker and Johnny Longden, and vowing never to go to the track again—"not until tomorrow." The customers loved him.

* * *

It was hard to believe that only three years earlier I had been living in a West German prison camp. How do you reconcile memories so wildly at odds with each other—Nikola sitting on my bed with a knife in his back, and Sinatra using my bed for a secret liaison with Marilyn Monroe?

The only explanation that made sense to me was soccer. In sports, you play in the moment. There's no dwelling on mistakes, no replaying who scored against you, no fixation on whether you're ahead or behind. You focus only on the present. As I often reminded myself: Let the ball do the running, Bata.

And run it did. I was studying regularly with Jeff Corey. One afternoon, I performed a scene in his class with actress Carol Eastman—who would go on to write *Five Easy Pieces* years later. A casting agent from Dick Powell's production company happened to be observing that day. It was spring of 1957, and Powell was producing and directing *The Enemy Below*, a World War II submarine thriller starring Robert Mitchum and Curd Jürgens. The casting agent was making the rounds of acting classes in search of young faces for smaller roles. After hearing my accent, he approached me as soon as class ended.

He said there were two parts for a young soldier on the submarine, either a helmsman or a sergeant. He asked if I would take a screen test at 20th Century Fox. I said sure and got the part two days later. Filming was scheduled to last eight weeks on the Fox studio lot. Could I be available? Yes, not a problem, I explained, before detailing my responsibilities as a soccer player with my San Pedro team.

"You're a professional athlete?" he said.

"Yes."

I think that made him even more interested in me.

"But you're going to have to change your name," he said.

I shook my head, startled. "I can't change my name. Dobrivoje Tanasijević. Everyone calls me Bata."

"That won't work," he said. "Go home, think about it overnight, and come back tomorrow."

Early next morning I telephoned my parents and told them about the offer to be in the movie but that it was conditioned upon me changing my name. My mother deferred to my father.

"Listen, son, I don't care what they call you as long as they don't break you. They can give you some other name. To me, you're Dobrivoje Tanasijević. But let me ask you this: Can they pronounce Tchaikovsky?"

"Yes."

"Well, Tanasijević is easier than Tchaikovsky."

"I'll tell them," I said.

I returned to the studio that afternoon and met with two guys in the casting department, the one I knew and someone else, while their secretary listened in the background. They started playing with names and came up with Danny as a first name. I did not like Danny. I was not a Danny.

"How about Dan?" the casting agent I knew said.

"That's okay," I said.

Now they had to find a last name.

"How about Turner?" the new guy suggested.

"No, he's not English, nor British," the girl said from her desk. "He's got to have a name that's more like his accent."

"How about Tchaikovsky?" I said. "Everyone knows how to say that."

The casting agent looked up at the ceiling and took a big breath. "When you become famous, you can be Dan Tchaikovsky."

Meanwhile, the secretary was busy scribbling names and crossing out letters on a pad of paper.

"How about Dan Tanana?" she said. "Like banana but with a T."

The two casting agents said the name a few times and looked at each other in a way that said it was good but not quite there. Their secretary kept writing and crossing out before looking up, pleased.

"Try the first four letters of your real name—Tana. Dan Tana."

I said the name out loud, Dan Tana, and looked around the room at everyone's reaction. "Wow. I like it."

So did everyone else. And that was how a small slice of my personal history was made (or rather re-made). There in that small office on the 20th Century Fox studio lot I was rechristened with the name I would use for the rest of my life, Dan Tana. But it was just the beginning of my life in the movies. Within a week or two, I was back on the Fox lot, where a detailed replica of the interior of a submarine had been constructed on a soundstage. Going to work was like playtime. Midway through production, I became friendly with the movie's star, Robert Mitchum.

We started talking one day after he became intrigued by my accent and asked about my background. When Bob heard my crazy story of being a soccer-playing refugee from Serbia via Belgium, Germany, Montréal, Vancouver, San Francisco, and Villa Capri, he said I had to meet his best friend, actor Peter Coe, because he had a similar story. The three of us met for dinner at La Scala and lasting friendships were formed. Both Bob and Peter were about twenty years older than me, but our age difference melted like the ice cubes in the glass of Chivas both men started their meal with.

The chemistry between these two friends could have easily made me feel like a third wheel, but I was immediately charmed by Peter, who was as colorful a character as I had ever encountered. Born in Dubrovnik, he had been in his late teens and working as a beach lifeguard when he got in trouble with the local police. Two gay guys visiting from England rescued him from the authorities and spirited him to England, where they were prominent theatrical producers.

Through their connections, they got him into the London Academy of Music and Dramatic Arts, where Peter learned English and discovered he had real talent and an interest in acting. Pursuit of a career took him to Toronto, then New York City, which was where he met Bob Mitchum, who was then another anonymous up-and-coming actor. Both were dating girls named Dorothy. In 1940, Bob married his longtime girlfriend Dorothy to get her to move to Hollywood with him; they remained married until he passed away fifty-seven years later. Peter also wed his girlfriend Dorothy, using it to help him get citizenship papers; it was the first of his eight marriages.

When I met him, Peter was married to Rosalee Calvert, a tall, elegant actress and model regarded as one of the world's most beautiful women. The *Los Angeles Times* dubbed her "The Face" and noted costumer John Hayles said, "I've worked with the best and most famous in the industry, but no one can match Rosalee Calvert in front of a camera." However, neither those looks nor their two little boys (they would eventually have three) could dissuade Peter from his insatiable appetite for the lithe dancers in the city's burlesque clubs he liked to frequent late at night.

About a year or two later I stayed briefly in the guest quarters behind Peter's home in West Los Angeles. Rosalee had a job out of town and Peter was taking care of their children, though their housekeeper did all the work. Peter went out every night, bringing home girls after the clubs closed, as was his practice. Most mornings I would go into their kitchen for breakfast and find the two small boys, the housekeeper, a young woman, and Peter, who would greet me with a wink and introduce his friend as my girlfriend even though I was seeing her for the first time.

It helped to be an actor. But who was I to judge?

* * *

I was starring in my own matrimonial charade with a woman who I knew about as well as I did one of Peter's overnight paramours. My Yugoslav-American team was having a terrific season, and as a key player the team's owners were looking out for me. They were concerned about my lack of citizenship status. They knew that I had come into the US on the flimsiest of German passports and with my profile growing in Hollywood, I was a potential target for deportation.

After practice one day, the lawyer who worked with the club motioned for me to join him on the bench. Mr. Martin waited until we were by ourselves.

"I have the answer," he said.

He described a woman who had been coming to our matches. She was thirty years old, a former army nurse who had served in Korea, and "she likes you," the lawyer said. Seeing that I did not understand where he was going with this, he cut to the chase. "You're going to marry her, and we'll work on your papers from there." As explained to me, she did not want anything from me or the club, but as the lawyer explained, "She has her own little house in Long Beach, and she doesn't like men," I realized both of us were benefiting from this arrangement.

A few days later I met her in the morning, and we stood before a judge in an empty room near the port in Long Beach.

"Where are your witnesses?" the judge asked.

My bride-to-be—I will call her Bonnie—was a very clever, quick-thinking woman. She saw it was 10 A.M. and said that she had mistakenly told our witnesses to show up at 10:30 A.M. We walked outside and she darted into a nearby coffee shop whose booths and tables were inhabited by mostly older people who looked like they were spending their last $1.50 on coffee and eggs and toast. She found two who agreed to be our witnesses for twenty dollars each, and a short time later Bonnie pulled two rings from her purse and the judge pronounced us married.

"Are you going to kiss your wife?" he asked.

I did not have to pretend that I forgot about that part of the ceremony. I grabbed her face, kissed her on the lips like I was the happiest man in the world, and we walked outside newly and legally husband and wife. Bonnie was a lovely girl, not especially beautiful but her good heart was evident to me even though we had just met, and if I was helping her be a little less frightened about her lifestyle preferences, it was a win for both of us. I knew the value of trusting the right people.

The two of us drove separately to San Pedro, a brief ten minutes away, where we met with our lawyer, who advised each of us to keep some T-shirts and underwear at each other's place on the slight chance that someone from immigration showed up asking questions. As instructed, I also slept at her house a few times so her neighbors could see me coming and going. It was when I questioned the lawyer about my papers that he mentioned that marriage did not completely solve my problem.

"Your German passport has expired, and it wasn't stamped when you came into the US," he said. "You're here illegally. You have no proof. You married Bonnie, but how'd you get here in the first place? We have to get you out of the country and then get you back in."

"How?" I asked.

"Mexico," he said.

Mr. Martin, who claimed to have helped twenty-five thousand people get in or stay in the US, had contacts on both sides of the border and knew what he was doing. Twenty-five thousand was a big number to swallow, but I just had to trust him and follow the script, he said. During our drive to Tijuana, I flashed back to the train ride I had taken from Belgrade to Hanover when I sat amid soldiers and snitches worrying that my dream of freedom could end at any moment. What if I was stopped at the border and sent back to Canada and then to Yugoslavia? This remarkable life I have been living could easily end up seeming like a figment of my imagination.

The ocean air as we drove down the coast helped clear my head of those dark thoughts. We crossed into Mexico without incident, and I met with an immigration officer in Tijuana as my lawyer had arranged. I presented him with a letter Mr. Martin had given me before I went in stating that I was in Mexico to meet with the Guadalajara team about a spot on their roster. The officer was a football fan. He read the letter carefully twice before stamping my expired passport and saying, "Don't play in Mexico. We need you in America."

I walked outside holding my passport in the air. My lawyer was across the street and could not tell if I was happy or upset.

"You got through?" he asked.

"It's stamped," I said. "Now we can go back, right?"

No, the plan changed while I was meeting with the immigration officer. Apparently, Mr. Martin's contact on the US side of the border was taking the day off and would not be back on duty until tomorrow. So we spent the night in Tijuana. Mr. Martin got blazing drunk. Before he passed out in his hotel room, he warned me to hide any cash I had under my mattress in case a bandit broke in and tried to rob me. I had two hundred dollars cash, which I left in my pocket, thinking a thief would have a rougher time trying to get it from me than the mattress. I hardly slept.

We wasted no time the next morning heading home. Mr. Martin felt much more confident about this leg of the trip. He explained that he knew a particular officer at the border who was on the lookout for us. The officer wrote screenplays, and he had two that he wanted to give me in exchange for stamping my passport.

"Why me?" I asked.

"I told him that you just made a movie with Robert Mitchum, and you're going to give his screenplays to a producer at Fox."

"I don't know anyone at Fox," I said.

"Just tell him that you're going to read his screenplays and pass them to the right people."

After I sailed through the border crossing, receiving both an official "Welcome to the United States" and two screenplays, I believed that my lawyer was telling the truth when he said he had helped twenty-five thousand people. As we passed by the Camp Pendleton Marine Corps base along the highway, I tapped the screenplays. I could not think of who I was going to give them to.

"Give them to me," Mr. Martin said, holding out his hand.

"Now?"

"Yes."

He put the scripts in his lap, opened his window, and tossed them onto the highway. I looked back and saw them sitting on the asphalt near the center of the highway, the pages fluttering in the breeze. After that, I saw Mr. Martin at my games, but we never spoke of our adventure south of the border. It was not until I had been married to

Bonnie for three months that he brought any of this up again, and then, as seemed to be the pattern with him, he confused me.

"You're going to be a free man," he said.

"What do you mean? I am not a free man," I said. "I am married to Bonnie."

He touched his forefinger to his nose. "You have problem. You married a Catholic girl and you're Greek Orthodox and you and Bonnie can't decide what religion to raise your kid if you have one. It's a serious religious problem."

"It is?"

"It is." He nodded. "Leave it to me. I'll take care of it."

A few days later, he put a legal document in front of me and told me to sign. It was an annulment of my marriage due to irreconcilable differences. Once my signature was on the paper, Mr. Martin congratulated me with a firm handshake and a self-satisfied grin at his own handiwork that would not only let me stay in the US without fear of deportation but also start me down the road toward legal citizenship.

The whole episode taught me something about life in America: It pays to have a good lawyer.

20

La-La-La Scala

In January 1958, I got a part in the movie *Imitation General*, a military comedy about an Army sergeant who impersonates a general to boost his company's morale. The MGM production starred Glenn Ford and Red Buttons and featured a rising young actor named Dean Jones who was represented by my agent. About two years earlier, my agent had heard that MGM was looking for the next Fred Astaire or Gene Kelly, and he lobbied to get Dean a screen test.

To prepare, Dean had to learn how to tap dance. As a favor to my agent, I partnered with Dean in tap dancing classes. After two months of study, Dean aced his screen test and signed with MGM, where his guy-next-door likability landed him in several movies, including Elvis Presley's *Jailhouse Rock*. From what my agent told me, though, the studio's producers thought I was a better dancer.

Now both of us were working on the same picture. Dean was an American GI, and I played a German soldier pursued by Glenn Ford's character after he finds out that I killed the general whose shoes he was pretending to fill. During production, I became friendly with Glenn Ford. After filming ended, we would get together either at his beach house in Santa Monica or for dinner and drinks at La Scala. What did we have in common? A fondness for beautiful women.

Jean Leon loved seeing us come into La Scala. Jean was afflicted by the same weakness for the ladies. If Schwab's was the place hopeful young actresses went in the afternoon to be discovered, La Scala was where they went at night to find a rich boyfriend. The restaurant's mix of celebrities, studio executives and producers, Vegas heavies, and Chicago mobsters was unrivaled until Frank Sinatra and Peter Lawford opened Puccini's in 1959.

Sinatra attempted to raid La Scala's staff but only succeeded in taking his boyhood pal Matty Jordan, who lasted a scant three months at the South Beverly Drive restaurant before Jean Leon let him have his job back. However, at the time Matty left, Jean was about to take his family on a twelve-week trip to France and Spain. Suddenly he didn't have a maître d'. Without Matty, he had no idea who was going to negotiate the delicate task of seating the famous, those who thought they were VIPs, and the others who came so they could brag about having dined at La Scala.

I volunteered. My days as a football player were winding down as I was getting more acting work on television series like *Peter Gunn* and *The Untouchables* and the shows had difficulty insuring me given the chance I could get injured on the field. I had to choose one career or the other, and since acting paid better, I went with Hollywood. Like most actors, though, I had free time between jobs, which made it easy to help Jean. He was comfortable leaving me in charge of the door knowing that I was already on a first-name basis with most of his regulars.

The only excitement while Jean was gone took place behind-the-scenes. On Friday and Saturday nights, the staff wound down from their stressful shifts by shooting dice into the small hours of the night after closing. I played with them a few times. One night, maybe at about 3:30 A.M., four Beverly Hills police officers who had noticed cars parked behind the restaurant came in and found a bunch of guys sitting on the kitchen floor with stacks of money and a pair of dice in front of them. A quick-thinking Croatian waiter named Tony picked up the dice and dropped them into a silver water pitcher. With the evidence gone, the cops were told the crew was merely dividing up the night's tips and there was no proof otherwise.

During the day, the bookkeeper took bets from the staff on the horse races at Hollywood Park and Santa Anita Raceway. Sometimes he called the bookie and placed the bets, but other times he kept the money, explaining it was too late by the time he was able to make the call. One day Pasquale the chef got a tip and put fifty dollars on a horse that was 75 to 1. At 5 P.M., he went to the pay phone in the kitchen and called the bookkeeper, who had already left, to see if his horse had come in.

It turned out his longshot had come in first, but the bookkeeper said it was one of those days when he had not been able to make the bet. Pasquale was in a state of shock from hearing he had missed out on a $3,800 payday. There was a giant pot of boiling hot marinara sauce, enough for the next two or three days, cooling against the wall beneath the pay phone, and Pasquale, as he was hopping mad in disbelief, stepped into the vat and burned both his legs and feet. He had to be rushed to the hospital, and we went through the night with only one cook.

I was a natural out front. Marlon Brando came in and I ushered him straight to his booth. I did the same with Paul Newman, Robert Wagner, Dick Powell, and Fred Astaire. It was the 8 P.M. rush, no different than any other popular restaurant, except that these people were the biggest stars on the planet. What I noticed, though, was that everyone, whether they were famous or not, wanted to make a reservation at 7:30 or 8 P.M. and I had to turn people away to keep tables available for the celebrities. Jean was not going to make Lauren Bacall and Humphrey Bogart wait for a table.

I knew the non-celebrities who came to La Scala, from the lawyers and doctors who lived in Hancock Park and Beverly Hills to the tourists, wanting to see Brando and Newman and whoever else was at the restaurant just as they did at Villa Capri, so what I started doing was booking people at 6 P.M. when it was empty and telling them that we needed the table back at 7:30. Most people respected that and still got to see the stars on their way out. The staff loved it; their tips increased.

* * *

When Jean returned, the restaurant was making double the money it had been taking in before he went to Europe. He was ecstatic, but seeing ordinary people in booths that he normally kept empty until the stars arrived made him nervous. One night I saw him anxiously watching three women in a front booth. He did not recognize the powerful gossip columnists Hedda Hopper and Louella Parsons, and Princess Mirushka, the owner of a luxury boutique in Beverly Hills.

I knew what was going on. It was 7:30, and he *needed* their table. Paul Newman and Joanne Woodward were coming in at 8 P.M., and that table was reserved for them. It should not have been a problem since the ladies had finished their dinner, but they were not getting up. They ordered cappuccinos. Jean told Matty to tell them they could enjoy it at the bar, on the house—"we'll pay for it, but I need that table."

They said thanks but no thanks, they wanted to sip and talk right where they were. Jean kept checking his watch, growing more agitated by the minute. He handed Matty their check. They did not budge.

Now it was war. The busboys were ordered to clear their table. Everything was taken off and still the women did not make a move to pay the check. Matty returned to their table and politely but sternly asked them to vacate the table. "We don't want to leave," I heard Hedda Hopper say. Jean heard her, too. He marched over to the table, grabbed the white tablecloth, and pulled with all his strength. The trio of ladies held onto their end and a tug of war ensued.

Suddenly, Hedda, Louella, and the Princess let go and Jean flew backward, landed on his head, and was out cold. I took him to the hospital.

As I recall, his recovery was quick and his threat to ban those three women from La Scala for the rest of their lives was short-lived after he found out who they were. This was part and parcel of his crazy life. A friend of his, David Goodman, a prominent writer from New York, thought Jean should open a French restaurant. Here he was running a Mediterranean restaurant that was impossible to get into, imagine what he could do with a place that reflected his native France.

Except I knew Jean was born and raised in Spain and arrived in Los Angeles via New York after stowing away on a ship he thought was taking him from France to Guatemala. This was typical of our generation of immigrants; none of us traveled in a straight line. None of which mattered to Jean's new benefactor. Goodman raised $100,000 for the venture, and Jean renovated a building across from La Scala that opened a few months later as a classy French restaurant called Au Petit Jean.

The restaurant was Goodman's dream, and Jean did his best to make it sparkle. He hired authentic French waiters and a kitchen staff shaped by renowned Chef Jean-Paul Broulard, who soon brought in young Chef Jean Bertranou, who would open one of the city's great restaurants, L'Ermitage, in 1975. And thus, Au Petit Jean helped plant the seeds for what eventually became nouvelle cuisine in Los Angeles.

But that history looks best in retrospect. La Scala was a dump compared to the sophisticated splendor of Au Petit Jean, but one was packed every night and the other would close within a year and a half.

* * *

While Au Petit Jean was undergoing its remodel, Jean heard that a team in the Greater Los Angeles Soccer League was teetering on insolvency. In Spain, he had been swept up in the excitement of Real Madrid's fourth consecutive European Cup victory, and he returned even more fanatical about the sport than before. So, after making some inquiries, he purchased the Los Angeles Scots for a few thousand dollars. He became president and asked me to run the club as the general manager.

The Scots were one of a dozen or so professional teams in the Greater Los Angeles Soccer League, one of the oldest soccer leagues in the United States. They had won league championships in 1950, 1952, and 1954. The local nemesis at this time was the Los Angeles Kickers, a team of mostly Germans led by the great Al Zerhusen. The Kickers captured the league championship for seven straight years, beginning in 1958. The competition was very high.

I threw myself into the job of running the Scots, which we renamed the United Scots, recruiting strong young players from all over, including a young German waiter at La Scala named Hans-Jörg Gudegast. He was a world-class athlete who later changed his name to Eric Braeden and spent fifty-plus years starring on the soap opera *The Young and the Restless*, among many other TV and movie credits.

The twists and turns of fate are beyond explanation. Who would think that Eric, the son of a Nazi party member, would come to Los Angeles, play for the Jewish LA Maccabees, proudly wearing a Star of David on his jersey, before I recruited him to United Scots, then have an acting career that spanned from *Combat!* to *Titanic*?

I felt that way about my own life when, in March 1960, I became an official US citizen. Even with all I had been through up to that point, it was still another beginning. I had spent months studying for my exam, which I passed without any problem, but when

I was being interviewed, I noted two things to the official: First that the date, March 4, was the day my boyhood club Red Star had been founded in 1945, so it was very fortuitous, to which the official muttered, "Wonderful, wonderful for you"; and second, I pointed out that I was born May 26, 1935, but my citizenship paper said 1933. That was risky and probably stupid because the official could have questioned the veracity of my papers, which could have derailed my eligibility.

Instead, he tapped his pen on the desk and leaned back. "Young man, if I were you, I would leave it as is right here on the paper. It might save you from being drafted into the army. And you might also get your pension two years early." (That explains how I ended up with three passports with three different birth years: a German passport that says 1931, a US passport that says 1933, and a Yugoslav passport that says 1935.)

As a newly minted US citizen, I could vote in the next presidential election, which was fast approaching and something everyone discussed. Nixon or Kennedy? Tricky Dick or JFK? There was no question who I was going to check off on my ballot when the time came later that fall. John F. Kennedy and his team ate dinner at La Scala two or three nights a week when they were in Los Angeles. I had been around a lot of charismatic stars, including Sinatra, but I never felt the kind of magnetism JFK had when he walked into the restaurant.

Of course he was never alone. I saw him with Angie Dickinson. I saw him with Marilyn Monroe. I saw him with Judith Exner. They were all around him. So was Peter Lawford, who was married to JFK's younger sister Patricia. Occasionally his brother, Bobby, was with him, too.

With the campaign in full swing, they asked me to visit Serbian churches in San Francisco and Sacramento to talk about Kennedy.

After several weeks of travel up and down the coast, I reported back to the Democratic Party: Don't spend any money on the Serbs, I said. You won't get any votes from them. They hate the Catholics because of the Second World War.

One memorable night, Sinatra came to La Scala to meet with Bobby Kennedy and Peter Lawford. Sinatra had never set foot in La Scala because of his beef with Jean Leon at Villa Capri, so just seeing him there was significant. Later that evening, after he left, Peter Lawford filled me in on the details of their meeting. "Sam has got a million dollars waiting for us in Chicago," he said. "Frank said the money is there. Send someone from the party to pick it up." Judith Exner was also at La Scala that night. She was the Chicago mob boss, Sam Giancana's girlfriend. I connected the dots.

Five years later, I was having dinner with Clarence "Dan" Martin and his wife, and he recalled being sent to Chicago to pick up the money and deliver it to party headquarters in Washington, DC. By then, he had served as Kennedy's under secretary of transportation and also played a pivotal role in my acquisition of Dan Tana's restaurant. But back before the election, he owned a car dealership in Santa Monica and was active in Democratic party politics. He remembered flying with his wife to Chicago, where he was given a briefcase containing a million dollars in cash. Back at their hotel, his wife noticed the briefcase.

"Darling, where did you buy that?" she asked.

"I didn't buy it," he said. "It contains a million dollars. It's for the Democratic party. We're going to fly to Washington, DC, and give it to headquarters."

His wife balked. "I'm not going to the airport with you," she said. "We'll be robbed and killed before we get there. Chicago is the biggest Mafia town in the country."

"Don't worry about it," he said. "They gave me the money."

Some months later Peter Lawford met with Jean Leon and said that Jack and Bobby would be at La Scala even more if he could solve a couple of minor issues. First, they needed a private dining room for their meetings. Second, the staircase leading up to the bathrooms did not have proper handrails and JFK had a problem going up and down with his bad back. Until then, Jean had resisted putting up handrails even though customers routinely stumbled. "This is not a place for cripples," he would say.

However, two days after Peter's request, Jean's office upstairs was remodeled into a private dining room seating ten people and thick handrails were installed on both sides of the staircase. Ironically, Kennedy won the election and never returned to La Scala as president.

* * *

I was talking to Jean one night at La Scala's bar. Even though I was no longer working there, he liked having me around in case something happened, and I lived nearby, in West Hollywood, so it was easy to drop in at night for a drink and something to eat. I felt at home there. I had felt that way at Villa Capri too, and lived above the restaurant. But this was my first real awareness of a restaurant assuming the role of home—for the customers, for the staff, for those like me considered friends of the family.

Indeed, it was like being part of a family, something I would be very conscious of later when I had my own restaurant. Jean was complaining about his restaurant across the street, Au Petit Jean. It wasn't doing any business. He asked me to take some of my friends there for dinner to give it a little boost. "It won't cost you anything," he said. "Just leave a tip."

So that Friday I went there with Robert Mitchum, Glenn Ford, and Peter Coe. The restaurant was half full, maybe three-quarters at best, and this was prime time. We were commiserating about Jean's poor luck with this place, but the food was delicious if you liked traditional French food and were not that hungry. Around 10:30 P.M., the four of us were finished with dinner but lingering as Bob, Glenn, and Peter worked on their after-dinner cocktails. I was not a heavy drinker, and a teetotaler compared to their prodigious consumption of alcohol.

By this time, the restaurant was almost empty. Suddenly, in walked one of the most beautiful women I had ever seen in my entire life. She looked like a combination of Sophia Loren and Gina Lollobrigida, only more stunning. I guessed she was eighteen years old from the way she was so full of life ready to be lived and enjoyed. The maître d' took her to a table with three men—one in a suit and two generals in heavily decorated military uniforms. The man in the suit was her father, I learned later. He was the head of production at Universal Studios and meeting with the generals about a war-related movie they wanted to put into production.

The three guys I was with all remarked on this young woman's bewitching attractiveness. Nothing crude was said, but all three said they would give anything to have a girl that looked like her. I raised my hand like a police officer halting traffic and said, "You guys are married. I'm the only one at this table who is single. So, you know what? I will bet you that I am married to her within two years."

Glenn Ford took out a one-hundred-dollar bill. "Okay, we bet you one hundred dollars each." They were drunk and figured I was just having fun, but something about this girl had reached inside me in a way I could not explain. I had to force myself to stop staring at her across the room. I got up, slipped the maître d' a twenty-dollar bill, and gestured inconspicuously toward her.

"Did she come in her own car or a taxi?"

"Her own car."

"When she goes to leave, tell the valet to say that he can't find her keys. Have him look around for a few minutes."

A short time later, she walked out with her father and the two generals, then came back inside and sat at the bar presumably while the valet searched for her car keys. We asked her to join us, but she politely declined, though she did say hello to Bob Mitchum, who she had met through her father. I walked her out to her car and learned she was studying art at Santa Monica City College, taking dance classes, and working part time at a Santa Monica coffee shop.

"You are a beautiful girl," I said. "I would love to take you out to dinner."

She offered a half-smile. "I don't date."

The valet arrived with her car, a Nash Metropolitan that had not been washed in God knows how long, with clothes, newspapers, and magazines littering the seats plus a surfboard sticking up in the back. The incongruity of this beautiful girl and her neglected little sports car took the conversation out of me. I got her name at least. Andrea. I wrote my phone number on a piece of paper and handed it to her.

"Andrea, if you change your mind about dating, here's my phone number. I will be happy to take you out."

A couple months passed without hearing from her. She was still very much on my mind though, and not only because of the bet. Tired of waiting for a phone call that might never come, I drove into Santa Monica and found the coffee shop where she worked. I had lunch and asked the cashier, another young woman, if she knew of someone who worked there named Andrea. Her face immediately brightened.

"Andrea! Yes, she's so beautiful. Such an angel. We were in an NBC *Matinee Theater* together. She works mostly Saturdays and Sundays as a waitress."

I wrote my name and number on the back of my bill and asked her to please give it to Andrea. The following week she called me and agreed to go out with me. We met at Au Petit Jean, and she brought two girlfriends with her. On our second date, she showed up with her best friend, Lynda Harris, a sharp young woman who ran her own advertising agency and would later earn renown in the corporate world as Lynda Resnick, the self-made billionaire behind the Wonderful Company. But the group dates did not last much longer.

The next time I asked Andrea out, I made it clear that I wanted it to be just the two of us, and fortunately she agreed. For the next six months, we went out to dinner, danced, and enjoyed each other's company. I was different than anyone she had known. Whether talking about my family, soccer, or my arrival in Hollywood, she was fascinated by it. My connection to the Kennedys through La Scala sounded even more intimate after the botched Bay of Pigs invasion in April 1961 when I told her about having overheard conversations about getting rid of Castro.

She had her own Hollywood connections through her father, but she was still greatly amused when I picked her up one night wearing a new sport coat and shoes and explained that Robert Wagner had come into La Scala that afternoon, offering his entire wardrobe to Jean. His wife, Natalie Wood, had caught him having an affair and thrown all his clothes onto the front lawn of their home on Canon Drive. The sprinklers had come on; everything was soaked. "Give it all to your employees," he said.

I was among the lucky recipients. Everything fit me perfectly, as if it had been tailored for me instead of RJ. "Only you, Dan," Andrea said. RJ felt the same way about me. For years afterward, whenever he saw me, he would crack, "Are you still wearing my clothes?"

I was Andrea's first serious romance, and the spell she cast on me that first night I saw her at Au Petit Jean retains its grip on me all this time later. But both of us had too much going on to move hastily. That is, until the day Andrea called me and said she wanted to meet for breakfast at Schwab's the next morning.

21

Come On, Baby, Let's Twist

Until then, the only drama in Andrea's and my relationship centered around the soccer team Jean and I were involved in, the United Scots. Management took up most of my time. Practices, recruiting, player issues, games, and trying to build enough of a fan base to keep the team in business. Every day was a struggle.

The team did not perform particularly well in league play during that 1960–61 season, coming in seventh place out of nine teams. But we caught fire during the playoffs for the US Open Cup and found ourselves in the finals against arguably the best team in the country, the Ukrainian Nationals out of Philadelphia.

Due to the expense of travel and the shoestring finances of both clubs, we agreed to play one game in Los Angeles on June 11 and split both the expenses and the gate. Even though the rules called for two games, it would be winner-takes-all. The Ukrainian Nationals—having dominated play in the East Coast's American Soccer League—were heavily favored, but we outplayed them and went up 2–0 until the last five minutes when they scored two goals to even the score. The match ended in a draw.

The Ukrainian Nationals insisted the Scots had to travel to Philadelphia for another game. If we did not agree, they threatened to declare themselves champions. The federation backed them. Jean and I conferred and agreed we could lose the cup on the field, but we were not going to be bullied into giving it away, so we traveled back east. We stayed at a hotel outside of New York City.

On game day, most of the team flew to Philadelphia with me, but the five best players took a bus with Jean, who was deathly afraid to fly (and only made the trip east because the players carried him onto the plane). The bus got lost on the highway, forcing us to start the match at McCarthy Stadium without them. The Ukrainian Nationals jumped out to a 3–0 lead.

Once our players arrived, we scored two goals and fought valiantly to even the score. I lost my voice on the sidelines, screaming instructions and encouragement. In the end the Ukrainian Nationals had too much all-around strength and talent. They topped us 5–2 in the game and 7–4 in the aggregate score.

But this was in the past when Andrea asked me to meet her for breakfast at Schwab's. She was waiting for me in a booth. I spotted her as I walked through the door, and ordinarily every person in the place would be stealing a look at this beautiful girl, wondering who she was and which studio had signed her. But I could tell from her expression that she had made herself practically invisible. A moment later, I was sitting down opposite her, and she was in tears.

"I'm pregnant," she said, crying even harder.

I did not say anything. I did not need to. Andrea blotted her eyes and cheeks with a napkin and continued.

"I've never been with anyone else. I was a virgin when I met you."

"Okay," I said, ready to take acknowledge my part in this equation and talk about next steps. But Andrea beat me to it.

"You don't have to worry about anything," she said. "My parents know about it. They don't want me to have an abortion. You don't have any responsibility."

I leaned forward over the table and took Andrea's hand in mine. "Listen, if I am the father, let's get married."

Andrea's eyes filled with tears, but she did not cry. Then her lips formed a tiny, timid smile. "You have to ask my parents."

First, I had to meet them. Although Andrea and I had been dating for seven or eight months, I had yet to be introduced to her family. Her mother, her sister, and her aunt knew about me, but they had been sworn to secrecy around her father, Sam Wiesenthal, a larger-than-life personality who was twenty-one and an accounting whiz when film pioneer Carl Laemmle brought him to Los Angeles from New York (they played gin rummy on the train all the way across the country). At twenty-seven, Sam became head of production at Universal Pictures, overseeing early film classics such as *All Quiet on the Western Front*, *Dracula*, and *Frankenstein*.

In 1935, he met Naomi Schwartz, a dynamo in her own right. A New Yorker, with a degree from Parsons School of Design, she worked as a press agent with Warren Cowan and Henry Rogers, founders of the PR giant Rogers & Cowan. Then gossip columnist Walter Winchell hired her to be his eyes and ears at all the best parties and events in the city. For a while, she even dated Clark Gable.

Recognizing the power of her allure, beauty *and* brains, Winchell sent her to Hollywood, where she met Sam. They married four days later. Sam was that kind of guy. Larger than life. He filled the room. You could not help but love him. But Naomi had second thoughts after realizing Sam was a studio executive, not a celebrity, and she went back to New York, thinking she could have the marriage annulled.

Winchell wanted her in Hollywood, though, and ordered her back. She moved in with Sam, who she really did love—and he adored her. Soon she was pregnant with Andrea. Two more children, John and Bettina, would follow. Naomi and Sam were living in Fullerton, in Orange County, when I drove to their house for that first meeting with them.

* * *

I got terribly lost and arrived two and a half hours late and embarrassed. Sam and Naomi put me at ease. "Calm down. Don't worry. You're here." Sam hugged me, and Naomi sat me down on the sofa and spent the next two hours telling me her family's history. Naomi's sister, Pearl, also lived in Hollywood and was married to the writer Rowland Barber. Sam had hired him to write a screenplay about the infamous Joe Louis–Max Schmeling championship boxing match at Yankee Stadium before World War II. The project turned into the bane of both of their careers. Every time they got close to starting production, the mob somehow managed to derail the film and it never got made. Sam lost a lot of money.

Sam noticed me trying to break into his wife's monologue. He planted himself on the sofa next to me and squeezed my leg. "Just let her talk." When Naomi finally said, "So tell me about your family," I knew I couldn't compete. I didn't even try. "You know, if my mother was here, she could tell you everything for hours. My family were farmers. My father ran a restaurant."

Naomi and Sam nodded. Theirs was a very different world. At forty, Sam left Universal to work for Howard Hughes at RKO. He could talk about movies forever. *Frankenstein.* Making *King of Jazz* with Paul Whiteman. Going to China in a race with "boy wonder" producer Irving Thalberg to signing Pearl Buck for rights to her book *The Good Earth.* He just couldn't outtalk Naomi. She was magnificent in her own right. I sensed that she had wanted a bigger career for herself, as an actress or journalist, but once with children, she poured her considerable aspirations into Andrea, whose beauty was equaled if not surpassed by her talent. Andrea could act, dance, paint, and charm. By any measure, she was a star. Just waiting for her break—until she met me.

I would have understood if Sam and Naomi had greeted me with anger and disdain for romancing their eighteen-year-old daughter and getting her pregnant. Yet I only felt warmth and affection from these two big-hearted, generous individuals welcoming me into their family. Maybe they sensed something in me that I wasn't fully aware of.

All Sam wanted to know was what religion Andrea and I were going to raise our baby. When he asked, I saw that he was serious.

"I'm not religious," I said.

"Well, the mother is Jewish," Sam said. "The baby will be Jewish."

"Okay," I said, "the baby will be Jewish."

In September, Andrea and I exchanged vows in a low-key, backyard wedding ceremony hosted by friends of Sam and Naomi. Our guest list was mostly Andrea's extended family and a few close friends of mine, including two United Scots players and actor Paul Stewart, who had been in *Citizen Kane* with Orson Welles. Paul had the shock of his life when he saw Andrea's mother and whispered to me, "I dated your mother-in-law when she was nineteen."

It was true. Naomi had dropped him for Clark Gable, and I don't think Paul ever got over it.

My best man, Jean Leon, was a no-show. He did not even call to let me know. We'd never had a serious disagreement before, so his absence was hurtful. I later found out he was upset with me for getting married because I was his regular alibi to his wife when he snuck out or did not come home until very late. He would say he was out with me. Now that I had a wife, he had to come up with some other excuse.

Though he never said as much, I also think he was jealous of how good-looking and sweet Andrea was.

Several years passed before we sat down together and cleared the air, and then, the animosity I imagined turned out to be fabricated nonsense. Jean had never told his wife that they were invited to my wedding or that I had asked him to be my best man, and she held a grudge for what she thought was a personal snub, which he let fester to the detriment of our friendship.

Only one other time in our friendship did Jean really get as mad at me. It was because of Elizabeth Taylor. One night she called La Scala distraught over one of her romantic entanglements. She asked Jean to bring an order of veal piccata, a side of fettuccine, and a bottle of Dom Pérignon to her house, which was not far from the restaurant. Jean was busy and couldn't leave. I was at the bar, and he asked if I would do him the favor of making the delivery to Elizabeth Taylor.

This kind of personal service was unusual but not unheard of. I arrived at Elizabeth's house with a basket of food and a bottle of Dom packed in ice. Less than a minute after I rang the bell, she opened the door wearing a transparent negligee with nothing underneath. She might as well have been naked. I could see her entire body. I explained I was bringing her the dinner she had ordered and extended it toward her, but she made no effort to take it and instead said, "Would you help me with the meal?" Then she turned and led me inside to her dining room.

"Would you like a glass of champagne?" she asked.

It was the first of several we shared that night as she ate and drank and cried and told me about her complicated love life. Sadly, and pathetically, she lamented being alone in her home.

"Would you hug me?" she asked.

It seems like a dream now, one of many incredible dreams accumulated over ninety-plus years, but it was very real—and too real for Jean. After several hours with Elizabeth, I went home. The next day Jean wanted to know why I didn't return to the restaurant after delivering Elizabeth Taylor her food.

"She asked me to stay," I said.

Jean's eyes narrowed. "What did you do?"

"I didn't do anything."

"Come on. You're there with a beautiful woman. You did something."

"Nothing," I said.

"Did you drink champagne with her?"

"Yes."

"Did you eat the piccata?"

"No."

"So, what did you do?"

"We talked. Well, she talked. I listened."

"Did you hug?"

"A couple of times."

"Kiss?"

"No."

"Come on, you must have kissed her."

"I did not. Nothing else happened."

Jean did not believe me. He was sure I had sex with Elizabeth Taylor. Even though that did not happen, I could not convince him otherwise. It was lodged in his imagination. Knowing Jean, he was mad that he had sent me instead of going there himself and he took it out on me.

* * *

Periodically, I wondered whether I would have ever gotten married if Andrea had not been pregnant. My parents did not have a happy marriage, so I was not motivated to follow in their footsteps. I was also something of a drifter, a dreamer perhaps. I still had the mindset of a rootless refugee, meaning no matter what, including my American citizenship, I was followed by a shadow of impermanence.

I was in pursuit of a fortune, not a family. Yet on May 3, 1962, Andrea gave birth to Gabrielle, or Gaby as we called her. Two years later, Katerina, or Katy, arrived. These children and my marriage would become the priceless blessings of my long and fortunate life, but those first couple years of trying to support a new family were hard. Very hard. Not only did I wonder what I had gotten myself into, I wondered how I was going to make it all work.

My break came from an unlikely source: Princess Mirushka, the doyenne of Beverly Hills fashion who Jean had banned from La Scala after she, Hedda Hopper, and Louella Parsons would not give up their table. However, when I had worked there while Jean was in Spain, I let her back in. She made a reservation at 6 P.M. with the understanding I needed the table back by 7:45, and I never had a problem with her. After I married Andrea, she became a big fan of mine.

From what she told me, she had married a so-called Russian prince mainly for his title, so she could call herself "Princess." I had teased Jean for spending $25,000 to be able to call himself a Baron in Spain, but as I told Jean, in America, you could call yourself anything you wanted, and somehow "princess" fit Mirushka more than Baron did Jean. One day, Princess Mirushka approached me about a business opportunity. She had just returned from New York where she had seen Chubby Checker perform his hit, "The Twist," live at the Peppermint Lounge, a red-hot dance club that saw the likes of Sinatra, Monroe, Truman Capote, and Audrey Hepburn twisting on the dance floor. Jackie Kennedy even had a Peppermint Lounge party at the White House. She could not have been more excited.

"Dan, we're going to open a twist place in Hollywood," Mirushka said.

I was acting and managing the soccer team. I did not know about the latest dance craze. "Hold on," I said. "What is *twist*?"

"I will show you," she said. "I want you to go to New York with me and George Hamilton and I will show you the Peppermint Lounge and Chubby Checker."

"I can't afford to go to New York," I said.

"I'm taking you," she said. "You'll see what I'm talking about. We'll open a club. You'll run it and be a third partner."

The next week Mirushka, George Hamilton, and I flew to New York. Before going to the club, the three of us went out to dinner. Midway through, the maître d' came up to our table and said he had a problem. A famous athlete was there by himself, but he had nowhere to seat him. Would we mind if he joined us? The athlete was Wilt Chamberlain, who had recently scored a hundred points in a game. He and I became great friends; in fact, ten years later, Wilt was staying at my vacation house in Split, Croatia, when he decided to retire from the NBA. He wished us good luck with our club.

Mirushka had rented a stretch limo and we pulled up in front of the club on West Forty-Fifth Street. The line to get in wrapped around the block. I could not see the end of it. Of course, they knew Mirushka at the door and had a table waiting for us. The place was packed. I think the club's capacity was less than two hundred people and there were at least triple that outside waiting to get in. The music was loud and lively.

"No one is touching," I said. "They're twisting but they aren't touching. This will never work."

"I want to open in three months," she said.

That timeframe not only seemed impossible to me, but the whole gambit struck me as ridiculous. But Mirushka was a force not to be underestimated. By the time we returned to Los Angeles, she had replaced George as our third partner with a Texas oil heir who bankrolled the club and signed Chubby Checker to play our opening weekend. She found a building on Cahuenga Boulevard, in

Hollywood. Half was a motorcycle garage and hangout for the Hells Angels, and the other half was a dance club where they had ballroom dancing one night, country and western another night, and so on. The club's promoters had a two-year lease. Mirushka bought them out at a premium and the club was ours. We painted the exterior with red and white stripes, like a candy cane, and Peppermint West was born.

When Chubby Checker canceled just before we opened, I sensed a disaster on the horizon. Everything was too good to be true. However, Mirushka booked Joey Dee & the Starliters, a group out of New Jersey who had a huge smash called "Peppermint Twist," and from the moment we opened the doors that first night, the place was a gold mine. Celebrities called to get in. People waited in line for hours. We only served liquor, no food, but that was enough to fuel fun and scandal. One night, Jayne Mansfield took her clothes off on the dance floor. Two months later, Pamela Mason stripped down to her bare essentials while twisting the night away.

Even though Los Angeles Police Chief William Parker had a table reserved for him every Friday, we were still busted several times for violating the club's capacity. We held 150, and we let in 300. On Christmas Eve, the police came in and rounded up a bunch of people including Warner Brothers' head of television William "Bill" Orr, his wife, who was studio boss Jack Warner's stepdaughter, and Jack Warner's daughter, who was not yet twenty-one. As they left, Bill insisted I go with them.

"Why do I want to get arrested?" I said.

"You aren't being arrested," he laughed. "We are. It's going to be Christmas soon. Come on."

I don't know why I agreed, but I did and the five of us—three women, Bill, and myself—were put in a cell together at the Wilcox Station. We were allowed one phone call each. Bill went first and called

California Governor Pat Brown. Within minutes of him returning to the cell and telling us that he had woken the governor, we were let out and wished a merry Christmas by the LAPD's boys in blue.

* * *

The club made a fortune. At the end of the first year, Mirushka, the Texas oil heir, and I split $300,000. I had my first taste of real money, which provided a sense of security about supporting my wife and one-year-old daughter.

I told Mirushka we should sell Peppermint West. New private clubs and discotheques like The Daisy were opening in Beverly Hills and it was only a matter of time until the celebrities, always thirsting for the next new hot thing, went there. Once they did, the lines would disappear outside Peppermint West. It was just like Villa Capri. When Patsy expanded, Sinatra stopped going there and soon so did everyone else.

She did not want to sell and instead they bought me out for an additional $20,000. The Peppermint West lasted another year before they lost everything. But I was free and flush with enough of a cushion that I was able to ask myself how I could begin to give back to America for all that America had given me. This is something unique to those of us who immigrated to this country with empty pockets. It is easy to share when you have nothing or very little, the way Bogie had invited me into his apartment. It is a generosity of spirit, a willingness to open your door to others—something I would never forget. Once people have wealth and accumulate things, they change.

I know some will say, but Dan, you became a rich man. Yes, I did, but I accumulated friends and acquaintances, not possessions.

My dream was to own a professional soccer team and help build the sport in the United States. The timing seemed better than ever. In 1963, after two years of negotiations, Jean Leon managed to bring

Real Madrid, the best soccer team in the world, to Los Angeles for an exhibition game against a team of All-Stars from our Greater Los Angeles Soccer League. I contacted William Cox in Philadelphia and followed up on his entreaty to expand his International Soccer League on the West Coast. For $25,000, I purchased the rights to start the Golden Eagles in Los Angeles when the league was eventually launched.

I rented an office on Santa Monica Boulevard, hired a secretary and a few others on a part-time basis, and began promoting games with professional teams from Europe and Canada. Attendance at many of these matches was underwhelming, which puzzled me as the competition was at a very high level, especially for soccer in the United States. When we met in my office to analyze why, my promotion man, Hans Stierle, made an insightful observation: The kids in America did not play soccer, not the way they did Little League Baseball. If we wanted to grow the sport, we had to grow interest among young people.

I agreed, and as a result, I and a silent partner of mine, psychiatrist Alan Glasser, each gave Hans $3,000 to start a soccer program for kids. He used that as seed money to start AYSO (American Youth Soccer Organization) out of his garage in Torrance with a friend of his, Bill Hughes, who had organized a Southern California youth league a few years before. Since the founding of AYSO in 1964, it has grown nationwide to more than fifty thousand teams and an estimated six to eight million participants.

An interesting footnote: During one of those early meetings, we discussed how each team would manage the cleaning of the kids' uniforms after the games. Someone said each kid's mother would do their own laundry just as they would drive them to practices and games, which sounded right to all the men around the table. That was, in fact, the birth of the soccer mom!

I had a powerful ally for growing the sport professionally in Los Angeles, Rams owner Dan Reeves. An acquaintance from Peppermint West, Dan was immediately interested when I pitched him on investing in this new league with me. He thought it was an excellent idea and told me that people said he was crazy when he moved the Rams to Los Angeles from Cleveland in 1946. Now the Rams were one of the league's best teams, with star players like Roman Gabriel, Deacon Jones, and Merlin Olsen.

Dan's office with the Rams was on Pico Boulevard, by Rancho Park, close enough for him to visit me in my office several times a week. He added his friend and Rams Vice President Clarence "Dan" Martin as a partner in our new league. I had a vague acquaintance with Dan Martin through the Kennedys at La Scala. The three of us met every Friday over lunch at the Ringer, the restaurant next door to the building where my office was located. Before the league came into fruition, we bought the restaurant. It was given to me to run and eventually own. Clarence's Italian chef created a new menu and for lack of any better ideas, it was rechristened Dan Tana's.

My mother had once said, "Whatever you do, don't own a restaurant." Though Belgrade is more than six thousand miles from Los Angeles, and I had not seen my mother for a decade, I heard her voice loud and clear. But it was too late. I had a restaurant to run—and another crazy new chapter of my life to write.

Part Four

The Entrée

22

Open for Business

It was quick and easy to rename the Ringer to "Dan Tana's," but the full transformation of the restaurant into the phenomenon it became took many years. It involved the contributions of a lot of very talented people, and a long series of coincidences and episodes of such extraordinary good fortune that it seemed almost miraculous.

But one day, Dan Tana's was there, fully formed, with a sign just inside the front door that said, "Total Capacity 65 + Paulie." Of course, once the restaurant had become a success on any given night, there would be far more than sixty-five people in the restaurant; there might be thirty-five just at the bar. By then, it was home away from home for both regular customers and staff.

How or why that happened is a mystery best explained by my friend and Dan Tana's regular, actor James Woods, who said, "It's a great place to park your ass and eat the best food with a fascinating mix of people."

My staff felt similarly. "I get up in the morning, and I can't wait to go to work," chef Neno Engleski told me. "Everyone feels like a part of a big family."

But it was nothing like that when the keys were handed to me and the restaurant was mine.

Money, or rather the lack of it, was always top of my mind. I had invested $25,000 in the new soccer league and recently lost another

$25,000 in the stock market. I had just under $25,000 in my bank account, with a family to support and a pile of bills coming due.

"I'm going to be very short of money." I sighed one afternoon when Andrea, Gaby, and I were at our friend Deanne Mencher's house. "I don't know how I'm going to survive this."

Deanne was married to Maurice Seiderman, who was Orson Welles's makeup artist on *Citizen Kane* and *The Magnificent Ambersons*. She jumped up from her chaise and offered a quick fix: her engagement ring. "I hate it," she said, adding that it was only one of the many things she hated about her marriage. "I'll pawn it and give you the money."

The next day, she handed me six hundred dollars. I tried not to take it, explaining that amount was not going to help, but Deanne insisted. It was a wonderful gesture of trust and friendship. Within a few months, I got her ring out of hock and paid her back. I also renegotiated the lease I had inherited from the Ringer. The original terms were $350 a month plus 6 percent of the restaurant's gross for five years. "There's no way I can afford to give you 6 percent of my gross," I told the landlord. "Plus, I'm already paying you rent."

We agreed on five hundred dollars a month. Then he offered a second five-year lease at $750 a month and a third five years at a thousand dollars a month. We had a deal—or, as time would prove, a steal. We closed for two weeks to facilitate the changeover from the Ringer to Dan Tana's. Dan Martin's chef Michela created a fine but limited menu. Knowing we had to be economical, he came up with seven variations of pasta using spaghetti, seven variations of veal, and the same number of different ways to make chicken: parmesan, cacciatore . . . one had mushrooms, another had peppers, another had so much garlic my eyes watered.

The absence of steak and liver and other fine dining staples was on purpose. They were expensive. For me, the highlight was Michela's

Caesar salad. You would think a Caesar salad is the same everywhere, but no, Michela had his way of making it, and I have to say, I have traveled all over the world, and to this day, more than sixty years later, that Caesar salad is the best I have ever had.

Everyone had their favorites. One night in the 1990s, I got to the restaurant and saw a man in a booth by himself. It was early, not long after we opened. Since it was not busy yet, I sat down with him and said I thought I recognized him from a while back. He nodded and said he used to eat at the restaurant every other week, sometimes with friends but often alone. He loved the Chicken Parmesan. He said he had spent the last seven years working in China as part of the US State Department and dreaming about Dan Tana's Chicken Parmesan.

"Tonight is my first night back and I ordered the Chicken Parmesan. I hope it's going to be as good as I remember."

"Let's see," I said.

I got up from the table and visited a few other people before catching up with the staff. About twenty minutes later, I returned to that man's table. He was in tears. He had eaten about two-thirds of his Chicken Parmesan. He looked up at me and said he had been crying since the first bite.

"It's even better than it was seven years ago."

We could only dream about that kind of reaction as we got ready to open. I spent two days in the kitchen, writing down the recipes as Michela taught his new dishes to my chef, Constantino, whom I had kept from the Ringer. The recipes were backup in case Constantino left. As we worked, Michela told us his life story: that his four sisters became doctors and lawyers, and he was regarded as the black sheep of his family until he became Mussolini's chef in Florence. Soon after these two days of vital training, Michela retired and went back to Italy.

Michela had given his expertise and time as a gift, no charge, and I like to think that giving spirit is one of the secret ingredients that would always be a part of Dan Tana's. A new menu was designed by my friend Flo Walman, a graphic artist. The walls were painted red, and the sawdust was swept off the cement floors. As for the rest of the staff, I went to the restaurant and retail workers union headquarters and told them the positions I had open. They said it was too few for them to staff and gave me a dispensation. I did not have to hire union workers. The neon sign out front went up next.

I still had a long to-do list, but time was money, and money was in short supply, so on October 6, 1964, I opened the doors of Dan Tana's with just two waiters, a dishwasher, a bartender. We also had the benefit of Deanne Seiderman, who walked into the restaurant one day and announced, "I'll take care of desserts." Constantino was skeptical until he tried her cheesecake, which she has delivered to Dan Tana's every few days ever since!

Something was still off. I sensed it before figuring it out one afternoon while sitting at the bar that divided the restaurant into two sides. The existing booths were too high and too private; you couldn't see who else was in the restaurant, which was part of the experience of eating at Villa Capri or La Scala. There you could see Audrey Hepburn, Paul Newman, or Elizabeth Taylor. Sometimes you sat next to your doctor. Other times it was Humphrey Bogart and Lauren Bacall. It was exciting.

The high booths had to go—and eventually, once I had made a little extra money, they did.

* * *

I hung a dozen or so classic straw-covered bottles of Chianti from the ceiling. The same bulb-shaped bottles wrapped in straw, called fiascos, decorated the walls and shelves at Villa Capri and La Scala. In addition to being a practical part of the décor, I had my two waiters tell customers that we would write their name on a bottle and hang it from the ceiling if they purchased one. It was a good sales pitch, and I am sure it would have worked if we'd had any customers.

The restaurants that preceded Dan Tana's in the same spot, Domenico's and the Ringer, had never cultivated a nighttime business. Domenico was a real chef who served fine continental food, with a daily special that filled every table during lunchtime. But he was not a restaurateur. For twenty years, he closed at 6 P.M. sharp; he would not open the door a minute later for anyone, not even the president of the United States. The Ringer, which did a decent lunch business, stayed open until midnight, but those who came in in the evening only wanted to drink at the bar.

We were filled from noon to 2 P.M. Locals from nearby doctors' offices, a veterinarian, the Writers Guild across the street, the flower shop at the end of the block, the ironworks next door, and an art gallery—they all came for lunch. They welcomed our new menu of spaghetti marinara and chicken parmigiana as an upgrade from Domenico's hamburgers and hot dogs. And thank God they felt that way, because there would be no Dan Tana's without that lunch crowd. They covered my costs.

Dinner remained nonexistent. I did what I could to help bring in customers. I put up little red-and-white curtains in front of the windows to attract some of the people heading to the music club at the end of the block, Doug Weston's Troubadour, and those driving past who might simply be curious about a new Italian restaurant in the neighborhood; but it did not work. I framed a menu on the outside wall near the door. Maybe some of those heading to the Troubadour would want dinner before whatever show they were going to see. The club was generating buzz. Lenny Bruce had been arrested there, Bob Dylan had recently played a surprise show, and the Smothers Brothers were house regulars. People were constantly parking behind the restaurant or right in front on their way to the club. I tried not to get annoyed because I thought the traffic would be good for us. I was wrong. Nobody came in. A few people stopped and looked in the windows. All they saw were empty tables.

After thirty days, I met with Cyril, the former co-owner of the Ringer, who was now my bookkeeper and Dan Tana's major shareholder until I paid her back the $30,000 I owed for purchasing the restaurant. We were going over the books for the first time. She showed me a stack of receipts from lunch. And those from dinner? Her eyes drifted toward a handful off to the side.

"That's it?"

She nodded.

"What's the total?"

"Seventy-eight dollars."

"We only took in seventy-eight dollars the entire month?"

She responded with a pained expression, as if being pricked by a needle.

"Oh god."

Two months later I called a contractor friend of mine and hired him to board up the windows. I did not want people looking in and seeing empty tables.

* * *

Gradually, some of my friends began to come in for dinner. Paul Stewart and Miklos Dora Sr., a Hungarian who represented fine European wines and was the father of legendary surfer Miki Dora, were among the first. So was producer Sidney Beckerman. Actress Patricia Norman, who had been a dancer in *The Red Shoes*, brought in English writer Willis Hall, who became a lifelong friend and, years later, a partner in English soccer. The actor Harry Dean Stanton found his way in early on, too, and basically never left. Someone once asked Harry what brought him to Dan Tana's that first time. "I don't know . . . a car, I guess."

As I recall, Harry ordered a steak that first night. I do not think he even looked at the menu. If he had, he would have seen that we did not offer steak. Knowing Harry, though, he had already had a drink, maybe two, and a few cigarettes while conversing with the barman, and he was ready to eat. A steak was what tasted good to him. I was not in the business of disappointing our customers. I gave the busboy five dollars and told him to buy a steak from the little market across the street.

Harry got his steak, and that market became our go-to anytime a customer wanted something off the menu, like steak, lamb chops, or liver. We had the recipes but not the funds or the customers to maintain such a varied inventory. My best customer in those early days was Dan Reeves, my business partner in the ISL soccer league and the owner of the LA Rams. He came every night Monday through Friday to support me. He would leave his Rams office on Pico Boulevard at 5 P.M., stopped by his brokerage office on Rodeo Drive in Beverly Hills, and then come to Dan Tana's, where he would have two or three martinis before he headed to the Wilshire Country Club and eventually home.

He was a chain-smoker. I never saw him without a cigarette in his mouth, even when he was sipping his ice-cold vodka martini. I tried giving him the drinks on the house, but he always refused.

"Dan, you're my friend," I said. "I'd like to buy you a drink once in a while."

He flicked his cigarette into the ashtray on the bar. "I want to support you," he said. "I'd rather drink $10,000 of martinis than have to give you $10,000 if you lose the restaurant."

In early 1965, Deanne, my cheesecake lady, sent word that a friend was recruiting people to be contestants on the popular TV show *Let's Make a Deal.* Hosted by affable Canadian personality Monty Hall, contestants dressed up in zany costumes, hoping Hall would pick them to make deals for prizes of varying in value. They might get a refrigerator, jewelry, or a new car. Or they might get "zonked" with a bale of hay or a wheelbarrow full of dirt.

My wife called me at the restaurant. She, her friend Ellen Hoffs, and my secretary Cheryl had dressed up in goofy clothes and grabbed some stuffed animals and were on their way to CBS, hoping to get into the audience. I thought she was ridiculous. "How're we going to pay the babysitter?" I asked.

Hours later the three women burst into the empty restaurant, laughing and jumping around like they were still in the audience. I was at the bar, talking to Giovanni. Ellen gave Andrea a gentle push. "Tell him," she said.

Gio and I stared at them in their costumes, excitement bubbling over, like they were silly teenagers.

"Tell me what?" I asked.

"Tell him you won!" Ellen said.

Andrea was one giant smile. "I was on the show," she exclaimed. "I won!"

"I don't believe it."

"She did," Cheryl chimed in.

"What did you win?" I asked.

Andrea took a step back and shook with excitement. "I won one week in Paris, two first-class tickets on American Airlines, and $5,000."

"It was the biggest prize on the show," Cheryl said.

As I grasped the details, I grew almost as excited as my wife. But for another reason. Numbers raced through my head. This was the answer to my worries about the first of the three $10,000 payments coming due per the purchase agreement for the restaurant.

The deadline was a few months away. But here was salvation. My prayers were answered in the strangest way.

I told Andrea that we could sell the plane ticket and pocket the $5,000 in cash and let whoever bought the tickets have the free hotel stay as a thank-you. It was a beautiful miracle, I said.

Except it was not possible. We were told the prize was a use-it-or-lose-it proposition. We could not sell it. I told Andrea to go with a girlfriend because I could not afford to leave the restaurant. I must have griped about all this one night to Dan Reeves as he drank his martinis at the bar because somehow, he insisted that I should go on the trip with my wife and he would take over the maître d' duties from me. He looked around the near-empty restaurant.

"How hard can it be?" he said. "I'm here every night anyway."

So the owner and president of the LA Rams took over running Dan Tana's for two weeks while Andrea and I flew to Paris. We spent the week surrounded by elegance at the world-famous Ritz Hotel and spent the $5,000 prize money like we were rich people. It was unbelievable, a surreal departure from our life back home with two small children in a rental house. At the end of the week, Andrea and I used the remainder of our prize money, like $750, to visit my father in Belgrade. My mother and brother had both died in recent years—my mother from cancer and my brother in a car accident. I showed Andrea where I was born and baptized and introduced her to some people from my childhood who were still there. It was the best holiday ever.

Even better was returning to the restaurant to find the staff and Cyril in buoyant moods similar to mine. The reason? Dan Reeves had filled the restaurant with his players every night I was gone. They drank and ate incredible amounts. Everybody made record-breaking tips. We had our best two weeks ever! And I was able to make my first year's payment to Cyril.

* * *

Soon after came an incident involving three of Dan Reeves's former players. Dan and the three ex-Rams spent all night at the restaurant, eating and drinking—mostly drinking. I was with them, so I can attest. Around 3 A.M., everyone was hungry, and they asked if I could scramble them some eggs or find something else in the kitchen. I looked but everything was locked up. Dan borrowed two dimes from me for the pay phone, called his wife, who had been asleep, and told her to please get their cook up, he was bringing three guys over to eat a late-night meal.

I went home, but the players pulled out of the parking lot behind Dan, who was leading them to his home in Bel Air. A little more than two hours later, my phone at home rang. It was close to 6 A.M. Dan was on the other end.

"I need seven hundred dollars," he said.

"What?"

He explained the three players who had been following him had been pulled over by the Beverly Hills police for driving on the wrong side of Sunset Boulevard. They were arrested for drunk driving and taken to jail. Bail was a thousand dollars. He had three hundred dollars from his wife and cook but needed the rest to get the players out before the press found out. I found the cash and met Dan at the police station. One of the players told me that the officers who stopped them asked where they had been. Dan Tana's, they said.

When asked what they'd had to drink, each of the guys knew what they'd had and how much, but when questioned about what food they had eaten, none of them could remember. Dan's waiters just brought plate after plate, they said. One of the players laughingly told me that the cops asked if it was good.

"We said it was amazing," the player told me.

"We'll have to try it," the cop said.

I wanted to build word-of-mouth, but not that way. From years of observing at Villa Capri and La Scala, I knew that when people talked about a restaurant, they focused on two things, the food and the service. To build word of mouth, both had to be impeccable, delicious, and personal. The food we served was as good as anywhere in the city, but Dan Tana's took a major step forward in the hospitality department when I hired Giovanni as our first maître d'. He had been a fixture for years at Nickodell, a martini and steak joint that catered to the Paramount Studios crowd. Stars and studio bosses mingled and egos demanded attention, and Giovanni handled it with an unflappable combination of authority and charm. He was world-class. He made everybody feel good.

After working the lunch shift at Nickodell, he brought his mastery to Dan Tana's at night. If he had been younger, I maybe would have had ten restaurants in LA instead of one that was barely hanging on. Everybody loved this man. He came at five and left at about ten. He was sickly and arrived exhausted, but he transformed into the restaurant's leading man as soon as he stepped up to the desk by the door.

Many years later, in 2023, I got a phone call from Giovanni's daughter, Joanna. I was eighty-eight years old, so she was eighty at the time, and she wanted me to know a few things about her father. During the war, from 1941 to 1945, he was in charge of entertainment at the Croatian Embassy in Berlin. When Croatia was carved out of Yugoslavia by Nazi Germany during World War II, he met a German girl and had five children with her. When the war ended, the Catholic church helped them emigrate to the US. Three more children were born in America.

It was an interesting story, not that dissimilar to many of the immigrant stories of the men I knew from the restaurant business, but his daughter added a twist. Giovanni hated, I mean detested, Serbs. It explained why, over the five years he worked for me, he hired mostly Croats. Suddenly, after all these years, I had new insight.

"Daddy hated Serbs more than anything else," his daughter told me. "He was a devout Croatian Nationalist."

This was a man who I loaned money to before he died so he could buy his family a house. How could he hate Serbs? If he hated Serbs, he hated me.

"No," his daughter said. "I asked him that. I said, 'Daddy, how can you hate Serbs when you work for a Serb?' He said, 'Dan Tana is a better man than any Croat. He's the best man I have ever met. I love Dan Tana, but I still hate the Serbs.'"

A few weeks later, Giovanni's health took a bad turn. With his daughter at his bedside, he picked up that same conversation.

"I am going to die," he said. "But when I come back, I want to be Italian."

"Why Italian?" his daughter asked.

"Because I'm sure when Dan Tana dies, he will come back as Italian and the two of us can be friends."

* * *

Business picked up a little. A few more of my friends came in at night, like Carol Eastman, who I had gone with briefly before meeting Andrea. And she brought her friends, like Helena Kallianiotes, a beautiful Greek belly dancer, actress, and social magnet. She had tried to buy the Ringer and turn it into a dance studio, like Cyd Charisse, but the landlord wanted to keep it a restaurant, and he preferred negotiating with me, Dan Reeves, and Dan Martin.

One night Helena ran her fingers through my hair and purred, "That thick hair of yours. Those curls. You are a gorgeous man." She knew I was married, but that was her personality. From the first time she came in for dinner with Carol, she became a regular. She said the same thing countless people did: The restaurant felt like home. In that spirit, some customers created their own anything-goes policy. She sat at a table one night watching a tape that was going around called *Cookie and Dookie*. It was about a fictitious homosexual encounter between John Wayne and Walter Brennan.

"I learned how to do Walter Brennan from that tape," she told me.

A while later she was sitting in the restaurant with Dabney Coleman and his wife. The actor, then in his early thirties, had started eating at Tana's almost from the time it opened. He did not have much money then, but he soon would and eventually the menu would offer a New York Steak Dabney Coleman. Dabney told Helena that he knew how to do Gary Cooper, and the two of them proceeded to sit at the table, "relatively shit-faced," as Helena recalled, and trade lines as Walter Brennan and Gary Cooper from the 1940 movie *The Westerner*.

"It was hysterical," Helena told me. "And it was at that moment I thought to myself, *My god, the lure of this place is unlike anyplace else*."

She brought her friends, including Jack Nicholson, who was not anybody yet, producer Bert Schneider and director Bob Rafelson. They were all thick as thieves. This was 1965, early 1966, and they had nothing, but they found something they craved at the restaurant. By the end of the year, Bert and Bob were producing one of the biggest shows on television, *The Monkees*, and their stars, Davy Jones, Micky Dolenz, Michael Nesmith, and Peter Tork, were showing up for dinner whenever they were in the neighborhood, often after they hung out at the Troubadour.

"You step back into this place and it's kind of like where you left off and then some," said Helena. Indeed, a few years later, Carol Eastman was being celebrated for writing the script for the Academy Award–nominated movie *Five Easy Pieces*, which Bert produced,

Bob directed, and Jack Nicholson starred in. Did Dan Tana's have anything to do with their success? We fed their creativity.

Something was going on that was too early to notice at the time but obvious many years later. "We were witnessing each other's lives," said Bob Rafelson's wife, Toby. "The people who worked there, the people who went there, it was like this living, breathing organism that never stopped but was always there. Like a family."

* * *

And like a family, it grew. Giovanni hired Mate Mustać, a young Croatian cook to assist Constantino in the kitchen. Mate had been a chef on Italian cruise ships. About a year earlier, his ship was docked in LA and somehow, he met Giovanni, who tried to recruit him to work at Nickodell. Mate said he had a girlfriend in Croatia who he wanted to marry. He told Giovanni that he would go back, get her and return, and jump ship. Giovanni wished him godspeed.

It took him six months to return to Los Angeles, now married, broke, and desperate for a job. Though Nickodell had filled his position, Giovanni told him not to worry as he had another job for him, at Dan Tana's. Four years later, Mate would take over when Constantino retired and would assume the role of head chef for the next thirty-eight years without ever missing a day. I loved him.

Aldo, another Croatian who Giovanni hired to work part-time in the kitchen, was also an excellent cook. He had learned his trade on fishing boats and showed promise. Something would happen a few years down the line that would sour me on him forever. But that was a rare blip of negativity.

Giovanni made one more hire, only this one was done without my knowledge. He knew I would approve—and he was right. It was Bogie!

Somehow Giovanni knew Bogie—probably from Nickodell—and welcomed him into the restaurant. I was summoned from my soccer office up the block and walked into one of the biggest surprises of my life. Bogie was at the bar. We wrapped our arms around each other, me who owed so much to Bogie and Bogie who trusted me as a friend and knew he could walk in and find work. Our bond was forever.

"Bogie!"

"Bata!"

I had not seen or heard from Bogie since Jimmy Dean died, and he left Villa Capri for San Francisco. Jimmy's death had shaken Bogie in such a way that he needed a dramatic change in his life. Bogie knew this Yugoslav guy who had waited tables at Villa Capri two days a week and drove a taxi the other five days. He got caught taking two detectives to a house of prostitution that was run by the gangster Mickey Cohen and subsequently lost his taxi license.

This guy was a heavy gambler, so he divorced his wife and moved to San Francisco and made his livelihood gambling. He invited Bogie up to San Francisco and found him a job. After three months, Bogie moved to Las Vegas, and from there he went to Atlanta and then Boston, where he said he worked at a top restaurant serving some of the best lobsters in the world. He was like a gypsy.

"Do you need a job?" I asked.

"Giovanni already hired me," he said.

I clapped my hands, delighted. "Wonderful."

Bogie was the most capable restaurant worker I ever met, someone who could step into any position from busboy to chef to maître d', so he fit in seamlessly. This would remain part of the appeal of Dan Tana's: I only hired professional waiters, not actors like so many LA restaurants. I had to pay more, but I always paid my people extremely well. There was never a person who did not get what they asked for, and many times they got much more. It was the cost of excellence.

Waiter Tony Paccini turned the tableside preparation of our Caesar salad into a romantic adventure. He wheeled the salad cart to the table as if he were a Venetian gondolier picking up passengers. The romaine lettuce was already cut but the dressing was mixed at the table, olive oil, a raw egg, Worcestershire sauce, Parmesan, with anchovies added at the end with a flourish that reminded me of the way my friend conductor Zubin Mehta led the Los Angeles Philharmonic, with both drama and delicacy that made you hold your breath.

Customers would stop their conversation to watch and listen, completely enthralled. He mixed the salad with anecdotes of its origin in the Tijuana hotel where Italian Caesar Cardini was employed, his own travels, and observations from the night that made it all seem magical. Bogie learned these moves seemingly overnight and narrated the preparation with his own unbelievable ups and downs from a life of courting Lady Luck. He turned the start of a meal into theater. We were still not doing much nighttime business but those who did come in, especially the regulars, could not get enough of Bogie.

He could get away with murder. One night four women came in early, around 6:30 P.M., and sat in a booth next to a good customer, actor Buckley Norris, who was there with two or three friends of his, though I noticed him paying more attention to Bogie. Why? The reason was pure Bogie. The four women in the booth were gabbing and cackling and having a good time while drinking their cocktails and smoking cigarettes. (This was when smoking was still allowed). They kept ordering, drinking, and lighting cigarettes. After the second round of drinks, Bogie went up to the table and asked, "Ladies, are you ready to order now?"

"We'll have another drink," one of the women said.

Finally, after they had been there for two and a half hours, drinking and smoking, while Bogie became increasingly annoyed and agitated, he asked once more, "Ladies, are you ready to order?"

"Yes, we're ready," the woman closest to him said. "Thank you so much for your patience."

Bogie smiled.

"Now, I think I'm going to have the whitefish," she said. "Is the whitefish fresh?"

"Madam," Bogie said, "it was when you sat down."

That was Bogie—and in a way, it was Dan Tana's, because every so often someone would complain that Bogie was curt or surly and I would simply shrug and say, "Well, there you are."

23

Open Till 2 A.M.

In the mid-1960s, my great friend Sidney Beckerman was not yet the prolific and powerful movie producer he would soon become with credits like *Kelly's Heroes*, *Portnoy's Complaint*, and *Marathon Man*, but he was already extremely successful in film distribution, and the work gave him important connections across the country. Sidney was about fifteen years older than me and much more worldly in business. He started coming into the restaurant for dinner and we became friends. He felt more like an older brother.

It was the summer of 1966, and I was stuck financially. I had only $5,000 of the $10,000 I owed Cyril in October and with business the way it was going, I did not see how I was going to come up with the rest or the last of my three payments the next year. The entire first year of business, from October 1964 to October 1965, I made $4,150. One afternoon I sat down with Sidney, who had come in for lunch by himself, and confided that I was having money problems.

I was trying not to look or sound desperate, but I am sure the expression on my face told the truth. I was not my upbeat self. My mood dragged two feet behind me. The restaurant was feeling like an uphill run.

"Sidney, I'm in a hard place," I said. "Would you . . . If you give me $15,000, I'll give you half the restaurant. I need a partner."

"Dan, I am in the movie business," he said. "I don't know anything about the restaurant business. But I'll find somebody for you. Don't worry about it."

A couple of weeks go by before he calls.

"I'm coming to lunch tomorrow with two people. I think one or both of them might be interested in helping you out."

I was waiting at the restaurant when Sidney walked in with the baseball great Joe DiMaggio, who I knew from Villa Capri, and a man called Sugar Brown, who I had never heard of but could not help noticing was dressed head to toe in brown—brown shoes, suit, shirt, tie, and hat. We sat in a corner booth, food was brought to the table, and we discussed the situation. I was clear that I was not looking to sell; I wanted a partner with enough resources to keep the restaurant going until dinner caught on—"like Villa Capri," I said to Joe.

"I'd like to help you out," Joe said. "But I already have a restaurant in San Francisco. I don't need another one. I'm doing very well there."

"I understand," I said.

"But," he interrupted, "if you're in real trouble, I will gamble on you."

Suddenly, Sugar Brown cut him off.

"I'll take it," he said, and pulled a wad of money, $15,000 in cash, from his pocket and put it on the table.

I looked at the money and thought, *I'm saved.*

"I'm from Vegas," Sugar Brown said. "I want you to keep three books. One for you, one for me, and one for the government."

"How do I keep three books?" I asked.

"I will get someone to teach you."

"Yeah, but I can get in trouble."

"Sure, you can get in trouble. But you get $15,000."

I turned him down and said thank you very much. Sugar Brown picked up his cash and put it back in his pocket. He was unfazed by my reaction.

"If you change your mind," he said, getting up from the table, "Sidney knows how to reach me."

About a month later, with the October deadline for my second payment getting even closer, George Swink came to the restaurant. George's secretary was the mother of the baby I had saved from drowning ten years before. I did not yet know that the kid was George's son. Over the years, George had befriended me and shortly after I opened Dan Tana's he said I should call him if I ever had a problem. He was meeting a friend for dinner. While he waited, the two of us stood at the bar and I told him the situation.

"Danny, I will give you the $5,000," he said. "If you succeed, pay me back. If you don't, you don't owe me anything."

"Thank you, George," I said. "That's very nice and generous of you. I don't need it for a month or so, and then it will take me four or five months to pay you back. But your offer is a big relief."

"Just call me when you're ready."

Because of a turn of events, what some might point to as more proof that I am one of the luckiest men ever, I never had to call.

* * *

It was about 4 P.M. when I got to the restaurant after playing eighteen holes of golf at Rancho Park, a beautiful public course a few miles from both my house and Dan Tana's. I had taken up golf as a way of giving myself two to three hours of relief from the stress of the restaurant and, to a lesser degree, the frustration of trying to get the soccer league off the ground. It was a mini vacation from real life, and I would get pretty good—good enough to notch a couple holes-in-one at Rancho Park and also win the Andy Williams Pro-Am with pro Billy Casper in 1973.

Bogie was waiting for me. We had only one reservation for the entire night, a party of four at 7 P.M.. I shook my head in disappointment and told Bogie that I was not going to come back the rest of the night if that was the case. But I wanted everyone to work until closing, I did not care if the place was empty. Bogie said fine, knowing it was not like any of the staff took off immediately after closing anyway. Many stayed and played cards and talked for a few hours to wind down from their shift before going home.

"But boss, this table coming in tonight, it's this Canadian jockey and his crew," Bogie said. "Wayne Harris."

I knew Bogie and his old Villa Capri pal Matty Jordan played the horses and had insiders' take on who was who and what was what at Hollywood Park and Santa Anita, whichever track was in season. Now it was Hollywood Park.

"A jockey doesn't eat much. I hope his friends order a lot."

"Boss, Wayne Harris brings in all these long shots. Can we buy him a bottle of wine?"

"Why should I buy him a bottle of wine?"

"He's running at Hollywood Park tomorrow. Maybe he'll give us a tip."

"Okay, buy him a bottle of wine."

I went home and phoned the restaurant a few hours later. Were there any new reservations? No, none other than the one Bogie had told me about. Were there any walk-ins? No. I exhaled, thinking I was going to have to call George Swink soon, then collected myself and took my wife and two daughters, Gaby and Katy, to Lucy's El Adobe Mexican restaurant across the street from Paramount Studios. It was a good, tasty, family-run restaurant, inexpensive, with strong margaritas.

The next morning, I was in the soccer office a few doors down from the restaurant when Cyril, our office manager, called me. She was in the office above Dan Tana's, clearing the cash register and comparing the sum to the slips the waiters wrote up. "Can you come here," she said. "I'm confused about something."

A few moments later, she was showing me a ticket that Bogie had written up. It said, "1-4-Mantro or Metro-something-or-other." I couldn't make out his writing.

"Let me call Bogie at home," I said.

Bogie's girlfriend answered and said he had already left for Hollywood Park, in a rush, intent on making the first race. It was Saturday, the track would be busy. I asked Cyril to get me a copy of the morning's *Los Angeles Times.* I opened the sports section and turned to the day's lineup of horse races listed in the back. My eyes widened with amazement. In the first race, Wayne Harris was riding horse number four, Metropolitan. The horse was a 50–1 longshot.

I started to shake with excitement. "Oh my God, this is the tip Bogie got!" I said. "I have to get to the track and bet on this horse."

I had never been to the track or bet on a horse in my life. Cyril called the Auto Club and got me directions to Hollywood Park. It was a little after 11:30 A.M. The first race was in exactly one hour. Taking a hundred-dollar bill from petty cash, I had very little time to get there and place a bet. I broke every speed limit law on my way only to find the place was packed. Sixty-thousand people. The parking lots were full. I had never been to the races, I did not know what to do.

I circled the neighborhood, looking for a parking space, and spotted a man watering his front lawn. For five bucks, he let me park in his driveway. If it was even his driveway. I did not ask or care. I handed him the keys and took off at a full sprint for the track. I made it to the betting window with a few minutes to spare and just enough breath left in me to say, "One hundred dollars on Metropolitan in the first race."

The teller at the window gave me an uncertain look. "Are you sure?"

"Please, please," I said, pushing the hundred-dollar bill closer to him.

People in line behind me grumbled and complained about the time it was taking me. "Hurry up or get out of line." "Come on, buddy." But it was the teller's fault. He was reluctant to take my money and give me a ticket.

"He's 50 to 1, pal."

"Please," I said, my expression imploring him to take my money.

Finally, I got my ticket, and the race started. There was no time to get to the track; I watched the race on the small television monitor near the window. I was surrounded by a crowd. The starting gun fired and horse number four, Metropolitan, stunned the field and all those watching, going wire to wire to win the race. My ticket paid $5,000. My hands shook as I stuffed it into my pocket. I would not need George Swink or anyone else's help. It was enough to make my next payment.

I wanted to thank Bogie. But where was he? I ran into a customer from the restaurant and asked if he'd seen Bogie.

"Yes, he's about a hundred yards that way," he said, pointing down the long, crowded corridor. "There's a bar. A Bulgarian named Wilson runs the bar. Bogie and Matty Jordan and their people are always at that bar."

After walking halfway around the pavilion, I spotted Bogie at the bar with a couple of guys whom I recognized as waiters from La Scala and Villa Capri. I walked up behind Bogie and put my hand on his shoulder. Bogie looked up, surprised.

"Boss! What are you doing here?"

I was trying unsuccessfully to hide my euphoria.

"Next time you get a tip on a horse, it would be fair and wise of you to tell me, your boss," I said.

Bogie had no idea what I was talking about. I pulled out the slip on which he had written the tip the night before at the restaurant when he was waiting on Wayne Harris. I showed it to him.

"I bet this," I said to him, pointing at his scribbles. "First race. Horse number four. Metropolitan."

Bogie shook his head in disbelief.

"Boss!" he exclaimed. "That's not a tip. It means table one, four people, and a bottle of Montrachet, which you said I could give them on the house."

"What?" I said, laughing at my mistake. "Oh my God. I thought it was a tip. I bet a hundred dollars on it and just won $5,000!"

Bogie was incredulous. So was the bartender, Wilson, who heard this and put a shot of something in front of me. Years later Wilson (his first name was Allan, but everyone just used his last name) asked me for a job. It was a favor, he said. His actress daughter was dating an actor who had asked what he did for work. He told him that he was the bartender at Dan Tana's. By this time, the restaurant was one of the hot places in LA. I gave him two nights a week—the two nights the track was closed—and told him to have his daughter and her actor boyfriend as my guest. Soon they had a reservation in the book: Rita Wilson and Tom Hanks.

* * *

Once I knew I was going to make my payment, the world looked brighter to me. But life did not get any easier or less complicated. One day I got a call from Dan Reeves's attorney, Alan Rothenberg, telling me to meet with the Canadian businessman Jack Kent Cooke. Cooke had bought the Los Angeles Lakers the previous year for five million dollars. Dan Reeves hated him. They had competed for rights to professional hockey in LA, with Cooke eventually outmaneuvering him to win the expansion LA Kings from the National Hockey League. Now they were battling over pro soccer in the city.

It was messy. Dan Reeves, Dan Martin, and I were working with William Cox to start the National Professional Soccer League (NPSL), and Cooke and his buddy, sports impresario Lamar Hunt, founded the rival North American Soccer League (NASL).

Then Cooke reached out to Dan Reeves about partnering on a local soccer franchise. Dan Reeves and Dan Martin did not want anything to do with him, so I was told to meet Cooke for breakfast at the Beverly Hills Hotel at 8 A.M. After waiting there awhile, the maître d' came to my table and said Mr. Cooke was unable to make it but had a car waiting for me in front to take me to his office where we would meet.

"Oh, and Mr. Cooke said to please finish your breakfast first."

Jack Kent Cooke was not a tall man, and when I entered his office, I found him seated behind an enormous desk that was set on a floor slightly higher than the rest of the room. He motioned for me to take a seat in front of him and put his feet up on his desk so that I was staring at the bottom of his shoes while he was looking down at me.

"Do you see my shoes?" he asked.

I could not miss them. They were all I could see.

"They're custom made by John Lobb in London, the world's finest shoemaker."

"I see."

"I only wear custom," he continued. "This suit as well as my shirt and tie, it's all Turnbull & Asser, also in London. Do you know them?"

I was wearing shoes I bought for eight dollars, a shirt I got in Hollywood for two dollars, and I had on Bob Wagner's old sport coat.

"No, I am not familiar," I said.

"It's extremely expensive," he said.

With that topic exhausted, he got straight to the point. He wanted to form a partnership with Dan Reeves, Dan Martin, and me. He proposed raising three million dollars between us, but he would put in slightly more and own 51 percent of the team. I knew that was not going to fly and said as much. My response sent him on a tangent about how he had made his fortune selling encyclopedias as a teenager in Canada. From there he sold soap, then stocks, and then TV and radio stations.

"I became very wealthy," he said.

I told him a bit about my road to owning Dan Tana's and said, "But I am not a millionaire."

He leaned forward so that he was looking down at me, while I was looking up at him, and what happened next ended any chance that I might see him in my restaurant. He tried to lure me away from my partnership with Dan Reeves and Dan Martin. We would be in business together, Jack Kent Cooke and I, partners, and he would make me a millionaire. I said no thank you, and our meeting was over. I could not be bought, and neither could Dan Reeves or Dan Martin.

But the meeting was not a complete waste of time. The next time I was in London, which was a few years later, I had some money and my friend Willis Hall took me to get several suits and shirts custom made by "sartorial wizard" Doug Hayward, aka "the Master of Mount Street" who dressed Michael Caine, Roger Moore, photographer Terry O'Neill, and all the other stars of the day. Forty-some years later, I still have those suits, and they fit wonderfully.

* * *

In 1966, my father came to visit me in LA. My mother had died in 1963, and I had seen him the following year when my old soccer team Red Star played an exhibition game in Los Angeles as part of an ISL tournament. They had come as a favor to William Cox, and as a surprise for me, they brought my father. I did not have the restaurant at the time, but now that I did my dad wanted to see it. He walked in just before we opened and was startled to see Bogie.

"Are you a relative of so-and-so?" my father asked.

"Yes," Bogie said. "That's my father."

It turned out Bogie's father got drunk at my father's restaurant every night. My father knew him quite well.

"They all think you're dead," my father said. "You have not written to your family for thirty years."

"That's right," Bogie said. "I stopped writing to them because they always asked for money in return."

My father was impressed with the restaurant. He liked to hang out in the kitchen with Constantino and Mate, and when he did, he always put on an extra set of chef's whites. "It's not correct to be in civilian clothes in the kitchen," he said. I do not know if I can give him credit for inspiring my next idea, but I thought of it around the same time he was there. I decided to keep the restaurant open until 2 A.M. Everybody thought I was crazy—and I knew from experience there could be a personal cost to it. My father kept his restaurant in Belgrade open until 2 A.M. and, as a result, we never saw him. He got up early in the morning to go to the market. Then he worked lunch and dinner and did not come home until 3 A.M. My father was a great man, a hard worker, an outgoing soul who was loved and popular in our town, but I grew up without knowing him. I did not want my daughters to feel that way about me.

On the other hand, I saw an opportunity to do more business. People went to the theater, to the various games in town, and after they finished around 10 P.M., there were no good restaurants open. You could not eat dinner unless you went to a hotel or a cheap all-night diner. Friends argued that LA was a one-industry town, early dining and early rising; everybody got up at 4 A.M. to work at the studios. Yes, but . . . that gave me an idea. At any given moment, most actors and writers were unemployed. They were going to be my late-night customers.

One night six people sat at the bar, having drinks before seeing a movie at the nearby Academy Theater. The restaurant was relatively empty, and I was on my way out the door, heading for a card game with friends before going home. But I saw those people with their cocktails and something about them caused me to turn around and go back into the kitchen. Constantino had gone home early, leaving Mate in charge. I told Mate to fix them a plate of stuffed mushrooms on the house.

"But, boss, we can't afford that," he said.

I shrugged. "Maybe they'll order another round of drinks."

This time on my way out, I stopped by the bar and told the group we had a little something on the house coming out of the kitchen for them. Soon after, Mate brought them the mushrooms.

"We're going to a movie," one of them said. "It starts at seven, and we will probably be out at nine or nine-thirty Will you still be open?"

Mate nodded. "We are open until two o'clock in the morning."

I came in the next day and as I went through the previous night's receipts, I saw that someone had spent $150. Cyril's eyes nearly popped out as she said what both of us were thinking: That was nearly half of our rent. When that night's waiter came in later in the afternoon, I asked who had spent that much money. He said it was the six people who had been at the bar. They came back after their movie.

"What did they order?"

"They tried this. They tried that. Everyone had a few things. It was more than usual."

"I can see that."

About a month later, my mother-in-law, Naomi, called the house early Sunday morning. Dan Tana's was open for lunch and dinner Monday to Friday, dinner only on Saturday, and we were closed Sunday. I was on my way to play golf. Naomi was excited. She told me to cancel golf and immediately go to the store and buy the Sunday newspaper "and read the Calendar section," she said.

"Why? What's in it?" I asked.

"Just go buy the paper. Read the Calendar section. You'll see."

I hung up with her, and the phone rang almost instantaneously. It was my friend Sidney Beckerman.

"Have you read the paper yet?" he asked.

"No, my mother-in-law just—"

He cut me off. "Read the paper."

As soon as I hung up, the phone rang again. It was Mace Neufeld, a talent agent who would become one of Hollywood's most successful producers. His wife and children were friendly with Andrea and our girls. Mace and I were on our way to becoming best friends. He said my "insanely upbeat personality" matched his "downbeat one."

"Congratulations!" he said.

"For what?"

"Have you seen Calendar?"

"No."

"Go get the paper. Read the restaurant column. Your life is about to change."

24

Feasting Italian Style

I came back home with the paper, my hands shaking with excitement. I also realized why that party of six at the bar a month earlier had caught my attention. One of the six was *Los Angeles Times* restaurant editor Art Ryon. Though I did not recognize him, which was unusual for me as I have always had a knack for remembering people, he had come in about a year earlier and, in one of his smaller columns, had mentioned the restaurant, including our phone number, which wasn't yet listed, in one of his smaller columns.

In that piece, Ryon had even exaggerated by describing business as "peachy." Subconsciously, I must have sensed he was important when I ordered his party stuffed mushrooms on the house. That three-dollar appetizer was probably the best investment I made in my entire life. Art was there with his wife, Patricia, and friends, and after they returned for a late-night dinner, at which they sampled various appetizers, antipastos, entrées, and Deanne's cheesecake, he wrote a review that was the centerpiece of the column that appeared in the February 6, 1966, edition of the *Los Angeles Times*.

The Sunday edition. In the Calendar section. The most-read section in the most-read edition of the week. And the review was fabulous. "FEASTING ITALIAN STYLE," it was headlined. It went on to say, "One of our more delightful dining experiences of the new year was enjoyed recently at Tana's, a comparatively new and charming Italian restaurant at 9071, Santa Monica Boulevard. Host Dan Tana offers a lively and varied menu. Complete dinners, which include antipasto, soup, spaghetti, and dessert, range from Lobster fra Diavolo ($4.95) to veal in half a dozen Italian variations ($4.00–$4.50), and the usual ravioli, lasagna, etc., plus Linguine clams ($3.75). In addition to minestrone, among the soups offered is tasty stracciatella (seventy-five cents a la carte). As far as I know, Tana's is the only restaurant in town that serves Chicken Lisbon. However, it is prepared only on Saturday and Sunday (only $2.95). For those who do not appreciate Italian food, there are a few offerings from the broiler, topped by a N.Y. cut steak ($5.95). Reservations might be wise. The number is CR5-9444."

On Monday night, we served two hundred dinners—up from our normal six to ten dinners. We were completely unprepared for such a sudden increase. Andrea and I both worked the entire night, helping our two waiters, and Constantino and Mate, Aldo, and the entire kitchen staff down to the busboy and dishwasher were exhausted at the end of the night. We closed at 2 A.M. and spent the next hour sitting in a stupor as the adrenaline that had fueled us was entirely spent. None of us had anything left. We wore the blank expressions of survivors of a natural disaster.

Except as the dust settled, the opposite was true. This was salvation, manna from heaven, answered prayers. From that night on, we never served less than two hundred dinners a night.

Overnight success brought changes. I needed more help. I went to the restaurant workers union and hired several more waiters and some additional kitchen workers. Because of the agreement I had with the union when I first opened Dan Tana's, the new workers were all union guys, but Dan Tana's remained a non-union restaurant. A few weeks later, a dozen or so union representatives marched in front of the restaurant with signs that said, "DON'T EAT AT DAN TANA'S!" and "DAN TANA'S IS NON-UNION!"

I was irate. Didn't anyone remember our arrangement? I met with the head of the union the following afternoon. I showed him the letter he had written me two years earlier giving me permission to operate as a non-union restaurant. I added that I paid all of my employees above-union wages so they could live well and pay union dues regardless of the restaurant's status.

"I'm a union man," I said, pulling a card out my wallet. "Look, here is my Screen Actors Guild card."

The next night there was a reservation for seven people: the heads of each division of the union—barmen, dishwashers, cooks, waiters—along with the head of the union himself. They came in to apologize for the pickets. Besides staffing the restaurant, I was able to address some long-delayed accoutrements, like the booths that always bothered me as too high to allow for the type of see-and-be-seen ambiance that I knew was crucial to Dan Tana's success.

I drove downtown to a restaurant supply store that sold everything from light fixtures, tables, and chairs to pots and pans from restaurants that had gone bankrupt. I found eight, low-backed, matching red leather booths and had them installed at Tana's the next day. The plain cement floors we inherited from the Ringer also went. I had heard the Mercedes dealership in Beverly Hills was changing their showroom carpet from red to blue. I bought their red carpet. It matched the red walls and new red booths.

In Hollywood, where looks are everything, Dan Tana's finally had one: classic, timeless, comfortable . . . and *crowded.*

* * *

For reasons that were never clear to me, my old friends from Villa Capri and La Scala stayed away from Dan Tana's the first couple of years the restaurant was open. Then, after the review appeared, I welcomed Patsy D'Amore, Matty Jordan, Bill Karan, and eventually Jean Leon, who finally let go of his grudge against me for marrying Andrea and resumed our friendship.

The restaurant began to attract more Hollywood luminaries. Bob Mitchum, Glenn Ford, Karl Malden, and other friends of mine who had not come regularly popped up more frequently in the reservation book. So did Cary Grant; boy wonder studio executive Robert Evans, who was put in charge of Paramount Studios at thirty-seven years old in 1967; Walter Matthau and his wife Carol; Shelley Winters; blacklisted screenwriter Carl Foreman and his wife Evelyn; and producer Dino Conte, whose mother gave Constantino her recipe for swordfish that is still on the menu to this day. My friends Paul Stewart and Peter Coe were regulars. Others brought their friends. Harry Dean often sat at the bar with actor Warren Oates. Helena brought in Art Garfunkel and world champion bodybuilder Arnold Schwarzenegger, who, in 1968, had just arrived in the US and barely spoke English. Dabney Coleman invited Ed Begley Jr. Rock stars, some known and others unknown, wandered in from the Troubadour. The Mamas and the Papas. Frank Zappa. And Joni Mitchell, who played the Troubadour for the first time that year. Giovanni famously bawled out Gene Clark of the Byrds for parking his car in front of the restaurant and blocking our customers all night when his band played at the club.

The entire city was buzzing with the electricity of change and, in a sense, revolution, with hippies and police clashing on the Sunset Strip and rock and roll blasting out of the Troubadour. At times, it felt like the neon sign in front of Dan Tana's was a lightning rod pulling in the old and the new. One night David Crosby was in with his girlfriend while across the dining room Robert Evans was in a booth with a woman who was a dead ringer for Sophia Loren.

Gorgeous. Voluptuous. But something about her was different than Sophia Loren. Was it that she was younger? Maybe . . . I kept staring at her.

Someone tipped off the paparazzi. Robert Evans, the young Hollywood hotshot, was cozied up in a booth at Dan Tana's with Sophia Loren. I do not know how word reached Bob, as everyone called him, but it did, and even though both of us knew his date was not Sophia Loren, we did not say anything to contradict the rumor. He asked me to help her out through the kitchen door in the back. *Gladly*, I thought.

Soon afterward, Cary Grant came in with the same woman. Every head in the restaurant turned in her direction. Together, they were gorgeous. Cary made no attempt to hide her. In fact, he introduced me. Her name was Ljubica Otašević, and she had been a star on Yugoslavia's national women's basketball team as a teenager in the 1950s. She moved to Italy to pursue acting and worked as Sophia Loren's double. There, in that enchanted country, she began a love affair with Cary, who flew her to Hollywood and helped get her a contract with one of the studios. She changed her name to Liuba Bodin.

Liuba and Cary went their separate ways when he married Dyan Cannon and she married a Texas oil heir, but both were relatively single when they came into the restaurant together. His marriage was over, and hers was on the rocks. I do not know whether they rekindled their affair, though I do know that the kind of feelings they once had for each other are not easily extinguished, and that was apparent by the way they sat close together in the booth.

On one of their dates at the restaurant, Liuba brought a can of beans and sausage from Yugoslavia. I took that can from her and we reminisced briefly about the food we grew up with back home. When I tried to give the can back to her, Cary put up his hand and asked if Mate would warm it up in the kitchen for her. We were amenable to special requests, but Mate drew the line when I showed him the can. He was horrified.

"What is this?" he said. "What if it's poison?"

I pleaded with him.

"Listen, boss, I will give them each a bowl of pasta fagioli."

I served them the pasta fagioli. Cary tasted the broth, then moved things around in his bowl and gave me a curious look.

"Where are the sausages?"

"There were none," I said.

He looked at Liuba and shook his head and in that famously suave voice of his said, "Fucking Yugoslavs."

* * *

At the time, I was living a double life. By day, I was managing the Los Angeles Toros, our team in the National Professional Soccer League, which we finally got off the ground after four years of work. At night, I was at the restaurant. Following the Toros' last-place finish, we sold the team before the next season and the new owners moved it to San Diego, ceding the Los Angeles market to our archrival, Jack Kent Cooke, whose team had won the league championship.

However, I remained involved in soccer and, if not for that passion, I never would have met Mike Gotovac, who spent fifty-plus years as Dan Tana's bartender and became almost as iconic as the Hollywood sign. He was another soccer-playing émigré who had left Yugoslavia to escape communism -and also his father, who was a bigwig in the Communist Party there. After finding his way to Los Angeles, he signed to play for a Croatian team in San Pedro, basically the same path I had taken.

Except his team did not find him an outside job that could supplement his player's contract, as mine had when I was put on the payroll of StarKist tuna. Then he crossed paths with Giovanni, who was in failing health and hunting for a house in San Pedro so he could be near the fresh ocean air. He met Mike at St. Anthony Croatian Church on Sunday, and we hired Mike as a waiter on Monday.

For six months, Mike waited tables and proved himself among the best. But when age began catching up with our full-time bartender, Armando, he asked Mike if he wanted to be the next bartender, and Mike found the role that would define the rest of his life. He learned the routine on Saturday and Sunday nights, then took over full-time six months later.

With Mike behind the bar, Dan Tana's began to feel like a great restaurant. We had All-Stars in the most important positions—Giovanni as the maître d', Constantino and Mate in the kitchen, and now Mike making drinks, making conversation with his regulars, and placating those sent to the bar while waiting for a table. He made a martini the way a master artist paints, by instinct. It was all gin, no vodka, skip the vermouth—and stirred, not shaken. Warren Oates and Robert Mitchum were among his early favorites. Harry Dean had a Manhattan waiting for him before he reached his seat at the bar. And Bob Rafelson's wife, Toby, always ordered a margarita.

"I don't know what it is," she once told me. "But once you've had his margarita, you don't want one from anybody else. There is no one else."

Filmmaker Henry Jaglom said he could taste Mike's margarita before he walked in the door. Mike's secret?

"My special mix," he told me.

I once asked him to let me watch him make one. Just as I did when Michela showed Constantino our original recipes, I took notes as Mike explained his margarita magic. This is my transcription:

"Tell me how you make one margarita."

"I start with two ounces of my special mix."

"What's in your special mix?"

"Fresh lime juice. Fresh lemon juice. Orange juice. And egg whites."

"Equal measurements?"

"No, a little bit of lime juice, half and half lime and lemon juice. Just a little bit of orange juice, a dash or a few drops."

"How many egg whites?"

"Just one for a lot of mix."

"So if I make your mix?"

"Eight ounces of lime, eight ounces of lemon, two ounces of orange juice, and one egg white."

"How long does that last?"

"It goes fast—but it can keep in the fridge for a week."

"So let's go back to making one margarita with your mix. What are the measurements?"

"Two ounces of mix, one-and-a-half ounces of tequila, and one-half ounce of Triple Sec or Cointreau. We use Triple Sec because it's cheaper, but personally I prefer Cointreau."

"Blended?"

"Yes, with five or six ice cubes. Count to ten. It can be longer, but the ice won't melt and it won't be cold enough if it's too short."

"What if someone wants it shaken?"

"Same mix. I shake it six or seven times and pour over ice."

"What about salt?"

"The glass must be cold, and I mean cold, so you dip the glass in the salt. You don't need water if it's cold."

* * *

For all this talk about margaritas, Mike was known for putting a shot of slivovitz in front of people waiting at the bar. Often this was on the house. On Mike. It was his way of saying welcome to my world. He started doing this when people said to give them whatever he liked. "I like what you like," they would say. He would shake his head. "You're going to hate me for that." They would insist and he poured them a shot of slivovitz. They smelled it, they made faces.

"What is it?"

"Plum brandy—a traditional Slavic drink."

"How do I drink it?"

"All at once. You'll enjoy it later."

I think Giovanni taught Mike a few tricks at the beginning. Then Mike came in his own. He cultivated friendships with the customers. He reminded people they were at a bar, and it was okay to get a little loud. "If you want peace and quiet, go to church or the library," he said. "Don't come to my bar." Customers loved his occasional abrasiveness. Like when someone did not know what they wanted to drink and asked Mike what he thought. He glanced up at the shelves of liquor bottles behind the bar and playfully snapped, "There's my menu, bitch." He knew how to read people. Ninety-five percent of the time he measured his drinks with practiced precision, but the other five percent of the time he would sense something in a person's eyes or in their body language and he would turn the bottle upside down.

Mike behind the bar was magical. The bar was in the center of the restaurant, a world within the larger world of Dan Tana's, and he was the ringmaster. Technique can be practiced, but instinct is something else. You can't teach greatness.

For much of the 1960s and 1970s, Mike's house cappuccino was the most popular drink we served. Over time tastes changed. Just like people ordered more martinis than margaritas, they stopped drinking cappuccino. But we used to sell hundreds every day. It was made with a little brandy, Kahlua, rum, the Italian liqueur Frangelico, espresso coffee, regular American coffee, and powdered chocolate and sugar. All mixed together. Then Mike added a bit of milk or cream or half and half and steamed it in the copper espresso machine behind the bar.

"People will die if they drink too much of that stuff," he would laugh.

Music publicist Bob Gibson probably consumed more of those cappuccinos than any other single individual. He insisted on the finest cognac; at that time, it was probably a Hennessy XO, meaning extra old. Gibson's cappuccino cost twenty-five dollars, which was a lot of money, and which was why he warned people not to buy him a drink. Gibson wanted to hire Mike to bartend on the private jets he took on tour with his rock and roll clients like the Rolling Stones and The Who. It never worked out, but the free-spending PR maven sent Mike and his wife on vacations to Hawaii, Cabo, and Acapulco.

I remember Mike describing their Acapulco trip as a disaster. It rained all week. He and his wife could not get out of their hotel room. Then he winked at me. "And that's how we had our third son."

Almost everyone who came into the restaurant seemed to leave with their own Mike story. I have my favorite, too. Mike had just gone full-time as our bartender when one afternoon Arnold Schwarzenegger came in. Arnold had won the prestigious Mr. Universe title in 1967 and moved to the United States shortly thereafter. He was like the rest of us, an immigrant looking for a better life, looking to turn his dream of becoming a movie star into a reality.

Mike still struggled with his English, but he spoke German fluently and got to know the outgoing bodybuilder in his native language, though the two of them mostly conversed in English. When Arnold told him that he was Mr. Universe, Mike snapped, "Bullshit." When Arnold expressed his ambition to rise to the loftiest ranks of Hollywood, Mike said, "You're going to have to learn to speak better English. Otherwise, you're going to have a tough time acting."

Arnold promised Mike that he was going to work hard on his accent. "You got any fresh-squeezed orange juice back there?" Arnold asked.

"Yes, I'll make you a glass right now," Mike said.

"How much?" Arnold asked.

"Fifty cents," Mike replied.

"Why that much?"

"These are the freshest oranges."

One night Arnold came in and ordered his usual orange juice but asked Mike to put two raw eggs in it. He did as requested, putting the orange juice and eggs in a blender before pouring it fresh and frothy into a waiting glass and serving it to Arnold. It was an Orange Julius à la Mike. While Arnold took a few sips, Mike went into the kitchen and asked Mate how much he should charge for it.

"What do you get for the orange juice?" Mate asked.

"Fifty cents."

"With two eggs, charge seventy-five cents."

When Mike returned to the bar, Arnold had put two quarters in front of him. Mike shook his head.

"It's seventy-five cents," he said.

Arnold stiffened. Something did not compute with him.

"How come it was fifty cents two days ago?"

Mike did not flinch. "Now it's got two eggs."

Almost forty years later, Arnold comes into the restaurant. Now he's Governor Schwarzenegger, with a bunch of hangers-on and squad of bodyguards. Though he was warmly greeted by waiters who had been at the restaurant back when Helena first brought him in and he fell in love with the place, he was no longer a regular. He's been busy. He became one of the world's biggest movie stars. More recently he had been re-elected to a second term as governor of California.

While his party was shown to a table, Arnold walked up to the bar. Mike stopped what he was doing and says hello to the governor.

"You remember me?" Arnold asked.

"I do," Mike says.

"And my drink?"

"Of course."

A minute later, Mike put an Orange Julius à la Mike in front of Arnold. Fresh OJ and two eggs blended into a refreshing froth and poured into an ice-cold glass. Arnold took a big drink, smiled, and slapped two quarters on top of the bar. Mike's eyes moved slowly from the coins to the governor's eyes.

"It's seventy-five cents."

25

It's a Family Restaurant

My youngest daughter Katy was born the year Dan Tana's opened, 1964. Her earliest memories of the restaurant, she says, were the smells and tastes. She remembers her mother Andrea taking her and her older sister Gaby for dinner at 5 P.M. and how the dim light always made her fall asleep at the booth or hide below the table. She also recalls sitting at the bar with Mike and dropping cherries in drinks.

Gaby recalls the "warm wonder and excitement" she felt as a little girl walking through the red door into the restaurant. The transition from the bright sunlight to the dark interior made her feel like she was stepping into an entirely different world—of course, it was.

She was five or six years old when she went to work there. Early on Saturday nights, she was the assistant salad maker. She sat on a chopping block and dropped olives on top of the Tana salads. She earned one dollar each shift. But the dollar was secondary to something else that interested her. His name was Jimmy Cano. He was a waiter at the restaurant and Gaby's first crush.

Handsome and charming, Jimmy was aware of his gifts and knew how to use them to his advantage. His father had been the maître d' at Musso & Frank Grill, another Hollywood institution, so the business was in his blood. Jimmy would spend thirty-seven years at Dan Tana's, twenty-five of them as maître d'. He kissed the hands of ladies and cracked jokes with the men. I understood why my daughter was infatuated by him. He didn't just serve, he seduced.

Jimmy had been poached from the Brown Derby by Giovanni, my first maître d'—and in many ways, the restaurant's guiding light or visionary. Giovanni told me early on that he had a vision of turning Dan Tana's from an arm-service spaghetti joint to a place for fine dining. It was a vision that required changes in both the food we served—like his Florentine dishes, his signature parfait, and an expanded wine list. But above all else, it meant hiring the right people. That was integral to Dan Tana's success and what it would become. Gio understood that food and service had to be excellent, but so did the spirit behind it. This was something coaches know in sports. A team can have great players, but if they don't know how to work together, if they don't mesh, if they don't put the team first, they will never contend for a championship. The people he hired didn't just work at Dan Tana's, they became Dan Tana's.

Giovanni knew everyone in all the restaurants, whether it was Nickodell or The Brown Derby or Chasen's or La Scala. He brought over several more waiters besides Jimmy. He added a line cook, Danny, who stayed for thirty years. He was responsible for putting Mate in the kitchen next to Constantino. He hired Mike. He understood Bogie. He wished Jimmy well when he left to be the maître d' at Chasen's. No hard feelings, it was a promotion. The door would be open if he wanted to come back—and eventually, he did.

I never met anyone who understood more about the things that made a restaurant work. Many who ate at Dan Tana's insisted their meal was not complete unless they hugged him or shook his hand on their way out.

So, it was an extremely sad day in 1970 when Giovanni's poor health finally took a long-anticipated turn for the worse. First, he began keeping an oxygen tank in the kitchen. Then he only worked a couple of hours at night. When he became too weak to show up for work, I knew the inevitable had arrived. He loved his family, but work was his life. Soon after he was cut off from it, he went to sleep and never woke up.

Word of Giovanni's passing quickly spread. Mike poured a lot of free drinks. Toasts to Giovanni echoed throughout the night. Men who had worked with him over the years came in after-hours and told stories.

Giovanni made sure that we were not left without a maître d'. Aware that he was winding down, he had mentored Bruno, one of the waiters he had brought over from Nickodell, to take over.

Bruno stepped into his new role as if he had been doing it for years. Likewise, Mate took over as head chef when Constantino finally retired, as he had been threatening for a couple of years. (Constantino had saved his money, and he moved to Mexico to open a restaurant.) Dan Tana's continued to flourish. One of my very good customers, the filmmaker Henry Jaglom, started coming in when he was working on *Easy Rider* with Peter Fonda and Dennis Hopper. I think Bob Rafelson, who produced that hippie epic, brought Henry in. He knew the gang of regulars who were making *Five Easy Pieces*, Jack Nicholson, Carol Eastman, and Bob, who directed that picture.

They mixed both old Hollywood—Loretta Young, Gene Kelly, and Fred Astaire, who was the first and one of the only customers I let run a tab—and new Hollywood - Mike Nichols and Al Pacino. We also had bookies, doctors and lawyers, the dancer Rudolf Nureyev, and basketball superstars Wilt Chamberlain and Jerry West. Then we had the music crowd drifting in late at night from the Troubadour—the Smothers Brothers, John Lennon, oil heir turned folkie Ned Doheny, and David Geffen. It was *the scene*, Henry said. Like Elaine's in New York.

Henry hated all the cigarette smoke before it was popular to object to cigarette smoke in a restaurant, and long before smoking was banned indoors. So much smoking and yelling at the bar, he complained. "I'm too much of a girl for that," he said. But he ate at Dan Tana's almost every night in the 1970s and once confided that one of the most exciting memories of his life took place at Dan Tana's.

He was standing behind a post in the front of the restaurant, watching Fred Astaire eat a steak. "I've never seen anything or anyone as graceful and gorgeous in my life as he was, eating his salad and steak. He cut his steak as if it were part of a dance, with an elegance and ease that was . . . It was unmistakably Fred Astaire. I spent forty minutes watching him. He ate as beautifully as he danced."

"And there was a girl with him," Henry continued. "I didn't know who she was. She was wearing the most beautiful dress I've ever seen. So, between this girl's dress and his eating, I was in heaven, watching this incredible scene. He was just tap dancing his way through that meal so beautifully."

* * *

Francis Ford Coppola came in. So did Roman Polanski, who was always with Jack when they were making *Chinatown* in 1974, though he had frequented Dan Tana's years before with his beautiful actress wife, Sharon Tate. One night I will never forget: August 9, 1969. Celebrity hairstylist Jay Sebring, who had dated Sharon Tate, was hosting a party of six people at the restaurant. In the middle of dinner, someone called him. He paid the check and left. I think he then met Tate and several friends at another restaurant and afterward they went to Polanski's house. Hours later, Jay and the others were brutally murdered by three members of Charles Manson's family.

That was not the only chilling last moment associated with the restaurant. On March 4, 1982, Robert DeNiro and Harry Dean

Stanton were eating at Dan Tana's, as they often did, and they invited their friend John Belushi to join them. Belushi was also a regular whenever he was in town. This was a completely different time at the restaurant. People routinely put mirrors on their tables or on the bar and snorted lines of cocaine, Belushi being among the most open about it. Belushi declined DeNiro's and Harry Dean's invitation to join them for dinner, but he did order a steak delivered to him at his bungalow at the Chateau Marmont Hotel, where he died of a drug overdose later that night.

Music producer Phil Spector was another famous last meal. A longtime regular, he always came in with a bodyguard. He barely spent any money, maybe fifty or sixty dollars, but he never tipped less than five hundred dollars. The staff loved him for that, of course, but since he paid with his American Express card, I had to pay 3 percent to the credit card company, which meant that I was basically paying for half of his meal. He ate dinner at his usual table the night before he went to jail for the murder of his girlfriend, actress Lana Clarkson. He ordered a steak and left a five-hundred-dollar tip.

For years O.J. Simpson came in once or twice a week with his friends or his wife, Nicole. I knew O.J. from the golf course. I played with him a few times. Then Nicole—by then his ex-wife—and her close friend, Ron Goldman, were murdered in her Brentwood condo and O.J. was suspected of committing the heinous crime. Though he was later famously acquitted of the murders, public opinion was against him from day one of the incident, especially on the west side of Los Angeles.

One of my customers flat out said, "If we ever see O.J. in this restaurant, we will walk out and never come back."

I knew they were not the only ones who felt that way. The next day I sought out O.J. at the golf course and told him that he could never come back to Dan Tana's. He heard me but turned and walked away without uttering a word. I never spoke to him again, and he never returned to the restaurant.

I took my customers' sensitivities as seriously as their preferences. One time someone complained that Mike told a Jewish joke at the bar. I delivered an immediate decree to the crew: no jokes about religion, politics, or ethnicity. Mike was confused, almost hurt. "I make jokes about everyone," he said. Not anymore. A careless utterance could destroy decades of loyalty—as happened in the 1990s to the Bistro Gardens, a staple of buttoned-down Beverly Hills, which shut its doors after an anti-Semitic slur was directed at a diner.

One of my early customers was a doctor who ate at the restaurant four or five times a week. He always drank until he was wobbly drunk. When I saw him in the reservation book, I knew that part of my rent was going to be paid. But he would get loud and surly with each drink, a problem we were able to manage until he got up from his table one night and yelled for all to hear, "The fucking Mexicans need to go back to their own country!"

Everyone in the packed restaurant stopped what they were doing and froze—except for me. I walked over to him, took hold of his arm, and guided him to the door. Before shoving him out, I leaned into him and whispered, "Dr. Vance, do you see this door? Please walk outside and never come back."

I shut the door behind him, and when I turned around, the entire restaurant erupted in applause.

All of us were from someplace else. This was our home.

* * *

One afternoon in August 1970, Doug Weston, who owned the Troubadour music venue down the block, called me and told me that I had to come down to his club right away. He said there was an English soccer player who was rehearsing for his show that night.

He was playing piano and kicking a soccer ball around his dressing room. I had to see this kid, he said.

This so-called kid was twenty-three-year-old Elton John, who was making his US debut. I watched him rehearse, kicked a ball with him, and talked about soccer until I had to go back to the restaurant. On my way out, I thanked Doug for tipping me off.

"But I hope he sticks with the piano," I said. "He's not a soccer player."

About a year later, Doug extended another urgent invitation. This time it was to hear a girl singer named Linda Ronstadt. I stood in the back during her soundcheck. Her voice gave me goosebumps. And she was gorgeous, just adorable. I thought I had seen her a couple years before when she first played the Troubadour with her old band, The Stone Poneys. You don't forget someone like her.

Indeed, I recognized her later that night. She came in late that night with three guys from her band, two of whom were the future Eagles Don Henley and Glenn Frey. The four musicians were pressed into a small booth. The guys were passing around a bottle of beer. One bottle! I stopped by and complimented Linda, explaining I had heard her sound check. She asked if they could order a plate of spaghetti with meat sauce and split it four ways, explaining they only had twenty dollars.

"Save your money," I said, "and tip the waiter. I'll bring each of you your own plate of spaghetti on me."

I knew what it was like to be hungry and watching every dollar, and my small act of hospitality started a friendship among all of us. Linda's paid off years later, and Glenn and Don came in so often over the years that Dan Tana's became the unofficial headquarters for the Eagles. They would tell their friends to meet them at the Yellow Submarine, code for Tana's.

Table 4 was their usual post. It offered an unobstructed view of the many beautiful women who came into the restaurant. The Eagles wrote their classic song "Lyin' Eyes" there one night. Glenn and Don were musing about couples that cheated on each other when Glenn spotted an attractive young woman who was with an overweight older man. Assuming theirs was an illicit mismatch, he scoffed, "She can't even hide those lyin' eyes." Don and Glenn and J. D. Souther also wrote another hit, "New Kid in Town" at the same table after seeing Bruce Springsteen play at the Roxy.

Like everyone else, they came for Tana's unique combination of intimacy, excitement, discretion, and familiarity. In other words, the home-away-from-home vibe with its own extended family, the regular cast of characters, the parade of beautiful women, the personal service, the late hours, and the excellent food. The scene fed on itself. You didn't have to be famous to be part of it. You just had to show up. Take this old man named Joe—everyone who ate at Dan Tana's, famous or not, knew Joe. In his nineties, Joe came in every night, sat at the end of the bar, and talked to whoever landed next to him.

"Hi, Joe, how're you doing?" I always said.

"I'm good," he always said, "I haven't seen you since last night!"

Joe was an ex-bartender who had worked all around town. He had grown up in Detroit. His father was a bootlegger. He landed at Dan Tana's in his retirement years like so many of the guys who made careers out of working in restaurants. It was comfortable, familiar, his home away from home. One Monday morning he fell and hit his head pretty hard. He saw a doctor. The doctor said he had bad news for him. He found some blood clots in his brain and needed surgery right away.

"Okay," Joe said. "But make it fast. I have to get to Dan Tana's in time to watch Monday Night Football."

* * *

I was not aware that my reputation extended beyond my little stretch of Santa Monica Boulevard until Yugoslavia's leader Marshal Tito visited Los Angeles in 1971 and I received a formal invitation to a dinner President Nixon was hosting for him at the Century Plaza Hotel.

Tito loved movies, especially American westerns, so the dinner, which Universal Studios chief Lew Wasserman was helping to organize, was going to be packed with Hollywood stars—and me. Except that I declined. Just imagining myself in the vicinity of Tito made me nervous. I called the RSVP number on the invitation, an office in Washington, DC, and explained that I could not attend. The person I was speaking to asked why.

"I ran away from Tito," I explained.

"You're not going to be in any danger," he said. "You're going to be there as a guest of President Nixon. The president wants to highlight Yugoslavs who came to the US to escape Communist dictatorship and became successful and have contributed to the country."

Persuaded, I agreed to attend. The next day I received a call at the restaurant. The caller threatened to burn down Dan Tana's if I went to the dinner. I reported it immediately. I also said I felt it was safer if I didn't go to the event. I was told the person who threatened me had already been apprehended by the FBI and I should attend the dinner without any concerns.

But I had concerns that I preferred to keep to myself. About two years before Tito's visit, I had bought some land on Hvar, a beautiful island off the Dalmatian Coast of what was then Yugoslavia. I had then commissioned the architect Ted Grenzbach to design a stone villa that would become my family's vacation home. Grenzbach, who was introduced to me by Wilt Chamberlain, had previously designed houses for Frank Sinatra and Johnny Carson.

Ted wanted to meet my wife before taking on the project, so Andrea and I met him for dinner at Tana's. He praised the Hvar property and described his vision: A stone house that would look as though it had stood for two centuries yet be thoroughly modern inside. I asked how much it would cost. His usual fee was $50,000, but he offered a trade. "I'm not famous enough to get into your restaurant. I'll waive my fee for $5,000 worth of food and a standing reservation."

The villa was mine—a magical place where the island met the Adriatic. The air itself was a tonic. It happened to be located directly across the street from Dr. O, the legendary soccer scout who had once been my guardian angel, rescuing me from Belgrade and opening the world to me. *Life is full of mysterious ingredients*, I thought. One day, I brought Wilt "the Stilt" to Dr. O's house for a pickup basketball game with some of the local boys. I'll never forget the look of amazement on his face.

However, with Marshal Tito about to arrive in LA, there was a good chance I could lose it. Foreigners were not allowed to own property in Yugoslavia. If Tito or his people found out that I owned it, it might be confiscated. Could I argue that the idea of buying property on Hvar had been the local mayor's idea? Would that get him in trouble? The situation kept me awake at night.

Then it was time for the formal dinner. Andrea and I dressed up. It seemed like about a third of the room were Yugoslavian ex-pats or Yugoslavs born in the US. We mingled in the crowded ballroom with Karl Malden, Brad Dexter, Peter Bogdanovich, even my old "boss," the owner of the StarKist tuna plant whose payroll I'd been on. Then the receiving line formed. It was time to meet Tito.

US State Department officials had alerted us beforehand that we were going to get a few minutes with Tito. Because he was an avid film buff, they advised us to welcome him to Hollywood. They also told me to ask if he wanted to converse in English or Serbo-Croatian.

He spoke both languages. So my turn came. He said he preferred Serbo-Croatian. I welcomed him to Hollywood as instructed and said it was an honor to have him visit us and be such a fan of the film industry. Blah-blah-blah.

Tito took it all in but a look of shock crept across his face. Still gripping my hand, he said, "You speak the language better than me. Where did you learn?"

I told him that I had left Belgrade in 1952.

"Defected?" he asked.

"Yes, defected," I said with a shrug. "What can I say?"

He wrapped his left arm around me and brought me close, like we were hugging. Then he whispered, "I would have done the same thing if I were you."

* * *

Before we sat down for dinner, I was pulled to the side by four men who were part of Tito's inner detail. Whether advisors or security or a mix I did not know. All I knew was they were keen on questioning me. Did I have a Yugoslav passport? No. Had I ever had one? When was the last time I had been in Yugoslavia? Yes, in 1965 when my wife and I were spending her *Let's Make A Deal* money, and again '69–'70 when I visited friends on the island.

"I even bought some land and built a house," I said, unsure why I was suddenly volunteering this information. "It will be finished later this year or next and I'll visit again then."

They looked confused, but the questions ceased, and Andrea and I were moved from our original table near the back to one closer to Tito. I found myself seated next to the US ambassador and the head of the Yugoslav consulate in San Francisco. The man from the consulate told me that Tito was fascinated by me but added, "How could you build a house as an American? It's not allowed!"

"Nobody asked me," I said, playing innocent.

"But you know what the law is?"

"I know the laws here, in the United States," I bluffed.

This went on for a bit. A couple hours later, following speeches and other formalities, the guy from the consulate, who had been up and down from his seat throughout the evening, sat back down and told me that Tito had ordered him to issue a Yugoslav passport to me. All I had to do was make an appointment with him in San Francisco.

The next day I had a chance to thank Tito in person. He stopped by the restaurant on his way out of town. I met him out front. He wanted to know where he could see some hippies and why they and the student protestors he saw on the news had beards. I guessed he was curious because during the Second World War, in Yugoslavia, the Partisans shaved but the Chetniks all wore beards. I had no idea why the hippies wore beards, but I directed him up to the Sunset Strip to see for himself.

As for my passport, it took a few years before I followed through and went to the consulate, where I paid seventy-five dollars and left with the official document. I no longer had to worry about losing my villa. But my friends were more excited than I was. Bert Schneider said, "You can fly to Cuba and get us cigars!"

For the kicker to this story, jump ahead to the late 1980s. I was in Belgrade, working with Yugoslavia's national football team. The team's secretary looked at my passport and saw it was going to expire in about six months. When I tried to renew it for another ten years, I found out it was no good. I had traveled on it for ten years and it had never been valid!

Apparently, the guy in San Francisco who issued it to me had pocketed my seventy-five dollars and voided the entry in the books right after he made it.

* * *

One evening toward the end of March 1972, I came into the restaurant and noticed four men seated at table 6. I didn't recognize any of them, but they all had the same look. Their suits and ties showed they weren't in the movie business. Bogie told me they had accents that sounded funny, like they were from out of town. Of course, most of my staff had accents and sounded like they were from some other place, including me. I figured these guys were in LA on business and had heard about Dan Tana's.

I was right. While they were being served drinks and salads, Bruno told me the chief of the West Hollywood Sheriff's Department was on the phone for me.

"Dan, there are four men sitting at the table in the back corner of the restaurant," the sheriff said. "I would like you to go up to the man on the end, the one sitting closest to the kitchen, and whisper that he has a phone call."

Interesting. How did the sheriff know such detail?

I delivered the message, which prompted a skeptical look, but the gentleman got up and took the call. On his way back to the table, he nodded to me to go back to the phone. I marveled at how much could be communicated without saying a word. It was like being back in acting class.

I picked up the receiver.

"Dan, everything is fine, everybody is fine," the sheriff told me. "Don't worry about it. Those men are from back East and I wanted them to know that I knew they were here in town—my town, I told them—and I had eyes on them."

Now things made sense to me.

Before Francis Ford Coppola made *The Godfather*, there hadn't been any serious movies about the mafia. The mob had shut down any attempt, including my father-in-law's efforts to produce a movie about the mob's involvement in the Louis-Schmeling fight. The Mafia boss Joe Colombo, head of one of the Five Families in New York, was not happy when he found out Paramount was producing Coppola's adaptation of Mario Puzo's novel.

Pressure was put on the studio to let them read the screenplay. Somebody high up in the Colombo organization got their hands on a copy and sent a message to the film's producers, Bob Evans, Al Ruddy, and Sidney Beckerman, all regulars of mine. It said that if they invited him to dinner at Dan Tana's within a week to discuss the script, they could proceed with the picture. If no invitation came, they would have to cancel production. The invitation was given, the Colombo organization came to dinner at the restaurant with the producers, and the movie got made.

Now, two years later, *The Godfather* was premiering the next day. The studio's PR machine had done a masterful job publicizing the picture. Mario Puzo's novel had been an international bestseller, and with Coppola, Marlon Brando, and Al Pacino involved in the film, plus the controversial subject matter, anticipation was high. Everyone wanted to see this movie—including the four men at table 6.

Toward the end of their meal, they asked to speak to me. Bruno, who was very handsome but not the brightest, was nonetheless tuned into their vibe. He looked at me and raised his eyebrows, a silent note to be careful.

"We were told that you could help us," the gentleman who had taken the phone call said to me.

"Tell me what you need," I said.

"Have you seen the movie *The Godfather*?"

"No, I know it is playing tomorrow. But at just two theaters. Then, I think in a couple days, it will be everywhere."

He nodded in acknowledgment. The three other men in his booth were staring at me with an unsettling intensity.

"We need four tickets for the ten o'clock show tomorrow morning at the Loews Theater in Hollywood," he said. "We want to sit in the back row."

It would have been easier to get them seats on the next NASA rocket to the moon. Maybe seated next to Neil Armstrong.

"All the tickets sold out weeks ago," I said.

He already knew this.

"The sheriff said that only one man can get us tickets, and that's you, Dan Tana. We are looking forward to seeing the movie tomorrow at ten o'clock."

I went home and told my wife about the men and their request. She asked what I was going to do about it. "Nothing," I said. "I don't even know their names. I don't know where they're staying. They didn't tell me anything." She strongly suggested that doing nothing would be a bad idea. I looked at my watch. It was midnight. I checked on my daughters who were sound asleep. I was wide awake, fearful, and realizing I was living a scene that could be in the movie.

How was I suddenly involved with the mafia? I called my father-in-law and told him what was going on. He put me in touch with his friend, Emmitt Shane, who managed all the Loews theaters. Now it's close to 1 A.M., and I was telling this man who I didn't know that I needed four tickets in the back for people whose names I didn't know.

"Don't worry about it," he said. "Leave it to me. If they show up, they'll have their seats."

"Okay, thank you," I said, and hung up.

Could I trust this man? I had no other choice.

The next night the same four men were back in the restaurant, at the same corner table where I last saw them. When I spotted them, out of the corner of my eye, my first thought was, oh shit. I had no idea if they had been able to get in the theater as they had requested or . . . Well, I didn't want to think about that. Then they saw me and waved me over to their table.

"We were just discussing the movie," the main guy said.

"How was it?" I asked.

"Great."

"Incredible," one of his tablemates said.

"You need to see it," another guy added. "We couldn't have done it better if we'd hired the director ourselves."

I asked what it was about.

"It's a family picture," the main one said, smiling.

"They cut the horse's head, but so what," another joked.

It was clear they had enjoyed the picture, and they thanked me with great sincerity for getting them seats. One guy offered introductions.

"I'm from Chicago," he said and then pointed to the others. "He's from New York. He's from Philadelphia. And he's from Miami. If you are ever in one of those cities and need anything, let us know."

I am happy to say that I have never needed anything.

26

Frequent Flier

On August 15, 1971, my friend and partner Dan Reeves died in his New York City apartment, following a long bout with blood cancer. He was only fifty-eight. I knew much of my success was due to his investment in me, both financially and through his belief in me.

My heart was heavy for months. I could not walk through the front door of the restaurant without thinking of the day Dan and Dan Martin told me that we were going to buy the place—and that I was going to run it! I have two angels in my life. One, Bogie who was a drinker and a gambler, and the other, Dan who was a chain smoker and who was just getting started after three martinis.

It was not until the next summer that I afforded myself a few weeks of vacation at my new villa on Hvar. Being at the villa with Andrea, Gaby, and Katy was exactly what I needed. However, while I was gone though, my old friend Peter Coe, bankrolled by a wealthy Texan, opened a restaurant in Beverly Hills and poached three of my key people—Bruno, my maître d'; Aldo, who was Mate's number two in the kitchen, and Mike, my bartender.

When I got home and learned more of the details, I was livid. I felt like my home had been robbed. I am pretty sure that Peter and his Texas backer had sat at Dan Tana's numerous nights, drinking heavily, while telling each other that running a restaurant was easy—and easy money. Anyone who has been involved in a restaurant at any level, from investor to dishwasher, knows otherwise.

Nevertheless, these two were willing to throw out good money and even better friendships for this booze-fueled pipe dream.

Their restaurant, Trieste, closed after just six months. Bruno called me and said he and Aldo wanted to come back. I said no thanks. Disloyalty had consequences.

Though tangential, I was reminded of the time Dan Reeves fired the LA Rams' head coach George Allen. Dan knew George Allen was one of the great coaches in the sport, but Allen had broken his bond with the team's owner when Allen banned him from the locker room after a practice.

Dan never got over that breach. I watched him stew for weeks. He told his friend, Pittsburgh Steelers owner Art Rooney, what had happened and asked if Rooney would hire Allen if he was fired. Rooney said no. "If he did that to you, he would do it to me, too." That was enough for Dan Reeves. On Christmas Eve, 1968, he was in the restaurant with three of the highest-ranking Catholic priests in the city. After the priests had their fill and left, Dan asked if he could use my phone.

It was close to midnight when he picked up the phone, dialed George Allen at home, and fired him. The news broke two days later. Fans were outraged. Dan hired him back almost immediately, but he fired Allen again two years later. The difference with my situation? No one missed Bruno or Aldo.

Mike was another story. He was too proud to ask for his job back and went to work at Jimmy's in Century City. In his absence, I brought in bartender George Samma from La Scala, a crazy little French guy who came in two nights a week. He was fine. He had a following and knew a lot of people, including Jimmy Connors, then a UCLA freshman tennis player on his way to winning the

NCAA men's tennis championship. I liked Jimmy. He was brash, a real scrapper, dirt poor—and hungry. He would come in, sit at the bar, and eat George's free meal.

But I missed Mike, and so did the customers. Harry Dean was among those who claimed it wasn't the same without Mike behind the bar. I knew why he and the others had left—the opportunity to own a piece of a restaurant—but still I would ask myself, why the hell did Mike leave?

After about four months, I contacted him and said I forgave him. I understood. No hard feelings. I wanted him back.

"For you, Mike, the door is always open," I said.

"What about the other two guys?" he asked.

"I'll stay friends with Bruno and Aldo, but I won't hire them back."

* * *

Bogie helped Mate in the kitchen until Mate could find a new second-in-command. A hardworking waiter named Ettore Perovich filled in as maître d' while I searched for a replacement for Bruno. Though Ete was one of the best workers I ever had—and twenty years later he snagged the local restaurant association's Service Person of the Year award—he lacked the people-pleasing panache the job required.

Bruno had been excellent, but Giovanni's shadow still loomed over the position. Then one day I found myself talking to a handsome, very polished man who walked in unannounced, asking for me. He heard I was looking for a maître d' and wanted to be interviewed. Then and there. His name was Guido Perry. It turned out he was Ete's brother.

Midway through our conversation, I realized Guido was interviewing me, not the other way around, and I was impressed. His good looks were matched by his charm. He spoke Italian, German, Serbian, and English. His wife was the daughter of the Romanian ambassador to West Germany. He had the gift. He could tell someone a bullshit story that would make them feel good about waiting an hour for a table.

I hoped he wasn't feeding me one of those stories. Later that day, Guido's brother met with me in private.

"I did not tell my brother to come here. He did that on his own. I just want to make one thing clear with you, Mr. Tana. If my brother does something wrong and gets fired here, I don't want to lose my job. I have a family."

I noted his concern and went ahead and hired Guido. He quickly showed that he had potential to be a great maître d'—maybe even better than Giovanni. After a while, I was confident the restaurant could run without me being there every night and I took my family on an extended trip to England, France, and Italy. We visited chateaus where I bought wine for the restaurant. In France, Gaby tasted Domaine de la Romanée-Conti, the world's greatest Burgundy. In Italy, Katy celebrated her birthday with a rum-filled cake at the Villa Medici.

I'll never forget, in Florence, our hotel bill and all restaurant charges were comped by a stranger who kept their identity a secret. Later, I discovered this beneficence came from a mafioso I knew from the restaurant who wanted to show his gratitude for the time I talked his daughter out of becoming an actress.

I had concerns of my own about my children. Gaby came home from school one day and showed her mother a marijuana cigarette that one of her classmates had given her. She wasn't even ten years old! Shocked, Andrea and I took that as proof the Los Angeles public schools were deteriorating. A friend of ours in London convinced us the English public schools were much better—and free.

An idea was planted—and it rapidly took root. Andrea wanted to paint and loved the notion of being an artist in Europe. I was more practical. I saw the culture of sex, drugs, and rock and roll at the restaurant and I saw the move as an opportunity to protect my daughters a little longer. Selfishly, I also saw the opportunity to be closer to the sport I loved. Arrangements were made.

Despite efforts to keep the move quiet, it still reached the two deans of fine dining in LA, Scandia's Ken Hansen and Chasen's Dave Chasen. They set up dinner with me and our wives at Dan Tana's. Before salads were brought to the table, I was listening to the biggest compliment of my life. They did not want me to leave. I was the best of the younger generation of the city's restaurateurs, they said. They were getting older, and they saw me as the person who could carry on all that we stood for. In other words, the torch was being passed.

But my mind was made up. I had already discussed the move with my employees. I knew that Guido and Mate had a firm grasp on their roles and most of the people who worked for me had been there from the beginning or close to it. Mike had the bar covered. Bogie could do anything. Pearl, my wife's aunt, managed the staff and handled the bookkeeping. And my father-in-law emptied the cash register every morning at 5 A.M. We were covered, and, as I explained to everyone, I would be back every other month. I said if customers asked for me between 5 P.M. and 8 P.M., tell them I was coming in later. If people asked for me after nine, tell them that I'd been in earlier and gone home.

The plan worked. We rented a lovely apartment in Kensington, the girls started school, and I phoned into the restaurant every afternoon—it was morning in Los Angeles—and got updated on the previous day's business. The numbers remained good and steady. I returned every other month. Not until my third or fourth trip back to LA, did I noticed subtle changes were taking place in my absence.

I answered the phone in the office one afternoon. It was Lew Wasserman's secretary.

Mr. Wasserman wanted to come in that night with his wife, she said, and he wanted to sit at *his* table.

"Mr. Wasserman has his own table?" I said, curiously.

I knew certain regulars had their preferences, which we tried to accommodate, but nothing was guaranteed, and I was not aware that Mr. Wasserman or anyone else had their own table.

"I'll have to check," his secretary said. "I will call you back momentarily."

The phone rang moments later, and she explained that her boss wanted the first table to the left as you walked into the smaller front dining room. Table 1. That would not be a problem, I told her. But I was irritated. For the rest of the week, I observed where Guido sat people and saw nothing but celebrities in the smaller of the two dining rooms. The other room was full, but not one famous face among them. He was copying Jean Leon at La Scala. Saving tables. Separating the famous and non-famous.

I met with Guido. No saving tables, I told him. Empty tables cost me money. And it irritated those waiting at the bar. To me, everyone was a VIP.

"I want a mix," I said. "I don't want celebrities with celebrities. I want everyone mixing and looking around to see who's here."

"But—"

"No buts," I said. "If I ever walk in and see this again, look for another job."

* * *

With each commute, I seemed to walk into some kind of situation. One night I showed up around 6 P.M., having come straight from the airport, and saw a handful of police cars with flashing lights in front of the restaurant. I figured there had been a fight or a robbery. I raced inside and straight into a mob of cops and employees, all of them talking at once. Naturally, Bogie was in the center of it. He pulled me into the fray.

"Boss, I'm so glad you showed up," he said. "We have a problem."

Before he could explain, the ranking officer, realizing I was indeed the boss, turned his attention to me. Everyone else stopped talking. The White House had been calling the restaurant repeatedly for the past forty-five minutes, the officer explained. Each time, the maître d', figuring it was a crank call, said "Fuck you" and hung up.

"Where's Guido?" I asked.

"He's not starting until seven o'clock," Bogie said.

"Who's been answering the phone?"

Bogie nodded. "I have, boss."

I turned back to the cop. "Is this for real?"

"Very real."

"Who's been calling from the White House?"

"President Nixon's chief of staff, Alexander Haig," he said.

I saw a look in his eyes that seemed to acknowledge this was out of the ordinary but not cause to hang up—repeatedly.

Then the phone rang. Everyone looked at it. It was like none of us had ever experienced this before. I picked it up. The man on the other end said, "Hello, this is Alexander Haig from the White House. Please don't hang up." I promised I wouldn't. We shared a laugh before I asked what I could do for him. He said he was trying to reach John Wayne. President Nixon had tried calling John Wayne at home, but his wife said he was on his way to Dan Tana's. The president wanted to speak to him.

I glanced around the restaurant. John Wayne was nowhere to be seen. Neither did he have a reservation. Then I saw John Wayne's agent was in a booth, clearly waiting for someone.

"I guess he's late," I told Mr. Haig.

"When he gets there, please have him call me," the chief of staff said, adding, "Every Friday, John Wayne and President Nixon bet on college football games. They select ten games, and they put ten dollars on each game."

"Mr. Haig," I said, "I don't know if you know this, but it's illegal to gamble in the US except in Las Vegas."

"Not if you're president of the United States," he said.

Just then John Wayne arrived. His timing was impeccable. I greeted him by holding out the phone and saying: "It's for you. It's the White House."

* * *

Life in London was a whirlwind. We socialized with friends from the restaurant, like LA transplants Mo and Lynn Rothman. Andrea studied art. I joined the Coombe Hill Golf Club in Surrey. A group of Hollywood exiles, most of whom had been blacklisted in the 1950s, urged me to open a Dan Tana's in Chelsea and even raised $100,000 to back the venture. I never liked the idea of trying to duplicate something that I knew was one-of-a-kind, and I was fortunate it didn't work out.

By the time I found the right location, the political climate in the US had changed and most of my investors and would-be customers moved back to Los Angeles. But I had rediscovered an old love by then: football. My playwright friend Willis Hall was president of the St. Albans club, though he was a fan of Fulham, and he invited me to the weekly gatherings of English football elite—players, owners, broadcasters—that he hosted. Suddenly, I was immersed in the world of English football.

It should not have been surprising—and I suppose it wasn't. In a sense, the ball was still doing the running. I played in pickup games on Sundays in Hyde Park. There I met Frank Blunstone, a star for Chelsea in the 1950s. Frank was working for Manchester United, but had previously managed Brentford, a club that was struggling in the fourth (and lowest) division of English soccer.

Sensing my interest, he stressed the club's potential and urged me to get involved. I took a look. It was love at first sight. Brentford wore red and black stripes, the same colors as the Red Star team of my youth. I saw the team did have potential. The problem? It was a mess off the field. Two rich families owned the club and ran it in a way that made continuity and a clear vision for winning impossible. They had one strategy: maintaining their power.

If I was going to work with the team, I wanted it to be as a board member. I needed a voice and actual influence. There happened to be one opening among the nine seats. To join the board, you had to be a stockholder in the club, so I purchased five shares for ten dollars and ran for election—with one stipulation. My election had to be unanimous. The room of shareholders buzzed. Who was this foreigner, setting his own terms?

A former player and co-founder of the professional soccer league in the United States. Big deal!

But I won. An impassioned speech about my instant love of the team and the stadium where they played, Griffin Park, earned me respect and votes. The following year, 1975, I was elected chairman of the board, the first foreigner to hold that position on any team in English football, and I stayed in that seat for the next seven years while upping my ownership of the team from five shares to 10 percent.

My first season was a disaster. Afterward, I fired the manager and hired a star, Bill Dodgin, who helped reshape the team on the field and began Brentford's rise to the First Division. Off the field, I focused on the team's image. I took my players to hospitals to visit with children. They made appearances at schools. I wanted attendance at games to be a more entertaining experience, not just a place where hooligans could get drunk and go at each other in the stands.

I raged against unruly fans who chanted racist slurs at Black players. I even made a citizen's arrest of a fan who was screaming obscenities during a game against Watford. "Not in front of my wife and children," I barked. The effort paid off. Season ticket sales rose. The press loved me. So did the soccer world. I was elected to UEFA, the body that governs European football, and put on the marketing committee.

We moved into a spacious five-bedroom home in Chelsea, where Andrea worked in a light-filled studio that quickly became a gathering place for local artists. Our girls thrived at school, and between my frequent trips to Los Angeles, football, and family life, I felt both busier and happier than ever. Still, when the opportunity arose to produce my first feature film, I couldn't resist.

Gasp was an anti-pollution political thriller about a microbiologist investigating a mysterious odor drifting across Belgrade. I partnered with the Yugoslav government's film agency, investing $50,000 of my own money in exchange for the Western distribution rights. The agency retained the Eastern Bloc. Production went smoothly—until the director decided to screen an unfinished cut to the Yugoslav film committee and submit it to the Cannes Film Festival.

It was a disaster. The film was pulled from Belgrade theaters after just four days, supposedly for political reasons, and the Cannes Festival rejected it outright. I was furious. I hired a lawyer, who made it clear that the film was incomplete and the director had no authority to enter the film into the Cannes Festival. I was invited to resubmit the film once it was finished.

I took charge of post-production in Hollywood, bringing in veteran composer Walter Scharf for an original score. When the picture screened for one night in Los Angeles, *Los Angeles Times* film critic Charles Champlin praised *Gasp* as "a powerful, original, and provocative work."

I had been told that screenings deciding upon Cannes Festival entries were not always the careful, considerate look a filmmaker might hope for their film. Those watching occasionally instructed projectionists to skip reels rather than watch a film in its entirety. Just in case, I slipped the projectionist a few hundred dollars to ignore any such requests with my film. Two and a half hours later, he returned the money, explaining the committee had watched every minute of *Gasp* and seemed to enjoy it. A few hours later, I was informed that *Gasp* passed. It would be included in the upcoming festival.

The film was part of the official competition in March 1977. It did not win the Palme d'Or, but we had a good time at the festival.

27

Dan Tana, Report to Security

Late one night in April 1997, I was asleep in my bed in London when the phone rang. I answered on the third or fourth ring, hoping it would not wake up my wife. I also wondered who would call at this hour.

"Dan Tana?"

The person on the other end did not sound like an official about to deliver bad news. I heard noise in the background. And music.

"Who's this?"

It was Glenn Frey of the Eagles. He was with his bandmate, Don Henley. They were in London on their *Hotel California* tour. They had phoned the restaurant in Los Angeles looking for me and Guido had given them my home number in London. They were at a party with Elton John and, as Glenn explained, Elton John had recently purchased the Watford FC soccer team and had some questions. Aware of my affiliation with Brentford FC, they wanted him to talk to me.

"He wants to fire the manager," Glenn said. "We told him that he needs to talk to you first."

Now my wife was awake. "Who's getting fired?"

"Watford's manager. Elton John," I said.

"Elton John isn't the manager of Watford," she said.

"Let me see what he wants."

Neither of the Eagles mentioned the late hour or the chance they might have woken me up or that the three of us who knew each other from my tiny restaurant in West Hollywood were in England at the same time. All they asked was if could I meet them now. I checked the clock on my nightstand. Almost 12:30 A.M. I said I would get dressed. They said a limousine was on its way to get me.

Within forty-five minutes, I was sitting down with Glenn, Don, and Elton, who greeted me warmly, remembering that we met before his groundbreaking US debut at the Troubadour in 1970. It was one of the most unexpected and enjoyable intersections of the different parts of my life. Elton jumped right into business, explaining that he was chairman of Watford but had to get a new manager who could help the team out of Division Four, the basement of English professional soccer. It was the same situation I had been in with Brentford.

"I want to hire Bobby Moore," he said.

"Bobby Moore was a great player, West Ham's greatest ever," I said, acknowledging the English soccer legend with a reverential tone. "Captain of the national team. World champion. It would be very prestigious to appoint him as manager."

"Agreed," Elton said.

"But—"

"But?"

"I love Bobby," I said. "I play with him in my pickup game on the weekend in Hyde Park. But he has no experience as a manager. Even if he did, I don't think he has the right temperament, which is true for so many great players."

"Who should I hire?" Elton asked.

"You need to get Graham Taylor at Lincoln," I said. "I've been scouting managers. Graham is the best out there."

It dawned on me that the two of us were grown-up kids. Talking about football teams and players and managers the way we might have when we were ten or eleven years old. But Elton took notes. Soon after Graham led Lincoln to a Fourth Division title, Elton hired him. Watford had never gone higher than Division Two, but Elton had grand ambitions for the downtrodden team he'd purchased, and it turned out Graham was able to help him realize those dreams. They won the Fourth Division that next year. They were runner-up in the Third Division the one after that. In his fifth year at the helm, he guided Watford to the First Division.

It got better. In 1984, Watford got to the FA Cup final, playing in front of 100,000 fans at Wembley Stadium. Elton called it the greatest day of his life. A few years later, Elton sold his stake in the team to refocus on music, but like me, he never lost his passion for the sport.

* * *

Most people had no idea where I lived, whether in London or Los Angeles. My answer depended on who asked and which side of the pond I was on at the time. The truth was that I lived in the first-class section on United Airlines' flight from Heathrow to LAX. I had a million frequent flier miles before I made my first million dollars.

I had other ways of keeping up. My regular Monday night poker game upstairs at Mr. Chow's in Beverly Hills was one of the best sources for gossip. So was my Friday night game, which moved around from one Beverly Hills hotel suite to another. The group usually included Walter Matthau, Sidney Beckerman, Dino Conte, David Begelman, and a few others. There were nine regulars. One night, FBI agents used our suite to surveil an anti-war protest across the street.

They ignored us until the pot swelled to several thousand dollars. Suddenly, our game was more interesting than anything going on outside. Zeppo Marx and I were the last two in. I held and he bought two cards. We showed our hands. Mine was terrible but Zeppo's was worse.

"I have never been so screwed in my life," he said. "I hope my wife is getting screwed by somebody just to make it fair."

"I heard she is," one of the guys at the table cracked. "By Sinatra."

Zeppo did not laugh. News of the affair did get out though, and soon Barbara Marx became Frank Sinatra's fourth wife.

There was no source of news and gossip like the restaurant itself. Stories from the night before were like Dan Tana's red sauce—there was never a shortage. One night Ringo Starr proposed to his girlfriend Nancy Lee Andrews, slipping a diamond ring on her finger for dessert. The whole place applauded. Their long engagement ended in 1980, though, when Ringo fell in love with actress Barbara Bach, his co-star on the movie *Caveman*, and married her the following year.

I was in the restaurant the night John Wayne ended a bitter feud with the brilliant screenwriter Carl Foreman. Carl had written *The Champion* and *High Noon* before being blacklisted by Hollywood studios for refusing to cooperate with the House Un-American Activities Committee during the anti-communist witch hunt led by Senator Joe McCarthy. Unable to work, he and his family spent the next twenty years in London, where he penned the big screen classics *The Bridge on the River Kwai* and *The Guns of Navarone* and produced the movie *Born Free.*

Wayne, on the other hand, was not just an arch-conservative but one of Hollywood's most prominent and ardent supports of the McCarthyite blacklist. He hated Carl Foreman and *High Noon* and had turned down the lead role in the film, calling it "the most un-American thing I've ever seen in my whole life." For Wayne, it was all about politics, and their falling out reverberated across Hollywood. Almost twenty years later, in 1971, Wayne told a *Playboy* magazine interviewer, "I'll never regret having helped run Foreman out of this country."

The two men did not have anything to do with each other until one Sunday night when they were both eating dinner at Dan Tana's.

Carl and his wife Evelyn, recently returned to the US from their self-imposed exile in London, had come to the restaurant with their children for an early dinner. They sat down in a booth near the front. Carl's son, Jonathan, spotted John Wayne—enormous, hard to miss, as Jonthan later remembered—toward the back. He asked his father if that was John Wayne. He said yes and walked his son and daughter, Amanda, over to Wayne's booth.

"Hello, Duke," he said.

"Hi, Carl," Wayne replied.

"My English children would like to meet you."

Wayne held out his great paw to Jonathan and solemnly shook the child's hand.

Carl's wife and I spoke about it long afterward. She described the moment as odd and sweet all at the same time—particularly after that brief handshake, when the two men stood looking each other.

"How are you doing?" Wayne asked.

"Fine," Carl replied. "How are you?"

"I'm good," Wayne said, adding, "Well, some bad things happened in the old days."

"They sure did," Carl said.

Carl and his family returned to their booth, and John Wayne went back to his dinner.

* * *

I hired a publicist to make sure Dan Tana's was mentioned in the press. He might have had one of the easiest jobs in Hollywood. Once, I was accused of paying Richard Burton to plug the restaurant. That was nonsense, but my friends would not stop calling to ask me if it was true.

I had just flown back into town, so I had no idea what they were talking about even though it seemed like the rest of the country did.

Earlier in the week, Richard Burton had called Dan Tana's around 7:15 and asked if we had a table for eight people at 8 P.M. He and Elizabeth Taylor had just come back from someplace outside the country and they wanted to take friends out to dinner. But the actor did not mention who he was. Guido answered the phone and said no, the restaurant was full. If it was only two or four people, yes, we could seat them, but otherwise we could only accommodate him at 9:30 P.M.

Richard Burton called back a few minutes later and asked again, this time making sure Guido knew it was "Richard Burton *the actor*" calling to make a dinner reservation. My maître d' laughed. "I know who you are Mr. Burton, and I know you want to bring in Miss Taylor, but I only have two tables that can fit eight people, and they're booked. They won't be out till nine."

Someone waiting for another table overheard the conversation and said, "Give him our table. We'll wait two hours. We want to see them."

The next night Richard Burton was on Johnny Carson's *Tonight Show*, which had moved to Los Angeles from New York in 1972, and for some reason, Johnny said, "I bet you and Elizabeth are so famous you can get in anywhere you want." Richard said no, not true, and he described being turned down at a restaurant just the night before. Johnny asked the name of the restaurant, and Richard Burton said he didn't want to mention it. So Johnny started to guess. His sidekick, Ed McMahon, also guessed. It was comedy gold.

Then *The Tonight Show* bandleader, Doc Severinsen, said, "Was it Dan Tana's?" Richard Burton said yes, and they all talked about the restaurant for ten minutes. Johnny said it was his favorite restaurant, too. My old friend Jean Leon was one of those who called me the next day.

"Son of a bitch, you got a million dollars' worth of publicity last night for not giving Richard Burton and Elizabeth Taylor a table."

They were not the only celebrities we turned away. Barbara Sinatra (formerly Barbara Marx) offered me $20,000 to close the restaurant so she could throw Frank a surprise birthday party. I politely refused. What was I going to tell all my regular customers, many of whom ate at the restaurant several times a week? Why would I want them to go elsewhere? Barbara and Frank never ate at the restaurant again. But his daughters, Nancy and Tina, continued to come in.

We had only so many tables. Once they were filled, what else could we say? Hang out by the bar until we call you or try another night. This was the situation with John Travolta one night as he was rocketing to the upper realms of Hollywood stardom. *Saturday Night Fever* had just opened, and I guess John—one of the nicest, kindest men in the business, and a frequent customer—thought the buzz around that movie would be enough to get him, his girlfriend, and two others a table without a reservation.

Maybe it would have been had I been there or Guido had been working that night. But I had already left, and Guido was off. John encountered Bogie instead.

"My name is John Travolta, and I need a table for four."

Bogie was unimpressed.

"I don't have a table for four," Bogie said. "Come back tomorrow."

"Do you know who I am?" Travolta asked.

"I don't know who you are," Bogie said.

"I'm John Travolta."

"I am Bogdan Sharich. And fuck you."

"Where's Dan?" Travolta said. "You're going to get fired for this."

"He's not here," Bogie said, losing none of his bravado because he knew that I would never fire him. "I am giving the tables here, and there are none tonight. You'll have to come back tomorrow, Mr. Travolta."

For years, the staff teased Bogie about not recognizing John Travolta. Of course, there was a perfectly good explanation for that. Bogie worked every night, slept, and spent his free time at the track. He never went to the movies and may have been one of the few people on the planet who had never heard of John Travolta.

To me, the funny part happened the next day. John called the office and asked to speak to me. I already knew what had happened and was eager to apologize to John for Bogie's rudeness. But John beat me to it. He was the one who had lost his temper. He understood Bogie was only doing his job.

"My girlfriend said unless I apologize to Bogie, she's not going to date me anymore," he said. "So please tell Bogie that I am sorry."

There were no hard feelings. John stayed my customer forever. In fact, in 1995, many years after this incident, he made the film *Get Shorty*, the story of a mobster who gets involved in Hollywood, and if you pay attention to last line in the final scene, you will hear his character asked, "Where do you want to go, Morton's or Dan Tana's?" To which he replied, "Let's go to Dan Tana's."

* * *

Writer Michael Mann was in one night and asked Mike at the bar if I was coming around that night. Mike told him that I was in London and would be back in a couple of weeks. He needed to get a hold of me.

From what I understood, he had heard that producer Aaron Spelling was looking for scripts to turn into made-for-television movies that, if they did well, could be developed into weekly TV series. He knew that Spelling and his production executives ate at the restaurant two to three times a week, and he wanted to give them a script he had written called *Vega$* about a Las Vegas private investigator who he had named Dan Tanna. He wanted my permission to use my name.

When I got back to LA, I read the script. It was excellent, and I said to Michael, "Once they see my name, they will buy this script immediately because they eat here all the time." I was right. Spelling bought it and put an hour-and-a-half movie into production. The day before it aired on ABC, I got a panicked call from one of Spelling's top guys, producer-writer E. Duke Vincent. I happened to be in London and, as I recall, the day he called was the only day in my life I played thirty-six holes of golf.

I got home and my wife said I had been getting calls from Hollywood every hour on the hour.

"I told them you'd be home for lunch and then you didn't show," she said. "What happened?"

"I played thirty-six holes," I said.

Then the phone rang. It was E. Duke Vincent. Relieved he finally got a hold of me, he wasted no time explaining there was a problem. The movie they had made—the pilot episode—was going to air and they did not have a release from me. He wanted me to give them the go-ahead right then, on the phone, and sign papers later. Even though I had liked the script, I didn't know. What if it was terrible? What if the name Dan Tanna became a joke?

"Can you send me a cassette?" I asked.

"There's no time," he said.

Vincent assured me the series was good and going to be a hit and I would be famous—"more famous than you already are," he added.

They wanted to pay me for the rights. He made an offer on the phone. It sounded fair; I told him to select a charity and give the money to them. Michael Mann went on to create *Miami Vice* and make some great movies, and as happens with many people early in their career, he felt his original vision was watered down by network executives—the "leisure-suit crowd," I think he once called them—but the show was a hit.

And E. Duke Vincent was right, or partially right. I don't know if it made me famous, but people were more aware of my name. Kirk Kerkorian, the billionaire businessman who owned two hotels in Las Vegas along with MGM studios, came into Dan Tana's a lot and marveled at how often I was in Las Vegas. I had only gone there one or two times to see the show being filmed.

"Don't BS me." Kerkorian laughed. "Every time I'm at the Sands Hotel, I hear you being paged."

I did not know what he was talking about. Years later, though, I really was in Las Vegas with friends. It was only my third or fourth time there. We were playing blackjack at the Sands Hotel where the TV series had been shot, and suddenly, over the casino intercom, I heard, "Will Dan Tana please report to security." I found the security office and asked if they had called me.

"No," the head guy said.

"Come on. The whole casino heard it. Will Dan Tana please report to security."

"No, you misheard," he said. "Go back and play."

A couple of hours later, I heard the page again. "Will Dan Tana please report to security." *This had to be a joke*, I thought. I went back to the security office, this time letting the guy there know I was not amused. I took out my ID and held it right in front of his face so he could see who I was. The character in the TV series, I said, was named after me.

That did the trick. I was invited into the office, where he explained that whenever there was a problem in the casino, they paged my name over the intercom. It was code for the casino's security team to address the situation. So, in a strange way, I guess I was in Vegas all the time.

Part Five

Dessert

28

Don't Change a Thing

It is said that imitation is the sincerest form of flattery. That might be true, but I was confused when Barbra Streisand asked me when I opened another Dan Tana's in Ireland. She had been in Dublin and seen the restaurant with her own eyes. Dan Tana's. Next door to the National Concert Hall. How could that happen without her or anyone else knowing about it?

She was not my only customer who asked about it. Don Rickles, just back from Dublin, walked into the restaurant one night and handed me a menu that looked exactly like mine. Same color and script. Same appetizers and entrees. Same name—Dan Tana's. Except it was located approximately 5,200 miles from West Hollywood, where the world's only Dan Tana's, as far as I knew, was located.

"It's not mine," I said.

"Then you should sue them," Don said.

I was not interested in litigation, but I was curious to find out more about this copycat. Was it true? A few months later, I was traveling with the Yugoslav national soccer team, and a game with the Republic of Ireland took us to Dublin. While the team settled into our hotel, I took a taxi to the National Concert Hall. I got out in front and stared in astonishment. Next door was a restaurant, my restaurant, Dan Tana's. I walked inside and it was as if I had entered a parallel universe.

It had red-and-white checked tablecloths. Red leather booths. Chianti bottles hanging from the ceiling. A menu exactly like mine. The only difference? The walls were green, not red, and they had neither a framed Brentford FC jersey nor Andrea's original oil paintings decorating the walls. I was stunned.

I sat at a table. A waiter approached, and I asked if the owner was present.

"Who are you?"

"I'm with the football team from Slavia."

"The owner's wife is here. But her husband is not."

"Can I speak to her?"

She came over to the table. A pleasant looking redhead, typically Irish, she greeted me in a confident voice. Once I introduced myself, though, she freaked out.

"Let me call my husband," she stammered.

Within minutes, he walked in, glanced at me, and disappeared into the back, an office I presumed, where he must have spoken to his wife, before he returned and introduced himself to me. Also Irish, he sat down opposite me and admitted that while he was slightly discomfited by having the authentic Dan Tana in his restaurant, it was an honor to meet me. Then he told me the story behind this Dan Tana's.

He had been managing a hotel in London, and his wife was managing a pizzeria there when the Irish government launched an incentive program encouraging Irish citizens working abroad to return to Ireland with their know-how and an idea that will attract tourists. He and his wife applied and received a stipend of £40,000 to open a restaurant. But they didn't know what kind of restaurant they wanted. So he sent his wife to the US, where she traveled from New

York to California, eating at restaurants in cities large and small and taking a menu from each one she liked.

Several months later, she returned with forty or fifty menus. She and her husband had to make a formal proposal to the Irish board. He asked his wife, "Of all the restaurants you visited, which one would you like to own?" She sorted through the stack of menus on the table in front of them and pulled out mine.

The man paused his story. I was tempted to order the chicken parm to see just how close they were able to copy my restaurant.

"I am aware I didn't pay you for the rights," he said. "We are able to make a living, but we aren't getting rich. I'd like to propose that you and your friends and your LA customers can come here and eat for free before you go to the theater."

I stuck out my hand. "It's a deal."

The next day, on the Yugoslav team's way to practice, I asked the bus driver to take a detour. We parked in front of the restaurant, and I led the team and coaching staff into the restaurant. There were about forty of us. Everyone took a seat. The owners came out from the back and surveyed the scene. They had just opened for lunch and saw their tiny restaurant was filled. I thought they were going to faint. The man came up to me holding a stack of menus, with a look of surrender on his face.

I stood up.

"It's just a joke," I said. "We're on our way to practice."

We all laughed. Then the team filed out and I never saw those people again. I heard the restaurant closed five or six years later.

* * *

In 1979, I had to fire Guido after evidence mounted that he was stealing—an all-too-common problem in the restaurant business but also one that stung in the wake of his brother's warning, which

I didn't take seriously until it couldn't be ignored. Jimmy Cano was the first to notice. Many customers tried to court my maître d's favor by slipping him money when they shook his hand. Instead of taking it, Guido whispered for them to put it in his jacket pocket. That way he could deny knowing about it.

Jimmy noticed this and got upset. He claimed this was money that should have been pooled along with all the tips the waiters and staff got each night. He accused Guido of stealing, and Guido fired him. As my maître d', Guido oversaw the waiters and captains, so I had to support him. At the time, I also believed him. We were close. He had thrown me a fortieth birthday party at his house. I had loaned him $20,000 to help him buy that house.

But more was going on. Guido had developed a gambling habit. Most of my guys played the horses or bet on various games, but the ten dollars Guido initially bet on football games turned into two-hundred-dollar and five-hundred-dollar wagers on all sports. His losses added up. With bookies breathing down his neck, something I learned after the fact, he began to steal from the restaurant, not just the employees. My accountant noticed first. We were making money, but not as much as we should have been. He suspected someone inside was skimming money somehow.

Pearl also noticed a discrepancy in the books. Things weren't adding up. Then one day I was showing our nighttime cleaning crew how I wanted them to clean the room where we stored wine. I took a broom, started sweeping under the racks, and discovered a bunch of wadded-up dinner checks. Something was fishy. I hired a company to investigate and after a couple months of undercover work, they found Guido was targeting the customers who paid in cash. He waited on these tables personally, wrote duplicate checks for lower amounts, and pocketed the difference. He had other tricks, too. But the point is, he was caught stealing.

I was crushed. I paid people well, more than they could make anyplace else. My people bought houses, raised families. They knew they could come to me for help without shame or embarrassment if they got into trouble. Finding out that someone was stealing was worse than a crime. It was personal.

I called up Guido and said I was coming over to his house for lunch. It was the house I had helped him buy. When I got there, I delivered the news the only way I knew how—with a firm, disappointed bluntness.

"I didn't come here to have lunch. I came to fire you. You're a thief."

His wife, who was taller and bigger than him, beat the shit out of him in front of me and his son and daughter, who were also nearby, watching in shock.

I was scheduled to go back to London the next day. So, now in need of a maître d', I went to see Jimmy Cano at the Bistro Garden, the Beverly Hills restaurant where he had gone after leaving Dan Tana's. He was the only person I could see taking over immediately. He had started as a busboy, then moved up to waiter and captain, and had gained valuable experience in his various sojourns away from Dan Tana's. He knew everyone, employees and customers, and he was respected and liked by all.

It was barely a minute after Bistro Garden had opened for lunch. I expected to run into Jimmy by the door. But the place was empty. Not even a waiter in sight. And no Jimmy. I sat at the bar and ordered a vodka martini. The barman apologetically said he could not serve me because I was not wearing a sport jacket. I asked if Jimmy the maître d' was there. He shrugged his shoulders, unhelpful, and nodded toward the door, indicating he wanted me to leave.

I walked out to my car. It was the only one in the parking lot. With the engine running, I sat there for a couple of minutes, thinking about what I was going to do. Suddenly, I saw Jimmy running toward me.

"Boss! Boss! What is it?"

I told him that I had been asked to leave. He said there was a jacket inside for me and escorted me back to the bar, where I explained what had happened with Guido. He felt bad for me but vindicated at the same time. I understood when he said, "I told you so." Even though it need not have been said, he had to. Then I asked if he would come back as the maître d'. He said yes, and it was a job he held more or less for the next twenty-four years.

I say more or less because Jimmy quit six times over the years. He claimed Bogie held the record for getting fired and he held a similar record among employees for quitting. First, let me set the record straight about Bogie. I may have lost my temper with him, just as he lost his with me. And I may have said, "You're fired." But he never walked out and always showed up the next day.

Jimmy was different. He did quit a half dozen times without returning the next day or the next, and the reason was always the same. He hated when, as he put it, I tried to "manipulate" the reservation book. Basically, he would be holding a table for someone with a reservation or a party that he had told to wait for the next available table and then friends of mine would come in and I would give them the table. It upset him, and he did not hold back on me.

"Dan, I was holding that table for those people at the bar."

"I'm the boss. I can do what I want."

"Yes, you're the boss, but you are paying me to run your restaurant."

"Well, I can do what I want."

"Okay, if you can do what you want, then you don't need me."

"No, I don't need you."

Both of us had tempers. Neither of us lost it often. But there were at least six times when we did. Then, a day or two or three later,

I would call him up and ask if he was ready to come back. Jimmy would come back the next day, and things would settle back to normal. Only one time did he seem to really leave for good—when he walked out and got a job a couple blocks down the street at The Palm.

The Palm was one of the top steakhouses in the city, with large, thick steaks, enormous lobsters, and strong drinks. When it opened in 1975, their ads in local papers, magazines, and Hollywood trades like *Variety* said, "Now Open. Next door to Dan Tana's." *Next door to Dan Tana's.* I took it as a compliment and maintained a good relationship with the restaurant's legendary maître d', Gigi Delmaestro. If we were overbooked, I sent people down the block to The Palm. I ate there myself when I craved lobster. That restaurant cost me a lot of money.

It also nearly cost me Jimmy. I sat down with him in an empty booth and said I not only wanted him back; I needed him back. The restaurant missed him. My customers missed him. I missed him, too. And truth be told, he was coming over after work with the boys from The Palm to drink and play cards with the Dan Tana's crew. God only knows how late they all stayed. Jimmy got up and found Gigi in the back, then both of them returned. Jimmy said that he told Gigi that I had offered him his old job back and if it had been anyone else, he would have said no.

"But it's Dan," he said.

Gigi understood—but only because it was Dan Tana's.

"If it were someplace else," he added, "I would be offended."

* * *

In May 1980, Yugoslavia's leader, Marshal Tito, died, and I bought drinks for everyone. Weeks later, two films I produced, *Days of Dreams* and *Special Treatment*, competed at Cannes—one of our leads even took home Best Supporting Actress. More drinks. In June, Andrea sold every painting in her first solo exhibition in Beverly Hills. Champagne all around. Life was good, and only getting better it seemed. In August, *Special Treatment* was honored at the Pula Film Festival, a dream setting of beaches, Roman ruins, and all-night parties.

My film was one of the hits, and after the celebrations, I treated myself to the ultimate indulgence: a yacht trip back to Hvar, where my family was waiting for me at our villa. I anticipated my daughters' hugs and kisses as the real treats of this most incredible week. Instead, Gaby and Katy ran toward me as soon as I came into view, with panicked faces and tears streaming from their eyes.

"Daddy, Daddy," they cried, "there was a fire at the restaurant. Dan Tana's burned down."

The rest is a blur. I only remember rushing to the island's post office—one of the few places with a telephone—just as Wilt Chamberlain had years before, when he called Lakers owner Jack Kent Cooke to announce his retirement.

We were nine hours ahead of Los Angeles. But time had stopped for me; it didn't matter. I tried Pearl and couldn't get her. Then I tried Jimmy, my maître d'. I couldn't get him either. Then I called the restaurant.

"Dan Tana's," a man answered.

"Who is this?" I asked.

"Mace."

It was my dear friend, producer Mace Neufeld.

"What are you doing at the restaurant?" I asked.

"What restaurant?" he said. "It burned down."

He explained that Pearl, knowing I was in Europe and not knowing who else to call, had phoned Mace in the middle of the night to tell him the restaurant was on fire. He got dressed and raced over to it. By the time he arrived, the fire had been extinguished, but the place was half burned down. What was left was charred inside and out. A disaster. Authorities on the scene, knowing that many restaurant fires are inside jobs to get insurance payouts, delicately inquired about my whereabouts. Mace rather indelicately set them straight. I was seriously underinsured.

Fire was every restaurateur's nightmare. I had to get back to Los Angeles. Flights off the island didn't exist. I needed to get to Split, where I could catch a plane to London. But there was only one ferry out in the morning, and one ferry back in the late afternoon, and it was already docked for the night. I turned to the island's mayor, a friend, who found the captain of the ferry. He rounded up his crew and they took me to Split. I was the only passenger on a ship that normally took two hundred people.

In Split, I went straight to the travel office. There was one last flight to London leaving later that night, but it was sold out. The manager, who knew me, told me to go to the airport anyway.

"You will get on the plane."

"There are no more seats," I said. "How am I going to get on?"

"Just go to the airport."

I followed instructions. The pilot was waiting for me at the gate. He knew of my reputation from world football and was aware of my emergency. He led me onto the plane and into the cockpit, where I sat behind him and his co-pilot. I got to London, and once there, I caught the next flight to Los Angeles.

The eleven-hour flight felt longer. I dozed off and on but was up and staring out the window as the plane flew over eastern Canada. The sun was starting to rise like a fire in the distance, promising light in the dark. I knew I had been through this and worse before. I knew how to survive, how to keep hope alive.

Once on the ground, I went straight to Dan Tana's. Sure enough, the restaurant was gutted. The smell of fire was still in the air. But the damage was not total. The kitchen and the upstairs office above it were intact; so were the bar and parts of the dining room. The rest was a charred shell of what had been there twenty-four hours before. For all practical purposes, the restaurant was gone. I understood why my daughters had cried.

Mace Neufeld and Pearl were both with me, offering support and encouragement. Their words went past me. I was in shock.

So were my employees as they began showing up for work. All stood and looked in shock and bewilderment, like me. And all asked me the same question. "Boss, what are we going to do?" The honest answer was, I did not know. Except for the obvious: I had to close the restaurant. How long was impossible to say. Short-term? Long-term? Permanently? I did not know.

* * *

I made an appointment to meet my insurance man the next day, and when I showed up, I found a note tacked to the door. It said, "PLEASE REBUILD AND DON'T CHANGE A THING!"

My insurance policy enabled me to pay my employees for six months, but rebuilding depended on the cause of the fire. My insurance man counseled me to be patient, explaining that many restaurants in financial trouble have kitchen fires; those raise suspicions and don't get covered. Even though Dan Tana's was filled every night and not experiencing any financial difficulty, the insurance company still had to investigate the cause of the fire, as did the fire department.

Investigators from both places arrived later that day and looked through every inch of the restaurant. Two men from the fire department told me that a pet store and a hardware store within blocks of the restaurant had also burned that night, both the result of arson. A day later, they concluded that Dan Tana's was part of that string of fires set by the arsonist. As a result, I would be fully covered and able to rebuild.

David Alpert, a general contractor and the brother of jazz trumpet player and A&M Records founder Herb Alpert, was a good customer. He had overseen the rebuilding of A&M's headquarters on the old Charlie Chaplin studio lot in Hollywood, and he offered to draw new plans for me. He said it would go faster if I had the original 1929 plans. It turned out the property's landlord had tucked them away long ago in the restaurant's office, in a crevice within a closet where no one had ever bothered to look. They were untouched by the fire.

David said this would be the time to expand the restaurant if I wanted, perhaps add a second story as many had suggested in the past, though if I did that, rebuilding would take a long time, maybe a few years. If I wanted to build it back the same, "like for like," as he said, we could get a quick permit. I chose the latter. I only wanted to make one change—have one table less than before. He laughed. Tables were not his field.

Working off the original blueprints, and obviously putting in long hours, David finished the new plans in two days. My builder was a man named Walter Vlada, a friend of Bogie's who I had met on my second day in Hollywood. He estimated construction could be completed in three to four months if we got crews to work around the clock, and if all the neighbors gave us permission, which they did. Everyone wanted Dan Tana's back.

All I needed was a building permit from the city—and that was where I ran into what seemed like an insurmountable roadblock.

I got to the West Hollywood City Hall early the next morning. Though I arrived shortly before the office opened, about forty people were ahead of me. Nearly two hours passed before my name was called. Then bad news arrived almost immediately. The clerk looked at his calendar, said it was August now and everyone was on summer break so it would be impossible to process the permit. September was already booked. Come back in October, he told me.

"But be aware the holidays will probably delay this into next year."

Frustrated and dejected, I was uncertain about Dan Tana's future. I also had no idea what to do next.

It had only been a few days since the fire, but news traveled fast—across the country and well into Europe and beyond. Calls came from Moscow and Tokyo.

What happened? Are you going to rebuild? When will you reopen?

I had no answers. Repeating the same painful conversation felt like pouring salt into the wound. And then—out of nowhere—a glimmer of hope. Suddenly, I was talking to Linda Ronstadt. Like everyone else, she had heard about the fire and wanted to know what was happening with the restaurant.

But unlike everyone else, she had a direct line to California's governor, Jerry Brown. When I told her about the trouble I'd had that morning trying to get a rebuilding permit, she asked casually if I had spoken to the governor yet, as though he might be someone I'd call for advice. I laughed—I didn't know him, had never met him. "Don't worry," she said. "I'll talk to him."

An hour later, Sacramento was on the line. One of Brown's assistants told me to return to the West Hollywood office right away—they were expecting me. "I was just there," I said. "They threw me out."

"Don't worry about that," he replied. "And don't take a number. Go straight to the counter."

So back I went. The same clerk who had dismissed me earlier that morning was about to call the next number when he spotted me. His entire face changed. He could not have been happier to see me.

"I just got off the phone with the governor's office," he said. "How do you know him?"

"We're best friends," I said without missing a beat.

He grinned, shuffled a few papers, and leaned in. "Listen, I'm up for a promotion. Between me and two other guys. Would you mind putting in a good word?"

"Of course," I said.

Boom-boom-boom—he stamped the forms, signed them, and slid them across the counter.

"You're all set."

I glanced down. "When can I start building?"

"Tomorrow morning, if you're ready."

We rebuilt in seven weeks and reopened in October. Andrea's new paintings hung beside fresh movie posters and a photo of me celebrating with Brentford FC. Pearl was back in the office. Sam was back taking cash from the register every morning. Naomi made new curtains for the windows, which were still boarded up. The place looked almost exactly as it had before—and all because of an extraordinary singer who once got a free plate of spaghetti. Proof, in the end, that generosity doesn't just feed people—it can rebuild an entire restaurant.

29

The Heart Grows Fonder

The reopening brought tears to my eyes. There was no invitation. We did not make any formal announcements. Still, people heard, and when we opened at 5 P.M. that special night on October 15, 1980, people were lined up outside.

The air conditioning was not yet installed, and it was as hot as hell inside all night. We never served fewer than two hundred dinners a night, but I think we almost doubled that number. The evening had the feeling of a family reunion—customers and waiters hugging, Mike pouring free drinks, Bogie shaking hands like he was a politician running for office, people walking into the kitchen to kiss Mate, customers hugging customers. Everyone was glad to be there.

The bar was still packed when we locked the door at 2 A.M. and drinks were still being poured an hour later.

In a way, what was old was new. A next chapter in Dan Tana's story began—and little did I know this was true of me, too.

It was the 1980s, and the decade ushered in a younger generation. New faces like Richard Dreyfuss, Larry King, and Christopher Reeve mixed with Jack Nicholson, Dabney Coleman, and Shelley Winters. Some things remained the same. Lew Wasserman was at table 1. Ron Perlman always asked for table 3 when he was in town. Phil Spector was at table 4. Fred Astaire was given table 5. Wilt Chamberlain remained a fixture at table 10. Barbra

Streisand enjoyed the privacy of table 12, which was hidden in the back. And the relatively new owner of the Los Angeles Lakers, Jerry Buss, who became like a brother, was easy. "Any table is good," he always said.

You never knew who you would see. One night it was Charlton Heston, the next it was astronaut Neil Armstrong, and then maybe it was Sidney Poitier leaning over his booth to say hello to Norman Mailer in from New York. But as I said, this was the 1980s. People were colorful and outrageous. Musician Ned Doheny told a story about driving to the restaurant on Halloween, a night of wild, uninhibited celebration for the gay community in West Hollywood.

He drove alongside two guys riding together on a motorcycle—the driver dressed in leather pants, no shirt, and a tiny leather cap, and the guy in back in glamorous drag cracking a small whip at onlookers. He thought this was weird—until he walked into the restaurant and came upon Harry Dean Stanton and banjo player Doug Dillard, friends from Bette Midler's movie *The Rose*, at the bar dressed like Washington and Lafayette. In full costume. Powdered wigs and swords.

"There's nothing like finding George Washington and Lafayette shit-faced at the bar," Ned said.

* * *

Actually, someone even more surprising came in one night—the extremely reclusive, famously idiosyncratic chess champion Bobby Fischer. I did not believe it until I saw him with my own eyes. But a journalist friend of mine in London wanted to interview Bobby. It had been ten years since he had beaten Russian Boris Spassky in Reykjavik, Iceland, to win the World Chess Championship. Since then, Fischer had dropped out of sight, reportedly living in a cheap hotel room filled with chess books somewhere in Pasadena.

My journalist friend informed me that Fischer's assistant coach in Reykjavik, Iceland, had been a Serb, so he thought I might know this guy and be able to contact the anti-social champion. I laughed out loud.

"How am I going to find Bobby Fischer?" I asked.

"I have some phone numbers," he said. "I don't know if they're good, but—"

I wrote down so many phone numbers I felt like I was copying a secret code. What was it going to unlock? Or rather who? Was I dealing with the CIA? Maybe. Nevertheless, over the next few days, I sat in my office and called the various numbers. Most went unanswered, and the few that were answered were picked up by men with heavy foreign accents.

When I was ready to give up, someone answered without saying hello or anything else. All I heard was silence.

But I had a feeling.

"Bobby Fischer?" I said.

More silence. But after a long moment, a man gruffly asked, "How did you get this number?"

I explained the connection and then introduced myself.

"I am Dan Tana, the owner of the restaurant Dan Tana's, in Hollywood."

"Dan Tana?" he said. "What the fuck? Why did you give your name to that stupid television show *Vega$*?"

I said nothing.

"How much money did they pay you for that?" he asked.

I told him the truth—nothing. They didn't pay me anything, not a nickel.

I could hear Bobby seething on the other end.

"I had some respect for you before I saw that show," he said, "and now, hearing this, it's all gone."

I didn't know the man beyond the picture the media painted of him as a nut, and here he was, seeming to live up to that reputation. But he had a point. I told him that he was not the first person who had criticized me for not making money off that TV series. Then I told him about my Serbian journalist friend who wanted to sit down with him in Los Angeles.

"Let him come," Fischer said. "Then call me and we'll meet at your restaurant."

Wasting no time, my journalist friend arrived in LA. He checked into a hotel across the street from the restaurant. I called Bobby to tell him my friend was in town and ready to meet. For three straight days, no one answered my calls. The phone rang and rang and rang. Around noon the fourth day I got a call in my office. It was Bobby.

"I'm willing to meet him," he said.

"What do you suggest?" I asked.

Bobby rattled off instructions that had to be followed exactly or else. I had to send a car for him. It had to be a four-door sedan. I had to tell him the make, model, and year of the car. He wanted the license plate numbers, too. I also had to give him the name of the driver. The journalist had to sit in the front seat with the driver and not in the back with Bobby. No one else could be in the car.

"I'll talk to him until we get to the restaurant. Then I want to come in and have dinner because I've never eaten there."

"Fine," I said.

"But I want to sit where no one can see me."

"I'll see what I can do."

I took care of everything, and the next night, as arranged, I sent the journalist with Nick, the man who cleaned our restaurant, to pick up Bobby. I saved table 17 for him. He would be able to walk from the parking lot in the back through the kitchen straight to the table. Then I waited, praying everything would go smoothly. And I waited. And waited. And I worried.

Nick was late. He finally arrived back at the restaurant two hours later than I expected. Later, he explained why. After pulling up in front of the address the enigmatic chess champion had provided, Bobby was nowhere to be found. So he parked the car and looked around. Suddenly, Bobby emerged from the bushes where he had been hiding and apparently making sure Nick and the car matched the information I had given him. Bobby had several disguises with him.

Then, on the way back to the restaurant, Bobby claimed they were being followed and insisted Nick drive through busy streets and dark back alleys in downtown LA to lose them. Only when Bobby was certain they were no longer being followed did they head for West Hollywood. Meanwhile, Bobby gave an interview to the journalist, who was not permitted to turn around.

I met them in the parking lot. Bobby was wearing a coat much heavier than needed on this temperate evening. But there was a reason. He put his hands in his pockets and pulled out two stones, one in each hand.

"If anyone comes near our table," he explained, "one of these is going straight in their head."

"Just a second, Bobby," I said. "This is a small restaurant. People might come to the table. They might want to talk to you."

"Well, I don't want to talk to them," he said.

He was amenable to continuing his conversation with the journalist. So the three of us went inside and made it to the table without Bobby needing to use one of his rocks. While my tablemates spoke, I got up to greet people on the other side of the restaurant. While I made my rounds, screenwriter Carl Foreman stopped me. When he came in for his 9 P.M. reservation, he thought he had seen Bobby

Fischer in the parking lot. Was it him? And if it was, Carl asked if he could meet him.

"He doesn't want to meet anybody," I said.

"Ask him," Carl said.

When I came back, I told Bobby that one of my best customers wanted to meet him. His expression immediately changed, like an animal reacting to danger. He looked like he was going to reach for one of his stones. But when I mentioned the name Carl Foreman, Bobby did a complete about-face. Carl was one of his heroes, he explained. A great writer. Blacklisted. He knew the whole story.

I brought Carl to the table and the two of them reached across to hug each other. It was awkward and thrilling at the same time, both saying, "You're my idol." Carl mentioned he owned a copy of Bobby's book and had a nice big chessboard at his home, which was just up the street. He said he would be honored if, after Bobby finished dinner, he would come over and sign his book. I expected stones to fly. But Bobby agreed.

Bogie was finishing his shift, and I asked him to drive Bobby to Carl's house and then back to Pasadena. He mentioned that he had played chess against ten-year-old Bobby Fischer in New York City and lost ten dollars to the kid in a few minutes. Once at Carl's house, the screenwriter suggested playing a game out of Bobby's book. The champion said sure, pick any game. I think Carl imagined Bobby might have forgotten a move or two. But Bobby wiped him out.

Carl said that between games he asked Bobby to explain the surprising move he made—giving up his queen—in a 1956 game he played as a thirteen-year-old against one of America's top chess players, who was double his age. Because of Fischer's daring move and subsequent victory, *Chess Review* called that match the "Game of the Century." Yet Bobby told Carl it was simply one of the worst moves he ever made, so bad it stunned his opponent into a state of disbelief, and Fischer took advantage of it.

Bobby came to the restaurant one more time a couple years later. He called out of the blue, said he was living in Europe, but was going to be in LA and wanted to have dinner with me again. "The same table," he said. "Send the same man to pick me up, too." That night he ordered a steak, very rare, and when it was served, he picked it up with his hands and ate it like you would corn on the cob, but with juice dripping down his hands and arms.

That last time I saw Bobby was 2004. I was in the airport in Tokyo, on my way back to Los Angeles. I was traveling with the Serbia and Montenegro National All-Star football team after participating in the Kirin Cup there. Suddenly, I heard someone call my name, "Dan Tana." I looked up and saw Bobby Fischer.

He was surrounded by Japanese police officers after having been detained for using his US passport, which had expired. He was not handcuffed but as I moved closer, they would not let him hug me.

"He's my friend," I said.

An officer put up his hand and ordered me to keep back. Bobby and I were able to reach out to each other and shake hands. That was it, along with one last "goodbye, take care," from me.

* * *

In 1982, I was ousted as chair of Brentford. The team was not winning, its finances had dipped into the red, and fans were upset. For three days in a row, fans protested outside Griffin Park, demanding the manager and myself resign. "What a load of rubbish," one yelled at me as I left the stadium following a shutout against a team we should have beaten. "We want football!" Other fans were more pointed. "Tana out!" They chanted. It hurt. No one wants to lose.

But this was part of the sport. What was I supposed to do—give up? Wave a white flag?

I was a realist but also an optimist, which put me in conflict with myself. I gave up the chairmanship but remained on the board. At the next game I attended, a match against Bristol City, I stood by a turnstile and gave kids badges I'd made that said, "Bees Can Sting," a reference to the potential of the team.

In sports, as in life, you do not fall out of love so quickly even when things sour, and I was only stepping aside, not going away.

The same was true of my marriage. It dissolved behind my back while I was producing my next movie, *Twilight Time*. The story of an older man who, after spending his adulthood in the US, returns to his birthplace on a farm in Yugoslavia to help raise his grandchildren, it starred Karl Malden. This was a labor of love my dear friend and I had cooked up nearly a decade before over dinner at the restaurant. It was a chance for both of us to explore our roots. In fact, Karl's character was named Mladen Sekulovich, which was my friend's given name, something he had long ago promised his father he would never forget.

We premiered the film in New York for the Yugoslav community there and then brought it to Los Angeles. *The New York Times* described *Twilight Time* as we intended, sweet and sentimental, and said of Karl's work, it was full of "compassion and humanity." I still love it. But when I finally went home to catch my breath from the constant travel and work and spend precious time with my wife, I experienced a harsh reality check: My marriage was over.

It was a shock. Andrea and I had been everyone's favorite couple for nearly twenty years. The two of us never fought. We had some rough moments in the beginning when money was tight, and everything was a struggle. But we always had a wonderful time together.

The problem now was we were not spending any time together—and that was my fault.

I traveled to LA every other month and spent the months in between, when I was supposedly at home, traveling with Brentford or making movies. I had a big, full, exciting life. Andrea painted in her studio. She was lonely. I was too involved in my own pursuits to realize this until it was too late. She fell in love with a fashion writer who had once been a painter. I knew they were friends but was unaware of her affection for him. What she seemed to have missed, though, was that he was gay.

I knew this because Andrea wrote him a love letter and then he sent it to me along with his own handwritten note professing his love for me. The situation was a mess, and the last thing I wanted was to see my wife hurt. But that was going to be for her to figure out. She said I should move to Los Angeles, and she and the children would stay in London. I did not argue. I walked out of the house with my clothes and left everything else for Andrea.

The girls insisted I get an apartment in London, which I did, so I could still see them. Our divorce was quick and uncontested. I gave everything to Andrea and arrived back in LA feeling like I had hit rock bottom.

The hurt persisted for a long time. Five years later I flew to New York one week to visit my daughter Gaby, who was studying at Sarah Lawrence College in Bronxville. I needed the hugs from family. We spent the weekend in the city. She bought me a teddy bear pin and fixed it to the lapel of my jacket. I smiled every time I glanced down at that cute little guy. Others remarked on it.

I asked Gaby to get me more so I could pin one on all my jackets. A box soon arrived in the mail. Gaby sent me a hundred. The teddy bear became my emblem.

* * *

But that was later. In those first days, friends swooped in to help. I borrowed money from Mace Neufeld and Sidney Beckerman to help me pay off the house in London and tuition for the girls' school. Being at the restaurant also provided reassurance. The routine, the people, the pictures on the wall, even Andrea's paintings, which hang in the restaurant to this day, reminded me that I was not a failure, no matter how I felt.

Pearl, my bookkeeper and Andrea's aunt, was very upset. The two of us spent many hours trying to talk each other into better moods. Several nights I landed at the bar, talking to people, with no pressing reason to go home. Whenever I found myself in conversation with a woman, Mike the bartender would find a way to quietly say, "She's not for you, boss." No matter, I wasn't looking.

I had a more pressing concern: the restaurant itself. On top of being confused about my life, I was worried about keeping the door open. Dan Tana's was my home and everyone who worked there was my other family. I treated them all the same, from my maître d' to my dishwasher. I said nothing about what I was going through, but they saw I was not myself. They were experts at reading people.

I did not want them to speculate. Rumors are like a cancer. People start to worry about their jobs. Their loyalty was essential to the restaurant.

Realizing I couldn't avoid telling them any longer, I called a meeting for three days later. I wanted to explain that I was going through a hard time personally and might have some short-term financial difficulties, and because of that I needed their understanding and help. I worked night and day crafting my speech. I wanted to convey the strong, reliable leadership people depended on, yet I also wanted to be honest. Admitting vulnerability was not something I was accustomed to.

I was scared. The entire staff gathered around lunch. They filled the smaller of our two dining rooms, some sitting, others standing, all facing the bar, where I stood. I greeted people softly in whatever language they spoke—English, Spanish, Serbo-Croatian, Italian. My handwritten speech filled a page and a half of legal-sized paper. I held it in my right hand, which everyone could see was shaking.

Finally, I cleared my throat, which quieted the room, and thanked everyone for coming. Suddenly, before I said another word, or even looked at my speech, one of my waiters, Ettore Perovich, raised his hand.

"Mr. Tana, can I say something?"

"Please."

"You have thirty-five of us working here. Most everyone is like me. We are married. We have children. Everything I have earned here has helped me raise my children, buy a house, go places with my family. I have spent more time with you at this restaurant than with my wife and children. I want you to know, you don't have to say anything. We know the situation you are in. I have spent twenty years in this restaurant. I hope to spend twenty more. We are with you 100 percent. You don't have anything to worry about."

I wiped a tear from my eye.

"Thank you. I have nothing more to say. This meeting is over."

The love I felt that day carried me through a very tough time. Within a couple of years, I found myself with someone who was navigating her own heartbreak. Eve Foreman had lost her husband—and my friend—Carl, to a brain tumor in 1984. Regulars at the restaurant since moving back to Los Angeles a decade earlier—Carl was a creature of habit, eating out at only two places: Shanghai Winter Garden and Dan Tana's—they were good friends with me and Andrea. Together they raised two wonderful, brilliant children, Amanda and Jonathan.

When Carl grew too ill to go out, I sometimes sent food from the restaurant to their home. After his passing, Eve hardly left the house for months. I understood—facing life alone is never easy, especially for a woman who had built her world around family. I gently encouraged her to come back to the restaurant, a place that had always felt safe and familiar. Six months later, she finally returned, bringing a girlfriend with her.

Before long, Eve and I were sitting down together, and from there a relationship began—one that lasted nearly four years. We were two lost souls, drifting through unwanted emptiness, and for a time we anchored our hearts to each other. It was safe, it was needed, and it was healing. I adored her children and felt proud watching them grow into remarkable adults: Amanda, an award-winning historian and writer, and Jonathan, a distinguished journalist.

Our friendship endured long past our relationship, which came to an end shortly after a walk along Santa Monica beach, where a fortune teller gently informed both of us that we were ready to move on. Eve needed someone more secure than I could ever be. She remarried, to studio executive Michael Williams-Jones, a perfect match for this chic British woman. I was a footballer at heart, too much of a free spirit to be tied down. When push came to shove, my deepest devotion belonged to the restaurant and to football and to my freedom. I was in love with life itself.

30

Everybody Comes to Tana's

It was Monday, January 20, 1986, a date I remember not only because it was the first time Dr. Martin Luther King Jr.'s birthday was a national holiday, but also because Santa Anita Park was beginning a tradition of holding races to honor the slain Civil Rights leader. In the past, the track was dark on Monday and Tuesday. But no longer.

I do not know if Dr. King was a fan of horse racing or gambling in general, and I am going to wager the answer is no, but Bogie and Mike were, and they were thrilled to have an additional day to go to the track. They invited me to go with them. So I asked my secretary to go to the bank and get me a couple thousand dollars. She reminded me it was a holiday. Banks were closed.

I had two hundred dollars in my pocket.

"How much is in petty cash?" I asked her.

She checked. "Nine hundred dollars."

"Give me the petty cash," I said.

The three of us got to the track around noon. There we met up with Matty Jordan, my old friend from Villa Capri who owned Matteo's, and my former bartender, Wilson. Matty and Wilson were agitated as we went into the clubhouse, where we had reserved a table thanks to some of our customers who had pull. It turned out, because of the large crowd, the races were starting a half hour early, at 12:30 P.M., rather than 1 P.M. Matty, Wilson, Bogie, and Mike had to figure out their bets on the early races.

I gave Bogie and Mike a hundred dollars to make some bets for me. I do not know anything about horses. I just have money.

As we talked, three guys stood nearby and occasionally had a back-and-forth with Mike. They knew each other. Just before they hurried off to place bets, Mike introduced me to the main guy, the only one of the three who was wearing a hat, a light brown fedora.

"Boss, this is Jimmy the Hat."

Then I was left alone with these three guys. One of them shook my hand.

"Mr. T, I'm one of your customers. I've never met you. It's a pleasure."

They were lovely men, and big-time gamblers. They were at the track every day. Jimmy asked if I had any money on me. He explained they had been analyzing the horses and had a ticket for picks in all nine races they wanted to activate for $3,600. But they were nine hundred dollars short. Did I have that much? And if so, did I want in?

I peeled off nine one-hundred-dollar bills and handed them to Jimmy the Hat. He shook my hand and said he had to hurry to activate the ticket before the first race. I spent the next few hours in the club with Mike and Bogie, listening to them chide me for giving a wad of money to Jimmy the Hat. They said he probably had dozens of tickets. Did I have a copy of the ticket? No. Any kind of receipt? No.

"Boss, you got suckered."

"He's going to bring you a ticket that's already dead. Sorry, Mr. Tana. Better luck next time."

"Well, you introduced me to them," I said. "If they're crooks—"

"You were probably going to lose the nine hundred dollars anyway."

That may have been true. By 3 P.M., I had given Mike and Bogie my remaining two hundred dollars to bet, with nothing to show for it except a bunch of losing tickets. I checked my watch. I had to get home, and they had to get to the restaurant. I wanted to find Jimmy the Hat and his buddies and leave. Bogie got up to look for them, and I sat with Mike. Suddenly, I felt a tap on my shoulder. It was Jimmy the Hat.

"We got the first three races," he said.

"Fantastic," I said.

Jimmy the Hat handed me the ticket.

"We want you to hold it," he said.

I put it in my pocket. Mike and Bogie left for the restaurant. Then the fourth, fifth, and sixth races came in, and we had them all. Now I had to stay with Jimmy the Hat and his two cohorts. We had a chance. I did not believe we were going to win, but one thing I had learned: You never know what is going to happen. Sometimes you get lucky. Which is what happened to us. The next three races came in exactly as we had picked on our ticket. We had a perfect day at the track! Unbelievable!

Jimmy the Hat and the two other guys were all over me. I was congratulating them. Our winning ticket was worth $1.2 million!

We asked for the money in cash. After taxes were taken out, the four of us split a million dollars. By this time, we were among the handful of people left in the racetrack. Two police officers escorted us into the parking lot, where the other guys hugged me before getting into their cars and driving off. In the excitement, I forgot that I had not driven. I stood there holding a shopping bag containing $250,000. The idea of calling a taxi made me uneasy.

"Where do you live?" one of the cops asked.

"West Hollywood," I said.

"We'll drive you."

As we got close, I remembered that it was Monday night and my friends were playing poker upstairs at Mr. Chow's in Beverly Hills.

Instead of going home, the police dropped me off there. The game usually started after lunch with nine players, and it usually went until about 10 P.M. So, six guys were still at the table when I walked in and asked if I could play even though I was late.

"Sure, but there's a $5,000 buy-in," someone said.

I emptied my shopping bag on the table and watched my friends react. Everyone thought it was studio money. After some laughs and a drink, I went to the restaurant. It was not yet 11 P.M. when I got there. The place was still packed. I went upstairs to the office and divided the money. I kept $100,000 for myself and split another $100,000 between my daughters. Then I put $30,000 in the safe and took the remaining $20,000 downstairs to the restaurant, where I gave Mike and Bogie $10,000 each.

"How much did you win?" Bogie asked.

"$250,000."

"And that's all you're giving us, $10,000 each?"

"No," I said. "I put $30,000 in the safe upstairs. I want you to give every employee $1,000."

"What do we say when they ask why?"

"Tell them thank you."

* * *

In August 1987, Jimmy hired Craig Susser as a part-time bartender for the two nights Mike was off. Craig was a young, aspiring actor who would come in on Thursdays after his acting class and got to know Jimmy, Mike, and some of the other waiters. Sometimes, he came in alone. He was broke. Mike would give him a shot of slivovitz and a beer, and Craig would be in la-la land.

After a couple of years of this, Jimmy asked Craig if he had ever bartended. At the time, Craig was working as a waiter at Antonio's, an old-school Mexican restaurant on trendy Melrose Avenue. Craig said no, but Jimmy placed a bottle, a pourer, and a shot glass in front of him and said all he had to do was learn to pour a shot with his eyes closed. Just like that, Craig was hired.

He spent weeks studying Mike before flying solo. His first customer was Paul Rosenfeld, aka Big Paulie. A sign in the restaurant read, "TOTAL CAPACITY: 65 + PAULIE." That was him. The marketing and exhibitor relations genius for movie distributor Ted Mann, Paulie weighed over 350 pounds and was roughly the size of two or three people. He came in at 5 P.M. and walked straight to the bar, as he always did. Craig greeted him politely: "Hi, can I help you?" Paulie shot back, "Who the fuck are you?"

Sweat immediately poured down Craig's face. By his own admission, he was the world's worst bartender. But he persevered, eventually moving up to waiter, then captain, and years later, maître d'. As a waiter, though, he faced a similar trial by fire. He'd approach a table only to hear, "Where's Tony?" or "Get me Abel." More than a few customers asked if he was wearing a tuxedo—or if the tuxedo was wearing him.

Dan Tana's was a steep learning curve, but Craig—like anyone who stuck—had the personality and tenacity to succeed. As he once put it, you kind of fight your way through and slowly pick it up. That's the restaurant business in a nutshell. Craig learned as much from the customers as he did from the staff.

The same was true of a young cook who would one day take over the kitchen. In mid-1989, Mate needed a new second-in-command, and a friend recommended Neno Mladenović. He was hired after a single phone call. I prided myself on knowing who would fit in, and within a minute of meeting Neno, I knew—like Craig—he was the start of the next generation of Dan Tana stars. He had worked in hotels and restaurants across Europe, mostly in Croatia and Italy, before immigrating to the US and rising through the ranks of the Marriott Corporation.

Neno understood the subtleties of food and the varied tastes of guests who came from the Adriatic Coast, the French Riviera, Northern Italy, and Beverly Hills. Though a little intimidated by Mate—which was understandable—he shared Mate's passion for fresh ingredients.

I'll never forget a customer once asking him why we didn't follow trends like California cuisine, fusion, or nouvelle cooking. Neno just smiled. "We are an old-school kitchen—like Mama used to make. We're not inventing here. We have our way of doing things. People are happy. We fill up the plate."

And then some. The menu boasted dishes like Veal Jimmy Woods, Steak Dabney Coleman, and Chopped Salad Nicky Hilton, but at its core, it hadn't changed much since the opening night. That was the key. While other restaurants chased fads and disappeared, Dan Tana's stayed the same—and both critics and customers agreed we were doing something right. As waiter Tony Paccini liked to tell his tables in an accent thicker than the cheese on our chicken parm: "You don't need a menu. You tell me what you like, and we gonna make it for you."

For the twenty-fifth anniversary, everyone expected a blowout. I wanted something quieter, more meaningful: a party for the employees and their families. It turned out to be just that. Many had been with me since the start—or nearly so—and when I walked in, I saw them gathered with their spouses and children, from newborns to medical students. I listened as they told me how the restaurant had helped them buy homes, pay for braces, send kids to college.

It overwhelmed me. In that moment, I realized Dan Tana's wasn't just about food and drink. We had created stability and hope for a better future. It really was the American dream.

And Hollywood. Craig usually had to point out the younger stars who had made Dan Tana's their second home. We knew Drew Barrymore, of course—her mother, Ildiko, had been a waitress at the Troubadour and brought baby Drew into the restaurant, even changing her diapers at the bar. But with Cameron Diaz, Sharon Stone, Leonardo DiCaprio, Matt Dillon, Renée Zellweger, and the rest of new Hollywood, there was a learning curve.

One night, Sean Penn and Madonna slipped in at the height of the tabloid frenzy. Their only request: not to be bothered. Easy enough—three-quarters of my staff had no idea who they were.

Even Jerry Seinfeld was just another face in the crowd. He came in when his sitcom was the hottest show on television. Telling Jimmy Cano he had a reservation, he expected recognition. Jimmy looked in the book.

"What's your name?"

"Seriously? You don't know who Jerry Seinfeld is?"

Jimmy shrugged. "No. Who is he?"

One day in 1989, Lakers owner Jerry Buss called and said he had a problem. He was on his way to the restaurant. He got there and asked Mike for a rum and Coke. Then he sat down with me shaking his head as if in pain. His problem? The Lakers general manager and former great player Jerry West had drafted a seven-foot-one center named Vlade Divac from a team *in Belgrade* whose name the Lakers owner said he could not pronounce. He said it like it was my fault.

"And he can't speak a word of English. He wanted to meet at the airport. So I went to LAX. He had no idea what I was saying, and I had no clue what he was saying. What am I going to do with him?"

I laughed.

"Jerry doesn't need a professor of English," I said. "He needs a basketball player."

Vlade, who had played for Partizan Belgrade and starred on the Yugoslav Olympic team in 1988, soon found a second home at Dan Tana's. The two of us became very close. One day he gave me one of his signed Lakers jerseys to hang on the wall. It started a chain reaction. When Jerry West, one of my very early customers, saw it, he asked why I did not have one of his jerseys on the wall.

It was not for lack of wanting one, I explained. But when I requested one from the Lakers, they said it would cost four hundred dollars. The next time Jerry came for dinner, he brought one of his jerseys. Up it went. Guess whose feelings were hurt? Magic Johnson's. I adored Magic and his wife, Cookie. They were special customers, dining together after Magic played his last game, always spreading their joy in the restaurant. They came in one evening and Magic took me to look at Vlade's jersey. Then he walked me to Jerry's. I saw mischief in his eyes. The man has one of the greatest smiles ever, and he was doing everything to suppress it.

"Do you have something against Black players?" he asked.

"I don't have anything against anybody," I said.

"How'd you get these?" he asked.

I explained.

"I'm going to do you even better," he said.

Sure enough, Magic walked in a short time later carrying a framed number thirty-two Lakers jersey. It was dedicated to Dan Tana and signed by Magic. He was smiling as he handed it to me.

"I bet those guys didn't pay for their own framing," he said.

"No, they didn't," I said, and we laughed.

For someone who enjoyed people as much as me, I knew owning this restaurant was a gift. The parade of world leaders and presidents (Ronald Reagan, John F. Kennedy), film stars, superstar athletes, and newsmakers of all stripes (I have in mind people like Norman Mailer, John Paul Getty III, Cristina Onassis, and Monica Lewinsky and her lovely parents who lived nearby in Beverly Hills) was endless. But there was that one special person who came in and sent my heart rate soaring. Jimmy Cano corralled me one night and said there were three ladies at table 14 who wanted to meet me.

Of course, I obliged. But as I neared the table, I almost had to stop and catch my breath. I immediately recognized June Allyson, who I had met long ago when she was married to Dick Powell. Next to her was Esther Williams, whose movies I had watched in amazement as a kid in Belgrade. And beside her was Jane Wyman, my first love, the actress who filled my heart with desire and affection when, at age fourteen, I sat in a movie theater and saw her in *Johnny Belinda.* I told her as much after the ladies invited me to pull up a chair.

"I'm still in love," I admitted.

"Well, I'm free," she said, playfully. "But I live in Palm Springs."

I shrugged. That wasn't going to work.

* * *

By 1990, my UEFA duties kept me in Europe, close to football. I also spent quite a bit of time traveling with the Yugoslav national team. I was with them in Italy when they got to the quarterfinals of the World Cup. Football is the most important sport in most of the world's countries, and that was evident at the event in Rome, the culmination of matches that began with 116 national teams in 1988. Yugoslavia had their work cut out versus a solid Argentinian team led by the great Diego Maradona, but I had even more pressure when I got a call that Henry Kissinger, Lee Iacocca, and Pete Rooney needed hotel rooms and tickets to the game.

One was more impossible than the other. I might as well have been asked to bring Michelangelo's David back to the US.

I was in charge of arranging the team's hotel accommodations, and I had informed the hotel that I did not want anybody in the hotel besides the players. So, I had to bend my own rules to get Kissinger, Iacocca, and Rooney in the hotel. I did not know Lee Iacocca personally, but Pete was my friend, and I owed Kissinger big time. Back in 1967, when Dan Reeves and I were launching our professional soccer league, we recruited more than two hundred players from around the world without remembering to get visas for them. Someone knew Kissinger, and he managed to get everyone into the US.

Getting him a hotel room was the least I could do. I think he did as much as anyone to help popularize soccer in America in those early days.

Then Kissinger's back went out. Our team doctor treated him for three days. He took care of the players and the former Secretary of State. But securing tickets for the game almost drove me six feet under. I had two VIP tickets for myself and a pass for a guest. We needed one more. Pete Rooney was ready to pay $10,000 for a ticket, but I could not find one on the black market. As game time approached, the entire team knew of my dilemma. Finally, the manager invited me to sit with him on the bench, which freed up my passes and got everyone into the game.

I spent the entire 120 minutes of the game with the manager. If I had not been fifty-five years old, I might have insisted I be put in, that is how caught up I was being so close to the action in this nailbiter of a contest. Despite being a man down thirty minutes into the match, Yugoslavia outplayed Argentina to a 0–0 tie at the end of regulation, before losing 3–2 in a shootout. It was a tough loss, at a time when the Yugoslav people could have used a boost. But you can't win 'em all.

31

Changes

It broke my heart as Yugoslavia gradually crumbled and broke apart until it existed only in the hearts of people like me. I loved my country—and all its people. I loved America just as much and cherished its freedom and democratic values even more as Yugoslavia suffered under Tito and succumbed after his death in 1980 to chaos and conflict. Warring ethnic factions, economic problems, and every-republic-for-itself politics culminated in the bloody Bosnian War.

I loathed the corrupt brutality of Serbian dictator Slobodan Milošević. I could not believe what I saw go down. Yugoslavia was such a beautiful country, such wonderful people. History was written by people casting blame for this on everyone but themselves. But they did it to themselves. It was like a good marriage that turned out to be a bad marriage.

In the mid-1990s, I returned to Hvar to see the effects of the fighting there and what I found was horrific: many people injured and without homes. It was a mess. Total confusion. Only one thing looked familiar to me—football. The sport was the connective tissue for Serbians, Bosnians, and Macedonians . . . everyone . . . and a reminder that what was shared could be stronger than any differences.

When Yugoslavia was bombed in 1999, during the Kosovo War, I closed the restaurant for a couple of nights. I was literally shellshocked and could not see feeding other people in an atmosphere of celebration when there was so much to mourn. After two nights, though, my employees, who formed their own United Nations of ethnicities, urged me to reopen. They needed to support their families.

I understood. But every customer who came in that week congratulated me for protesting war.

I was always up for a cause that made sense. Like when I removed a Rams football jersey from the restaurant's wall after the team's owner, Georgia Frontiere, relocated them to St. Louis in 1994. To local football fans, that was like moving the Hollywood sign to San Bernardino. I felt betrayed. Georgia—or Madam Ram, as she had been dubbed after inheriting the team from her sixth husband, Carroll Rosenbloom, who drowned in 1979—had been a regular for years. But the NFL was still well represented without her. Raiders owner Al Davis frequently came in alone and worked out plays in a notebook. Pete Rozelle, the league's longtime commissioner, met his wife in the restaurant.

I took great pride in Dan Tana's consistency. Several months shy of the restaurant's thirtieth anniversary, a *Los Angeles Times* food critic snuck in on a Saturday night. We were not the type of restaurant she was supposed to like. But her review opened by noting that "every table is full, the bar is packed, and there are about ten people jammed around the front desk, all waiting for tables. So much for our nine o'clock reservation." She remarked on her waiter's good looks and his instruction to ignore the menu and just tell him what she wanted.

She asked for chicken piccata (not on the menu). And her verdict? "Perfect: tender, lemony, one of the few truly inspired uses for capers."

In 1994, my bookkeeper, Pearl—my ex-wife's aunt—bid me and the whole crew a teary farewell. Her son opened a restaurant in Oregon and she moved with him. Nada Palinković took her place and proved herself up to the challenge of being my right and left hand and a beautiful person on top of that. In 1998, Jimmy Cano was runner up as Maître d' of the Year in the Los Angeles Restaurant Association's annual honors. He lost to his dad, Phil Cano, the eminent maître d' at Musso & Frank's. The next year, Jimmy won. And Ettore Perovich took home Service Person of the Year.

I could not have been prouder. People often asked me the secret to Dan Tana's success. Was it the food? The people? To me, those who asked would never really understand—it was always more than one or the other. So, I kept my answer simple: "Have just one restaurant and run it as well as you can."

The truth is a place like Dan Tana's thrives year after year because life happens there—the good life. I had a friend at every table. I wasn't the only one who felt that way.

In 2000, I said goodbye to one of those friends when Bogie called it quits. My loyal employee, untamable gambler, drinker, womanizer, and lifesaver was tired. He wanted to retire to Las Vegas. Life would go on, but it would never be the same.

How could I thank the man who had taken me under his wing fifty years earlier, when he spotted me sitting at the counter at Miceli's and said, "Bata?" Food, work, a place to sleep, a fresh start, fifty years of friendship—that was his gift to me. How do you express gratitude for all of that?

I looked into my heart and remembered one thing: Bogie had never spoken to or seen any of his family in all the years I knew him. "They just want money," he always said of his eight siblings. I never fully believed it.

Without telling him, I tracked down the only sibling still alive—his sister Danza, in Belgrade. I flew there, brought her back to Los Angeles, and after she recovered from the long trip, I arranged a surprise.

I invited Bogie to the restaurant for lunch, telling him it was someone's birthday. He arrived with his longtime companion, Barbara, and joined me, Nada, and Danza—who wore dark sunglasses.

For most of lunch, Bogie had no idea who she was. Danza, who spoke only a handful of English words, stayed quiet until she finally said two of them: "Coffee, please."

Bogie shot her a sharp look. "Go get your own coffee," he said. "I'm not working today."

Danza laughed, removed her glasses, and said, "Bogie, I'm your sister."

They both dissolved into tears. The rest of the day was spent catching up, and though I don't know everything they did, I knew shopping had to be part of it—Danza had arrived with one small bag of clothes but returned to Belgrade a week later with two oversized suitcases, one weighing nearly eighty kilos.

The last time I saw Bogie was at an Italian restaurant called Battista's Hole in the Wall in Las Vegas. I'd gone to visit him after hearing he was sick with cancer. He was in surprisingly good spirits. After a lifetime of drinking, smoking, gambling, and chasing women, he was resigned to his fate. His life had been good, one adventure after another, he said—he had no complaints.

As we reminisced, I heard someone call my name. I looked up and immediately recognized Battista Locatelli. Back when I was working at La Scala while Jean Leon was in Spain, I was down a waiter and hired a hardworking Italian guy with a handsome smile—Battista. He was a trained opera singer with a rich tenor voice, scrambling to support his wife and four children while looking for his break in Hollywood. He often sang for us before the restaurant opened, and he was good.

Months later, Jean Leon was back from Spain and, though I no longer worked there, I still hung out there. One night, around 7 P.M., La

Scala was only about half full. Jean had gone home. Groucho Marx, who ate there two or three nights a week, was among those enjoying dinner with his agent. I overheard them talking about his new talent-game show *Tell It to Groucho.* So did Battista.

"Do you know Groucho?" he asked me.

"Sort of," I said.

"Ask him if I can be on his show."

Why not? Without anything to lose, I approached Groucho and pitched Battista, our singing waiter.

"Where is he?" Groucho asked.

I pointed to Battista across the dining room, then motioned him over to the table.

"I hear you sing," Groucho said.

"Yes, I do. Opera."

"Okay, so sing. Let me hear."

Groucho loved what he heard and had Battista on his show. His singing took him to Las Vegas, where he opened a bar to have a place to perform. That became Battista's Hole in the Wall. It turned out his cooking outshined his singing and made him a millionaire.

That night in Las Vegas, with Battista and Bogie both at the table, it felt like a mini-Villa Capri reunion. Wine flowed, stories flew, and fittingly, our last meal together was on the house.

* * *

I took my dear friend Roger Lewis (aka Chicken Marsala Roger Lewis) to Belgrade. We had golfed and laughed together for decades. His family was like my family. I wanted to show him where I grew up. It was the most intimate thing I could add to our friendship. We walked through the old outdoor markets, down cobblestone streets, past the Saint Sava Cathedral, and along the

Danube, while I railed against what Tito and Milošević had done to the beautiful country.

One thing neither of them diminished: the country's obsession with Red Star. I took Roger to a match. It was impossible to truly understand me without experiencing the connection I had to this team. Roger loved it but even more, he loved describing how, during the match, I spotted Milošević's deadliest ally, Arkan, in a seat near us. A shiver of danger ran through me. Arkan was among the US government's most wanted international enemies.

I had a passing familiarity with Arkan, as I did many politicians and power brokers on all sides of the equation, those who inspired hope and those who caused fear. I couldn't resist asking Roger if he wanted to meet Arkan. "Of course," Roger said.

I don't remember if that's really what Roger said, but that's what he remembers saying. So be it. I introduced them. But just to add a measure of thrill, as Roger and Arkan shook hands, I added, "Roger is here to take you back to the United States." Instantly, three of his bodyguards pulled out guns and pointed them at Roger. Arkan did the same. I laughed. It broke the tension. And after a quick explanation, everyone relaxed and went back to enjoying the game.

A few months later, in January 2000, Arkan was assassinated in the lobby of a Belgrade hotel. Reports said he had run afoul of Milošević. It was a sign the regime was unravelling.

At the end of September, I was back in Belgrade, participating in protests against Milošević. I marched with all my old football friends and much of the country. When Milošević came to power in the mid-1980s, I was there working on a film and heard his speech in Kosovo, at which he famously said, "*Ne sme niko da vas bije!*" or "No one will dare to beat you again." Those of us with scars from World War II knew ethnic nationalism was never a winning strategy.

I called my friends and told them Milošević was the worst thing that could happen to Serbia. The man is going to destroy our country, I said.

After marching for a week, I returned to Los Angeles. It was October 1—I remember the date clearly because a message from my friend, political commentator Bill Press, was waiting for me at the restaurant. Bill had started in local Los Angeles news before gaining national attention on CNN's *Spin Room* with Tucker Carlson. At the time he was co-hosting MSNBC's *Crossfire* with conservative Pat Buchanan.

He was supposed to fly back to Washington, DC on a 6 P.M. flight but told me he'd push it to a redeye if I was willing to have dinner and a bottle of wine with him. A few hours later, we were sharing a good burgundy and talking about Milošević. I listened, incredulous, as he shared inside information.

"Go back to Belgrade if you want to witness history," Bill urged.

I shook my head. "I just spent fifteen hours in the air. Why would I go back?"

He leaned forward. "Milošević is going down on October 4."

"What?"

"He's finished."

"How do you know?"

"I know," he said.

Whether he noticed the joy rising in me, I can't say—but inside, I was dancing. The very next day, I returned to Belgrade, gathered my friends, and marched once more in front of Parliament, shouting against Milošević. His brand of nationalism had wrecked the country, just as I had predicted. Serbia was isolated, economically destroyed, and haunted by his crimes against humanity. Now was the moment to end his rule and set the nation on a different course.

Hundreds of thousands filled the streets. Workers went on strike. The country was poised. Something had to give—and then it did. A protester named Ljubiša Đokić drove a bulldozer through a police barricade. People stormed Parliament and seized the TV stations. Milošević was finished.

When I got back to Los Angeles, a letter from Bill Press was waiting: "*Didn't I tell you that was going to happen?*"

In the weeks that followed, I joined countless celebrations—some public, some private. One of the best didn't come until 2002, when I took Roger to Brazil to watch Yugoslavia play in a friendly match against Brazil. It was preparation for Brazil's World Cup run, but for us it was something more: The first major international competition for Yugoslavia since US sanctions had been lifted after Milošević's fall, something I had a hand in behind the scenes, believing that sports was a way to transcend politics, to celebrate, and forget the horrors of fighting if only for ninety minutes. Poignantly, it was also the last time the Yugoslav national team played under its flag. The 1–0 loss to Brazil was nothing compared to what else had finally been lost.

32

Goodbyes

For my seventieth birthday, Eve Williams-Jones hosted a small gathering in my honor. Sidney and Marian Beckerman, Ed and Danica Ruscha, Jimmy Wood, Nada, and my daughter Katy, were among the guests. My girls had tried to plan a large party, but I wanted none of that. I hated birthdays. And more than birthday parties, I disliked birthday presents. I felt the same way about Christmas presents. "Every day is Christmas," I said. "Why save it up for just one day?"

In lieu of receiving birthday presents, a $75,000 soccer grant-in-aid fund for student-athletes at UCLA was set up in my name. I liked to quote Andrew Carnegie. "The man who dies rich, dies disgraced." I always thought it was easier to help other people than to help myself. I think I knew that I would somehow benefit if everyone around me did well. Turning seventy did not seem old to me, but it did cause me to think about the future of Dan Tana's. People asked if I planned on retiring. Was I going to sell?

That never made sense to me. Why give up such fun? Why walk away from people I loved?

I have to be honest: Succession did cross my mind every so often, and when it did, I asked my daughters if they were interested in taking over the restaurant. The question made them both emotional. But neither was interested. Gaby was busy producing TV and movies, and Katy had her own successful interior design business with customers in London, Venice, California, and points in between. They were doing what they loved, and in that sense, they were following my recipe for success.

The restaurant was not for sale anyway. Many customers had inquired over the years, some serious and others merely making conversation between their martinis and their chicken parm. I came close in 2001 when director Ted Demme put together a group of investors and made an offer.

It was a solid group, people with Hollywood ties who I believed would keep the restaurant's ties to Hollywood intact. Ted was also talking with George Clooney, a longtime regular, who wanted to open a hotel in Las Vegas that would include a new Dan Tana's restaurant. I saw the potential of something more, something bigger and even more iconic than I could accomplish on my own. And maybe the gambler in me was intrigued. Could it work?

Ted and I agreed on a price of four million dollars, and in January 2002, I flew in from London to sign the papers. But tragic news waited for me at the airport. Ted had suffered a heart attack and died while playing in a celebrity basketball game. Since the deal was with him personally, not his investors, it evaporated overnight. Life at Dan Tana's went back to business as usual—or so I thought.

I commuted to Los Angeles and moved among the tables in what seemed to be slow motion when everything else was a bustle, as Helena Kallianiotes once said. But even without saying a word about the near sale to Ted, people seemed to sense a subtle shift. Like when a restaurant switches to a cheaper produce supplier. Customers can't quite identify the change, but they know something's different.

So it was at Dan Tana's. Change was in the air. Goodbyes followed. Mate, my chef and the best employee I ever had, retired. A fixture in the kitchen since 1966, he never missed a day of work in almost forty years. He knew that Neno—who'd been by his side for fifteen years—was more than ready to take over, becoming only the third head chef in the restaurant's history.

I gave Mate a generous sendoff. He passed away in 2019 and was buried in his beloved Zadar, where he had built a house. As one customer put it, "Such an icon. Before there were celebrity chefs, there was Mate!"

Next, Jimmy Cano left the restaurant. He and his wife moved to Bellingham, Washington, to build their dream home. Several years later, Jimmy called me out of the blue. He said he had carried something on his conscience for decades: He was responsible for the fire that burned down Dan Tana's in 1980.

He and Bogie had closed that night. Normally, they stayed late to play poker with other restaurant guys, but with too few players, they went home around 3 A.M. That much I already knew. I also knew we had just received a shipment of matches—four cases, thousands of them—stored in the wine room. What I didn't know was that Jimmy admitted to leaving a cigarette burning near the matches. He assumed it had ignited them, setting off the fire that engulfed the wine. Inspectors had found matches scattered among the bottles, but no one ever proved a cigarette caused it—except in Jimmy's mind.

"Boss," he said, "the funny part is, if we had played poker that night, the fire never would have happened."

Who knows what history might have had in store for us if it hadn't. Either way, I told him I forgave him—and that I loved him.

* * *

Craig took over as maître d'. By then, he had nearly fifteen years at the restaurant under his belt, having worked as a bartender, waiter, and captain before Jimmy took him under his wing and prepared him for the day he would step into the role of maître d' and manager.

He was perfect for the job—handsome, smooth, and immensely likeable. Born in Brooklyn, Craig spent his teenage years less than a mile from the restaurant and grew up steeped in both old and new Hollywood. He knew Sumner Redstone always came in through the kitchen, George Clooney favored tequila, and that "Paris" meant a gorgeous blond Hilton, not a city or a hotel.

His temperament fit the job exactly. "The only thing you can do is make 80 percent happy," he said of the maître d's challenge. "The other 20 percent . . ." He would often recall a night when one man lingered as his family walked out, stopping to say, "Craig, I gotta tell you, you made this night so special. Thanks for squeezing us in. You're the greatest." Ten seconds later, another customer stormed up, furious about the wait, and snarled, "You are the biggest son of a bitch I've ever heard in my life."

Like those before him, Craig built strong relationships with regulars. Clooney, for example, was the only guest for whom I ever closed the restaurant—shutting the doors in 2006 so he could celebrate his first Oscar win. Craig himself once went on a second date with his future wife, Lisa, when Clooney spotted him across the room and secretly paid for their dinner.

My favorite Craig story involves his wedding. A magazine had once mistakenly credited my chef Neno as the restaurant's owner, and for weeks Neno endured endless teasing from the staff. He apologized repeatedly, embarrassed. Six months later, when Craig got married, the rabbi stood before the packed room and explained that Craig had met his wife at "the restaurant he owns, Dan Tana's." Without missing a beat, Neno leapt to his feet and shouted, "I'm off the hook!" The room erupted in laughter.

Craig was unflappable. When Ari and Rahm Emanuel brought in presidential candidate Barack Obama, Craig handled it. When Novak Djokovic won his first title at Indian Wells and announced to the press that he was celebrating at Dan Tana's—something Jerry Buss tipped me off about—Craig made sure the night went smoothly, even though most of the guests spoke only Serbian. So it felt only natural that Craig would want to buy the restaurant, and that I would agree to sell it to him.

Craig was the obvious heir. I had literally watched him grow up. After we celebrated the restaurant's forty-fifth anniversary, I looked at Craig again and thought he could carry it for another forty years. He found a partner willing to put up most of the money, made an offer just a million dollars less than Ted Demme had once proposed, and I said yes. The three of us went around the corner to a little coffee shop to sign the papers. But once we sat down, Craig and his partner began arguing, nothing was signed, and the deal collapsed.

I walked back to my office in shock. Word must have spread that I was selling, because while I was at the coffee shop, a man—Middle Eastern in appearance, according to Nada—came by and left a certified check for five million dollars along with his phone number. He said it was for the restaurant.

"I told him he was too late," Nada said.

My attorney advised me to sit tight. If I wanted, I could always go back to Craig in a few days and tell him I had another offer on the table. But the whole episode made me realize that selling Dan Tana's was not going to be as simple as I imagined. For a restaurant so famous and profitable, I thought buyers would be lining up. Instead, one prospective buyer had died and another deal had collapsed right at the signing. I never did call the man with the certified check. As it turned out, I didn't have to.

My longtime manager and friend Nada, together with her best friend, Sonja Perenčević, had spent twenty years looking to buy a restaurant in Los Angeles. Their search finally ended at 9071 Santa Monica Boulevard, in West Hollywood. Sonja's husband, Mihajlo, a

Croatian businessman who had made his fortune in Russia, bought the restaurant from me in 2009. The price was six million dollars—a staggering figure when I thought back to the $30,000 I had scraped together to buy it in the first place, and the extremes I went through to pay back that debt. Even more incredible than the numbers, though, was everything that had happened in between: the lives lived and shared in that tiny space of twenty tables, a bar, and a kitchen. It had been more than a restaurant. It had been a home—a family home—where life happened.

In the weeks and months after signing away ownership, I would get emotional—but in a good way. It wasn't just because of the restaurant. In September 2008, I had become president of my beloved Red Star. Three months later, a reporter for the *World Soccer* website asked if I regretted it. "Every day," I said. This jewel of the country's biggest sport was mired in mismanagement and corruption. The previous season had been a bust: no league win, no cup, and no points in the UEFA Cup group stage.

I thought I could help. I was wrong. Despite pouring myself into the team, along with donating a million dollars to save what was a sinking ship, I came up short. We were in third place at winter break. By spring 2009, I was out. The challenges were too great. But oh my, what a thrill it was for me to reflect on how far I had come, from that boy who played for their youth team to president of the club. I sat in the stadium and saw the most incredible life pass by—and it belonged to me!

My friend, film producer Lis Kern, sent me a note whose simplicity said it all. "It was incredible that I could go there and see your picture in the museum—the beautiful game providing a thread so precious."

Speaking of precious threads: In 2011, Craig opened his own eponymous restaurant, Craig's, in West Hollywood. Backed by wealthy Dan Tana regulars Gary Winnick and Jerry Weintraub, Craig's became an instant hot spot. "A Contender Elbows In," declared *The New York Times.* Any bitterness I had toward Craig was replaced by pride. He had learned well. We would always be family.

I returned to the restaurant periodically. Many of the same people remained, as Sonja had promised nothing would change—and it didn't. I enjoyed being referred to as "Boss," only now the employees hugged me instead of asking for time off. I made the rounds of tables. For dessert, I enjoyed a piece of Deanne's cheesecake exactly as I had when she brought samples in for me, Giovanni, and Constantino to taste in 1964. One night I brought the Serbian football team's coaching staff for dinner. Vlade Divac joined us. It was a party.

With good wine and good food and good friends gathered around a red and white checked tablecloth, stories and jokes being told, it was as if time stopped . . .

Only it didn't.

* * *

One can focus on life or on death. When death arrives in the form of war—when you hear bombs dropping as a child and wake to learn that your neighbors have been killed—you spend the rest of your days choosing life. You know instinctively what others spend a lifetime trying to grasp: Every day is precious.

Let the ball do the running, Bata.

By the early 2000s, that lesson was never far from my mind. After decades of traveling between continents, I had finally once again settled into Belgrade. I was back in the apartment I had purchased there, a place I now called home. The years of soccer had caught up with me, and I was having trouble with my foot. My massage therapist sent over a specialist.

Her name was Biljana Strezovski—Bebe for short. She had the dark beauty of a movie star and the kindness of an angel. She worked her magic and eased my pain. Despite a thirty-five-year age difference, we slowly fell in love—with each other, with each other's families, and in her case, with Dan Tana's.

When I first brought her to America, she didn't speak a word of English, but everyone adored her. They recognized her patience and concern for me. She, Nada, and my cheesecake lady became inseparable. In 2006, Bebe and I married in a small civil ceremony followed by a lunch with fabulous *tzigane* music. Together we traveled, entertained friends, and expanded our family with a King Charles spaniel.

Love won't keep you young, but it will let you feel young at heart—and so very present.

That presence was a blessing as others departed. In September 2017, we lost Harry Dean Stanton, at age ninety-one. A group of friends spent two nights at Dan Tana's reminiscing for *Vanity Fair*. Ed Begley Jr. remembered how he and Harry had been there every night without fail, until they got a movie with Warren Oates in Macon, Georgia. "It occurred to me we should probably call Tana's to let them know we were still alive," Ed said.

"I called them up—I still remember the number—and heard Guido answer, 'Good evening! Tana's!' I said, 'Guido! Ed Begley here. I'm with Harry Dean.' Guido cried out, 'Oh Jesus Christ, thank God! We were gonna call the police! We thought you fell asleep and left the gas on and now you all dead!'"

Stories like that made it clear: Harry might be gone, but his presence would always linger at the restaurant. The same was true of Mike Gotovac, who died of complications from COVID-19 in May 2020. By then, more than fifty years after he started, Mike was as much an institution as the Dodgers and the Hollywood sign.

He already had bad lungs when he got sick. I spoke with his wife, Miljoka, and even a couple of times with him in the hospital. For a moment, we thought he might pull through. But after three months of struggle, he lost the battle.

He had a bartender's reservoir of wisdom. "Only two things change," he used to say. "We get older, and prices go up." It was his gruff simplicity and humor that made him a part of people's lives. "There were a lot of lonely people in LA and he did have a soft spot," his wife told the *Los Angeles Times.*

Outside, the neon sign said Dan Tana's. Inside, the bar was Mike's.

Dabney Coleman mourned Mike as hard as anyone, as would be expected given the many nights they spent together. In 2024, Dabney passed away. He was ninety-two. Among all the tributes I read, I remember one in *Variety* that mentioned Dabney had moved to New York briefly in the early 2000s before returning to Los Angeles. Asked what brought him back, he said simply, "Dan Tana's."

After 10:30 P.M., you can find his ghost at table 1.

And me? That same year, 2024, I was diagnosed with colon cancer. I nearly died on the operating table, but lived to celebrate my ninetieth birthday on May 26, 2025. The celebration in Belgrade was three days long and attended by my daughters, my wife, my ex-wife, friends, and the sons and daughters of many former Dan Tana's regulars. I took everyone to the little church in Čibutkovica where my mother was married and I was christened.

The church was built in the early eighteenth century, back when the Turks ruled the land, though the lesson is that no one owns anything over time. Years earlier, I had donated money to restore the frescoes inside the chapel. Like many benefactors throughout history, I had my family's faces painted into murals. My mother looked down from the ceiling.

When I was a boy, my mother told me that you must love yourself before you can love others. Now, as a ninety-year-old I heard her voice again, only this time I understood what she meant—that loving yourself is the first gift, and every other love, every memory you give, flows from there.

My cancer worsened. News got out and the phone rang nonstop. Calls came in from England, Russia, Spain, Portugal, Greece, Japan, Montenegro, Bosnia, France, and the US. People offered their doctor, recommended specialists. I told each person that I loved them, listened as they said the same to me, and I knew there was no better medicine.

I feel like the richest person who has ever lived on this planet. No one has had more. I did all the things I love—football, movies, friends, and family. I always say I am lucky I fell in love with football before I fell in love with women. Dan Tana's was one of a kind. People worked at the restaurant their entire adult lives. It became theirs as much as it belonged to me.

The restaurant was a small yellow house, with green awnings, and a neon sign confirming that you had arrived at Dan Tana's. You walked through the red door, and the outside world disappeared. Time stopped. The maître d' greeted you. Reservation or not, you were taken care of. Everybody felt like they belonged. Rich or famous or simply hungry, it was a home for those in need of a home. We collected people, stories, and memories.

The heavens are full of stars, and I am convinced there must be a star that has always shone on me. It's still shining on me.

But stars also die. No matter how brightly they have shined, eventually they lose their energy and collapse. But in one form or another, whether it's gas or dust or light, they remain. Some even help form new stars. I like that. I like to think that when my star is no longer visible, people will remember not only what I brought to the world, but also what I left. Good times. Good food. Good friends.

I am nearing the end as I write this. It is no longer a matter of having more years behind me than ahead—it is a matter of weeks, perhaps days. What does a person do with such knowledge? For me, the answer is simple: I say thank you.

I have lived well. I have loved well. I gave freely, and life always found a way to give back more. That, I believe, is the true goal—the so-called good life or life well-lived—to arrive at this point that none of us can escape and feel nothing but gratitude. The grown son of a dear friend, long gone but never forgotten, once told me that the only reason he kissed his father was because he always saw me do it. "How much joy you have brought into people's lives," he said. That is the true measure of wealth, in the hearts and minds of those you've touched.

My life has been one long table. Sometimes crowded with friends, sometimes with strangers who became friends, and sometimes set simply for family. I have been the boy in a field at war, the young man chasing a soccer ball down uneven ground, the actor lucky enough to speak a few lines, the partner who stumbled into owning a restaurant, and the man who stood at his own bar, surrounded by ghosts.

EPILOGUE

Always at the Table

Our earliest memories of our father are as a storyteller. While our mother read us fairy tales at bedtime, Daddy spun stories of his own life—adventures of courage, kindness, and gratitude. There were "shoes with holes," "snowy streets," and "marketplaces where fruit and vegetables were weighed and sold." Only later did we realize he was sharing his childhood—the early chapters of the remarkable life that would follow.

He was a very different man and lived an exceptional life. A professional footballer, a defector and immigrant, an actor, a restaurateur, a film producer, a gambler, and above all, a brilliant raconteur. He was a great joker, a great provider, a man of unbounded generosity and restless curiosity—a citizen of the world. He had his habits, good and difficult; his passions; and a heart of gold.

For Daddy's fortieth birthday in London, our mother planned a surprise party with a huge cake piled with strawberries and cream. It was too big for the refrigerator, so she left it on the terrace overnight. Little Katy couldn't contain her excitement and secretly showed it to him. Daddy promised not to tell. But the next morning, as our mother stirred awake, he asked if she'd heard the rainstorm in the night. Panicked, she ran to check on the cake—while he roared with laughter. That was our father: playful, mischievous, delighted by life. His humor, like his warmth, was contagious.

His love of life was matched only by his love of people. He believed in fairness, generosity, and hard work. In a world that often prizes material wealth, he valued friendship, loyalty, and kindness. He was not driven by money but by connection—by the idea that there should always be enough for everyone. His restaurant, his football clubs, his friendships across continents were all expressions of that belief.

He was astonished at his incredibly good fortune, that the hard work, risks, and acts of generosity would reward him so handsomely. Not just with prosperity but more importantly with treasured friendships, relationships amassed over his lifetime through football, family, food, film, and at every turn with an irrepressible sense of play and fun.

His passion for football carried him around the world again and again—from Belgrade to Brussels, London to Los Angeles—and everywhere he went, stories followed. At the restaurant, at the stadium, at home, he was always "holding court," telling tales with a sparkle in his eyes. He was a citizen of the world, traveling between Yugoslavia, Europe, and the US. He had friends and adventures everywhere.

People urged him for years to write them down, and in the final years of his life, he finally did. English was not his first language, but that never stopped him. He read voraciously—five newspapers a day, mostly sports and politics—and wrote the way he spoke: directly, phonetically, and with enormous heart. "Life is very simple," he often said. "We complicate it."

This book was his last great project, and it kept him going. Even from his hospital bed in Belgrade, he sent notes and edits, his mind sharp and his spirit undimmed. Less than two weeks before his passing, he was discussing publicity plans. He wanted to live long enough to meet readers, to tell his stories in person, to attend the 2026 World

Cup in Los Angeles. "It will be my eleventh World Cup," he said proudly. Only his body gave out; his mind and heart never did.

We were all able to gather at his bedside during his last few days in Belgrade. He told us with his eyes that he was nearing the end. On August 16, 2025—his nineteenth wedding anniversary with Bebe—he tapped his wrist as if to say, "It's time." The next day, he slipped away peacefully, surrounded by love.

Three days later, a ceremony was held at Red Star Belgrade's Rajko Mitić Stadium, where he had once played as a youth. He was laid to rest at the New Cemetery in Belgrade, in a service attended by hundreds—family, friends, dignitaries, and teammates. The graveside eulogy was delivered by his dear friend Žika Petrović.

> *Dan Tana was a dream come true—not for himself, but for all of us. He was a reminder that dreams are not meant to be owned, but shared. In every raised glass, every handshake, every glance, he left a piece of himself—and a piece of Serbia. Now we remain: friends and family, witnesses of his journey, guardians of his legacy.*
>
> *The bells at the church in Čibutkovica have been ringing for two days, echoing across the hills of Šumadija like a cry for their patron. Sorrow has spread to Ada Međica, where the waves now know they will no longer greet his footsteps. Silence has fallen over Madera . . . America has lost a true gentleman, England a friend, and Serbia one of her finest sons.*
>
> *Today, as we bid him farewell, we do not say goodbye but thank you.*
>
> *Thank you, Dan, for teaching us to love unconditionally, to live with passion, to remember our roots. Thank you for showing us that style resides in the soul, not in the suit. Thank you for writing the word Serbia on every map of the world—not with ink, but with heart.*

The following weekend, Brentford FC held a minute of applause before kickoff, twenty thousand fans and players standing to celebrate his life. A few weeks later, during a World Cup qualifying match between Serbia and England, fifty thousand fans stood in silence, then erupted in a roar. Millions watched around the world. Our father's spirit could not have been more alive.

He lived analog in a digital world—no cell phone, no computer—yet he was more connected than most people ever are. He left the world rich in friendship, laughter, and love—his true currency.

Following his passing, and through all the wonderful tributes, phone calls, cards, and stories that have come our way, we have cried, we have smiled, and our hearts have swelled. Daddy is gone, but his spirit is everywhere—in the laughter of friends, in the roar of the crowd, in the clink of a glass raised in his name.

He used to shake his head after a good story and say, "Can you believe it?" That was his magic. He lived every day with wonder. He wanted this book to carry that forward, to be a way of table-hopping for eternity, forever greeting old friends and making new ones.

And so he will be—always at the table.

Gabrielle and Katerina Tana
London & Los Angeles

Thank You to

Todd Gold
Brankica Ralić
Aleksandar Miletić
Lyn Rothman
Jonathan Foreman
Andrew Croker
Eric Braeden
Lis Kern Shaw
Ellen Hoffs
Joanna Adler
Toby Rafelson
Richard Arlook
Andrea Tana
James Woods
Marin Hopper
Nadia Ghaleb
Biljana "Bebe" Strezovski Tana
Roger Lewis
Robert Coleman
Zivojin Petrovic
Marko Miskovic
Vlade Divac
Carolyn Marks Blackwood
Andrea Tana
Roslyn Sulcas
Craig Susser
Nada Palinkovic
Sonja Perencevic
Erica Silverman
Simon Brook
Christian Kneedler
Alessia Bologna
Judith Regan
Marilyn Cadenbach
Erica Silverman
Everyone who ever worked at Dan Tana's in his lifetime and those that dined with him too.

"I have known Dan Tana for over 25 years. He has business activities in Belgrade, Los Angeles, and London – he is a man of truly international renown. But above all, he is a football enthusiast.

In his early years he played for Yugoslavia's Red Star team.

For seven years he was Council Member of The Football Association of England.

He was a Consultant to Alan Rothenberg in America, prior to and during the WorldCup USA/94.

While his base of operations remained in Belgrade, he continued his relationship with Association Football in England, and is still a constant visitor to England International Football games.

Dan Tana remains an active member of the Yugoslav F.A. and travels the world for them on football matters. He is a MULTI-LINGUIST, as well as a GREAT FOOTBALL MAN. I hold a deep and lasting respect for him."

SIR BERT MILLICHIP
Honorary Member, UEFA

"For over 30 years I have been fortunate to know Dan Tana in his role as a movie producer and friend. I have found him to have the rare qualities of being creative, loyal, reliable and honest. These wonderful qualities are part of the reason Dan sits on the Academy of Motion Picture Arts and Sciences two most important committees; one that annually chooses the five Best Pictures in English, and one that chooses the five Best Foreign Language Films.

The time I have spent with him on a personal and professional level enables me to highly recommend Dan Tana for a seat on UEFA's Executive Committee."

KARL MALDEN
Member, Board of Governors;
Past President of Academy of Motion Picture Arts & Sciences

"When Dan Tana kicked his first ball for the Juniors of Red Star, I was there. I remained in Belgrade, but Dan travelled the world with football as a Player, Manager and Owner. He has also been a successful business man, producing numerous feature films, and owning and running a world famous restaurant in Hollywood, California for many years, that bears his name.

No one understands football better than Dan. His experience on grass root, amateur and professional levels is an asset that will be invaluable to UEFA. Football must be governed by honest and brave men – this describes Dan Tana."

MILJAN MILJANIC
President of The Yugoslav Football Assn.